GW01338867

BURGHLEY

THE HORSES, THE HOUSE AND THE PEOPLE

Photographed by Mark A. L. Scott

Foreword by Lady Victoria Leatham
Introduction by Jane Wallace
Highlights by Jane Pontifex
Photographs of all the winners,
and results tables, for 1961 to 1992

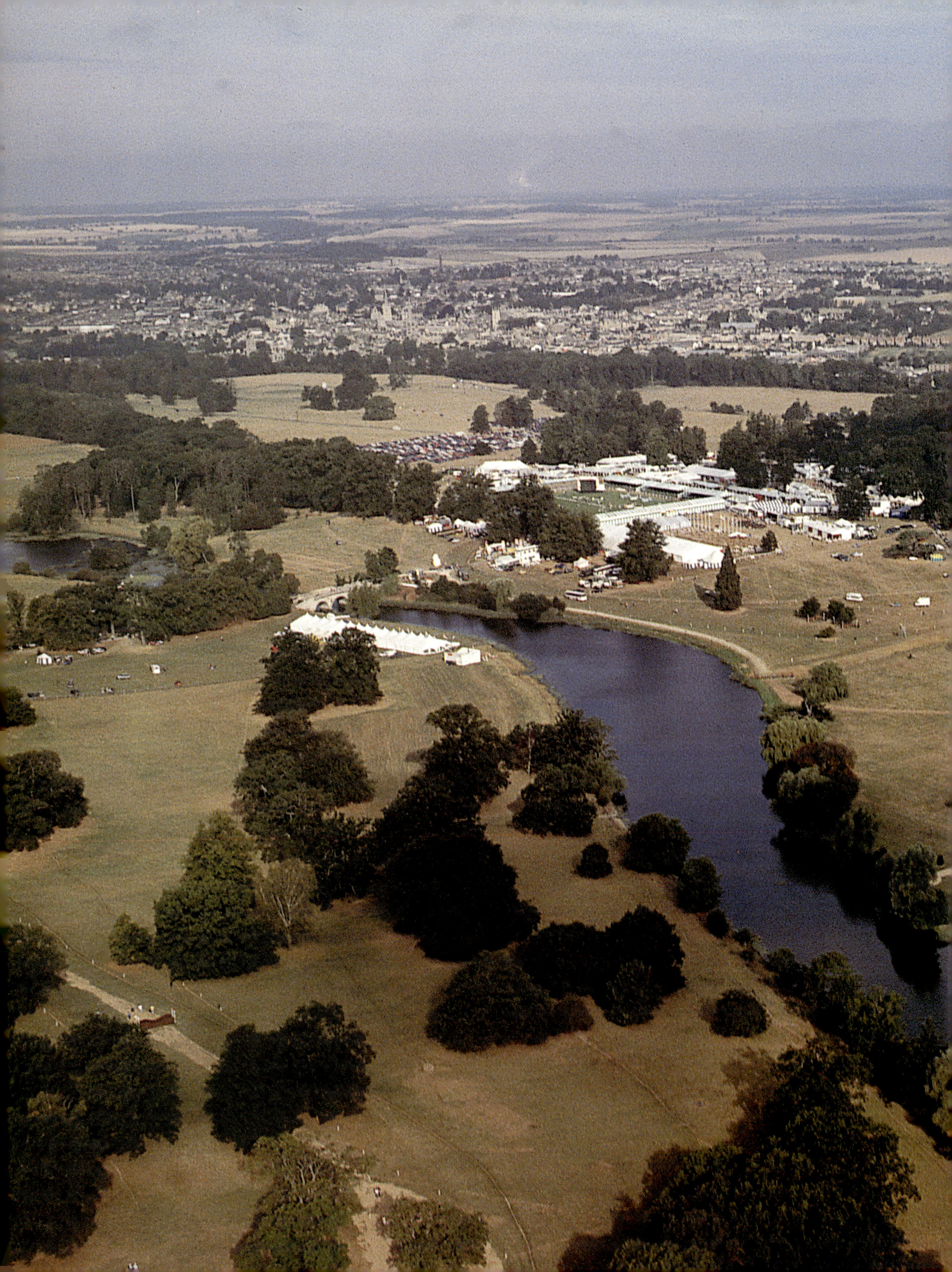

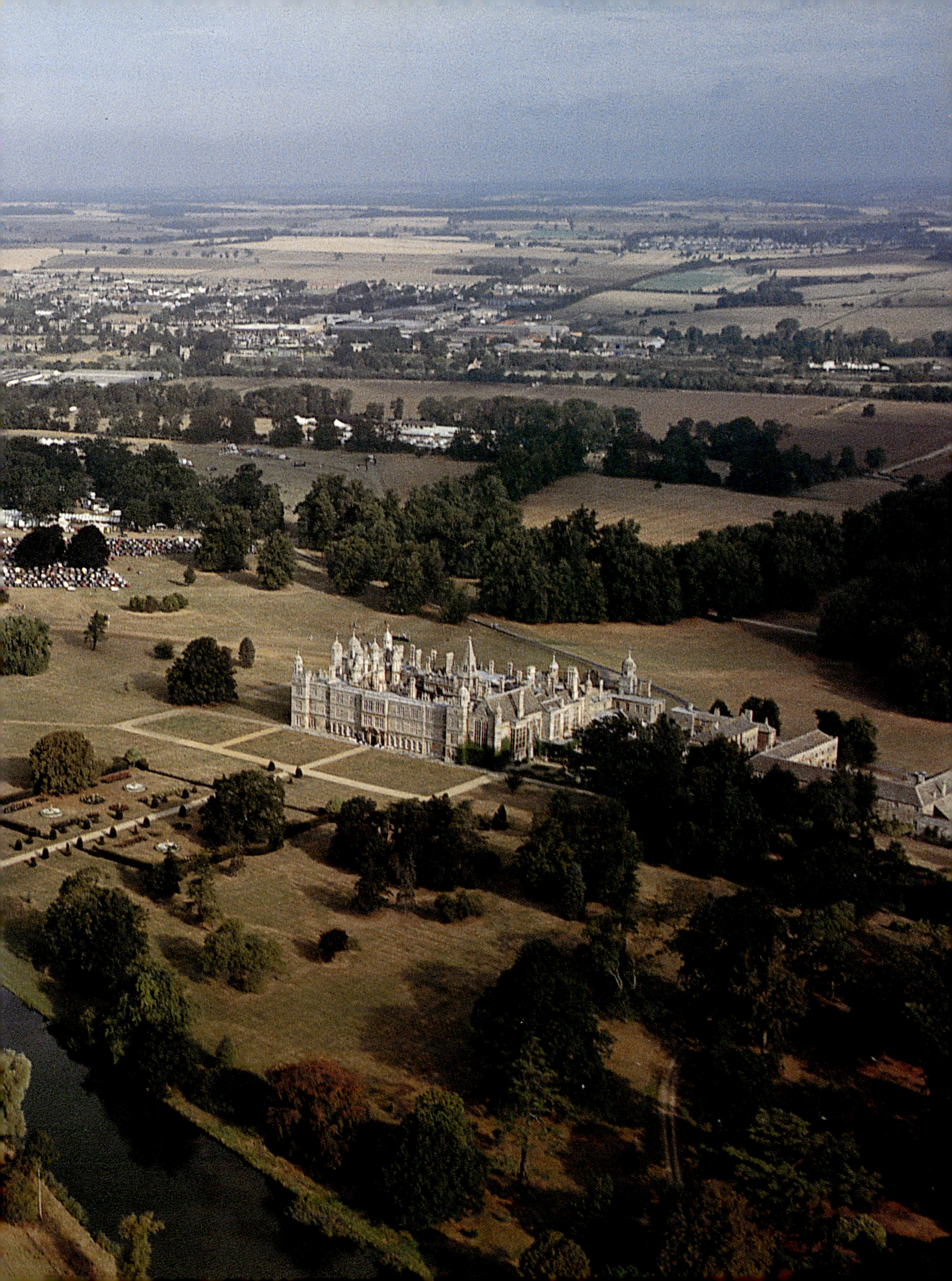

Published by The Burghley Horse Trials Committee
Stamford, Lincolnshire PE9 2LH

Devised and edited by Barbara Cooper
Designed by Adrienne Gear
Produced by Compass Books Limited

© 1993 Burghley Horse Trials Committee

All rights reserved. No part of this publication may be
reproduced, stored in a retrieval system, or transmitted in
any form or by any means, electronic, mechanical, photocopying,
recording or otherwise, without the written permission of the
Burghley Horse Trials Committee.

A CIP catalogue record of this book is available from the British Library.

ISBN 0 952 0899 0 4

Phototypeset in Ehrhardt by Intype, London.
Printed and bound by Mandarin Offset, Hong Kong.

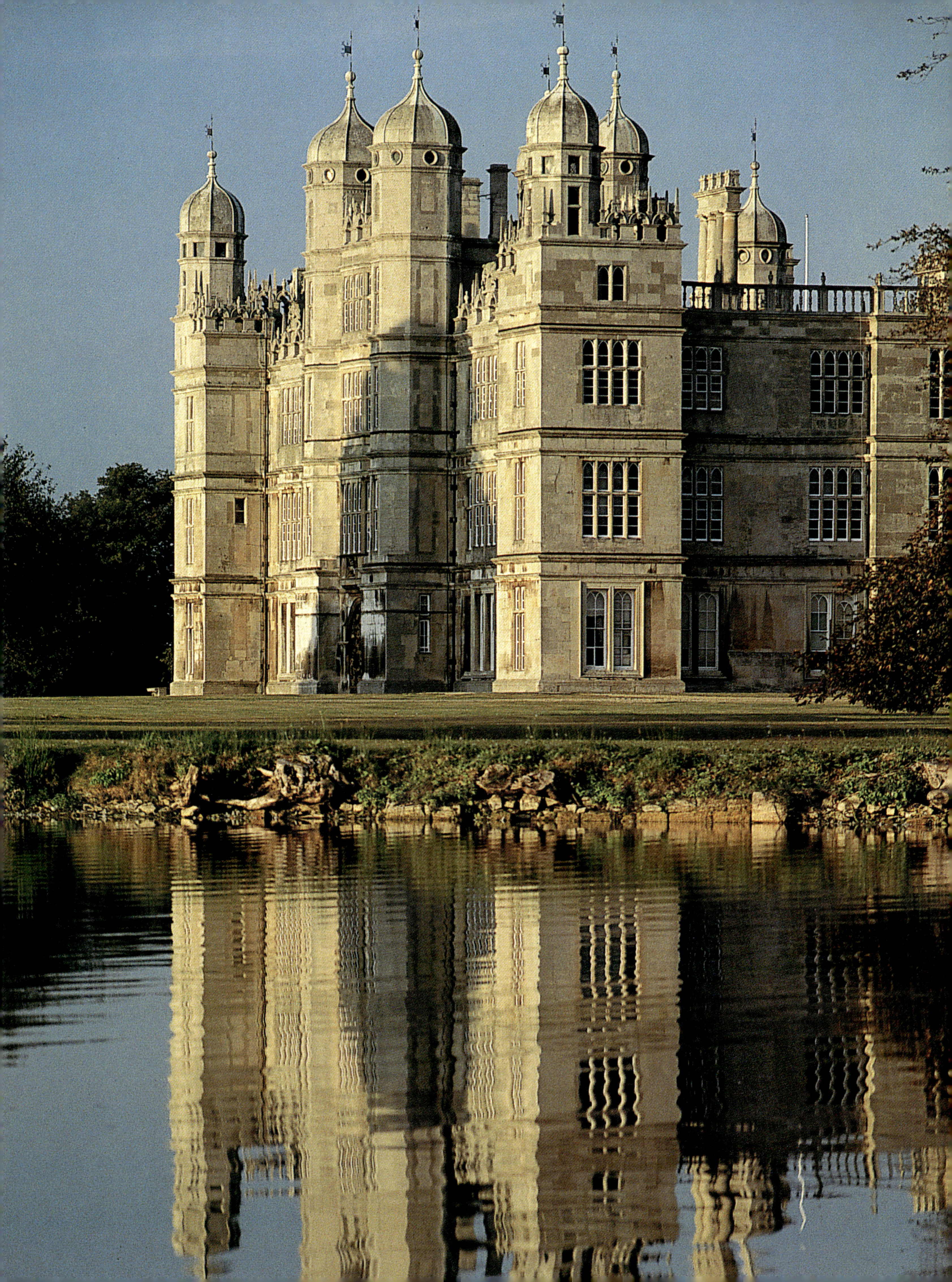

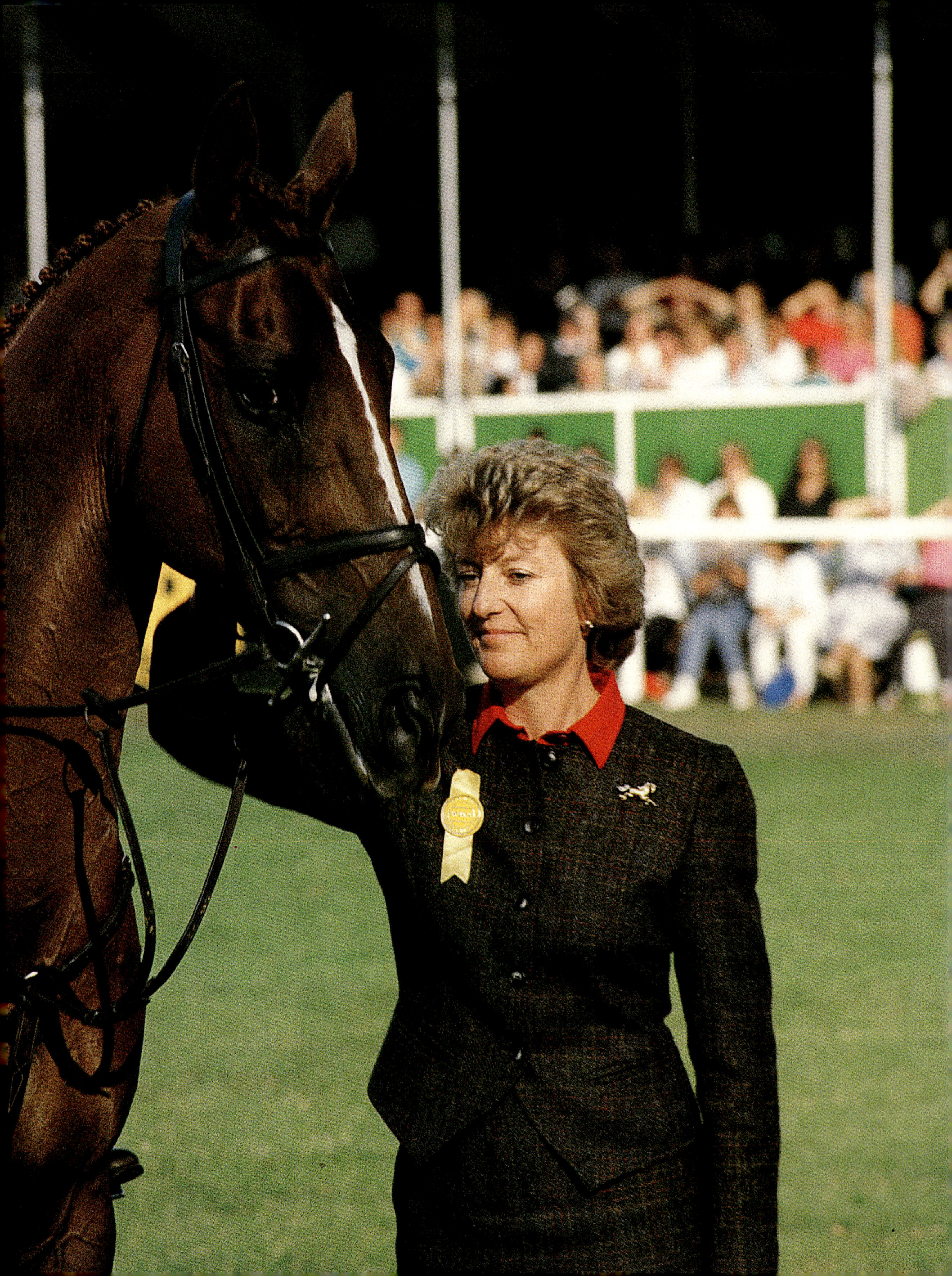

**BURGHLEY HOUSE
STAMFORD
LINCOLNSHIRE
PE9 3JY**

When I was originally invited to write the foreword to this marvellous book, it was but a mere twinkle in the editor's eye We have waited its coming with great excitement and we are not disappointed. It is intriguing to see how such a physical happening as the Burghley Remy Martin Horse Trials can be portrayed so successfully in photographs and prose.

It is all here, you can almost smell the bruised grass and sweating horses. You can empathise with the losers and join in the victory celebrations of the winners. Above all there is a sense of an intangible purpose, a sort of idealistic reason for it all which has carried on down the years since that great day in 1961 when my father took the decision to host the event for the first time.

Who would ever have guessed then, that one day there would be marquees with wall to wall carpeting; a giant television screen capable of taking us close up during a dressage test; flush lavatories in this 16th century park; a waiting list for trade stands even through the deepest economic gloom since the 1930's.

All this has to be viewed with understanding of all those who work so hard during the year to make the event special for everyone attending. It is this sense of achievement which comes over so strongly in this book, almost a celebration, you might say, of the "Unseen", the judges and the ground juries, the medical support teams, the litter pickers and the car parkers, let alone the office staff and the other organisers who make it all happen.

On reading this book I can only be grateful that in 1961 my father, who had enjoyed the company of horses all his life, made a bold decision to give back to the sport as much pleasure as he had received from it and decided to hold the first Burghley Horse Trials. The event made no money for several years during which time he underwrote the losses.

When asked by a reporter why he had decided to hold horse trials at Burghley, he replied without hesitation "Can you think of a better way to use the Park?" If I were to answer that question today, the reply would definitely still be "No"!........

Victoria Leatham

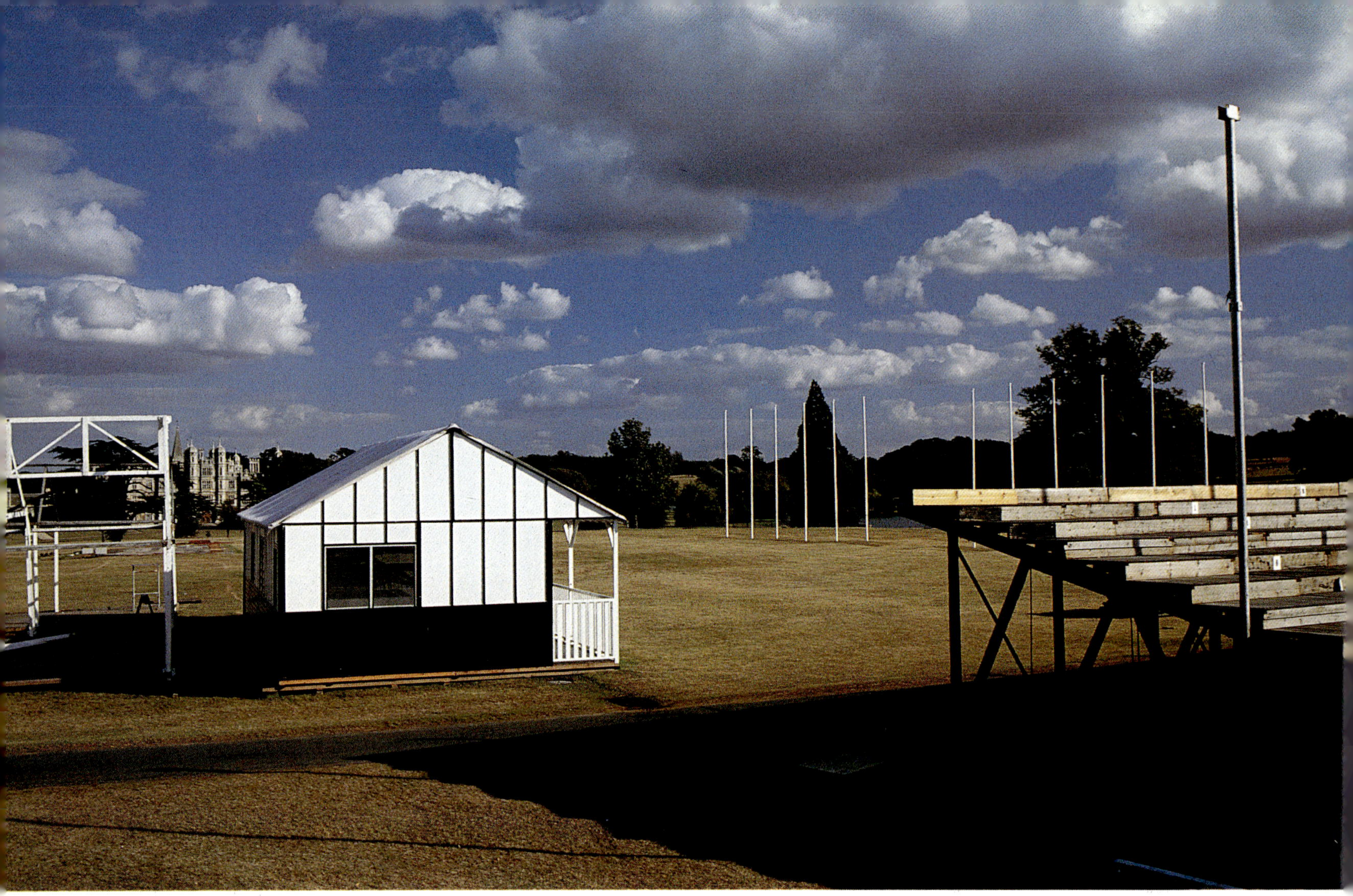

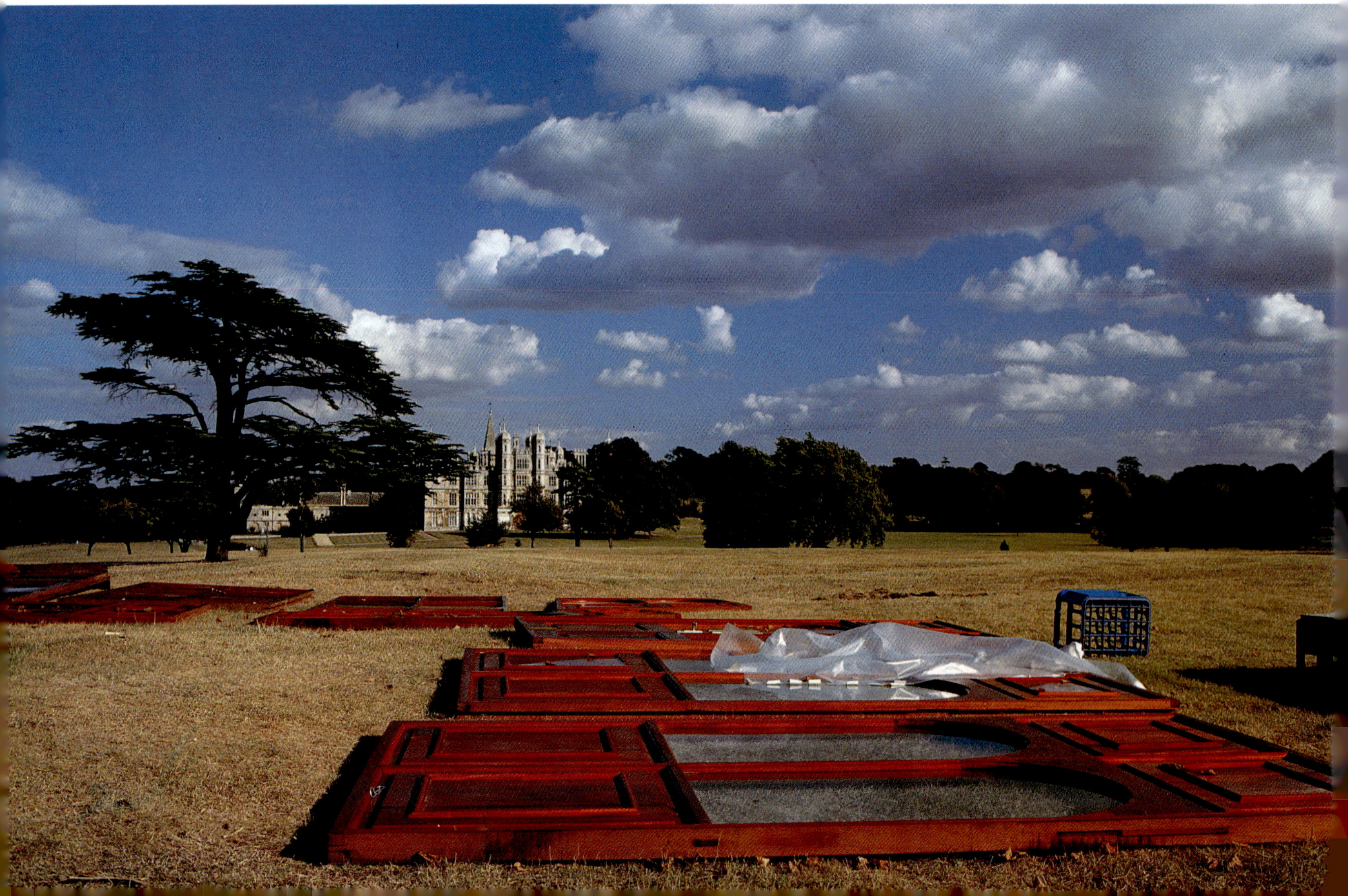

Introduction

by Jane Wallace

THERE CAN BE no more beautiful setting for a sporting occasion than Burghley. Every September the magnificent Elizabethan mansion with its fairy-tale turrets, chimneys, balustrades and mullioned windows; the stately park with its avenues of trees and gently undulating fields; and the ancient town of Stamford, are the focal point of one of the biggest gatherings in Britain: Burghley Horse Trials.

Burghley House was the creation of William Cecil (1520–98). Only son of a Northamptonshire squire, he was educated at Grantham School and St John's College, Cambridge. He served Henry VIII for a short period, became MP for Stamford in 1547, was Secretary of State to Edward VI, who knighted him. After the fall of Lord Protector Somerset in 1549 he was imprisoned in the Tower for several months. When Queen Elizabeth succeeded to the throne in 1558 she appointed him Lord High Treasurer, and until his death forty years later he remained her chief minister and most trusted adviser.

In 1552 he inherited from his father the manor of 'Burleigh' and a year later began work on redesigning and extending the original building: a task which was to take over thirty years. The house at which we still marvel today – one of the finest Elizabethan structures in England – is due to his inspiration.

Built of Barnack rag, a locally quarried stone, the house is centred around a rectangular courtyard, with an elaborate clock-tower at the east end. Work began on the east range in 1555 and the south in 1564. When building resumed in 1567 after an interruption, construction continued on the west side. Finally, the elaborate north front (over 200 feet in length), with its impressive central hall, was completed in 1587.

No architectural changes were made during the political upheavals of the 17th Century. During the Civil War the house became a refuge for Royalists, and was besieged by Cromwell's army. The south front was bombarded by cannon – fortunately suffering little damage. When John Cecil, 5th Earl of Exeter, inherited the title some twenty years later he embarked on major improvements. He had increased his fortune by marrying a wealthy heiress, Anne Cavendish, daughter of the third Earl of Devonshire. Advised by their friend the Grand Duke of Tuscany, the couple travelled extensively throughout Europe, acquiring many of the works of art that can be seen at Burghley today: paintings from Florence, tapestries from Paris and many other treasures.

Influenced by the Italian baroque style, John Cecil created a series of state rooms, the grandest being the Heaven Room on the south side, with wall and ceiling decorations by Antonio Verrio. The work took over eighteen months to complete and cost £500 – a considerable sum in the 17th Century. As a result of their extravagance, the Earl and Countess died heavily in debt, and the state rooms were left unfinished – but their influence on Burghley is clearly to be seen, both in the house and the park. During the 5th Earl's lifetime many trees were planted – mainly limes and oaks – and some of them still grace the park.

The 9th Earl (1725–1793) made four grand

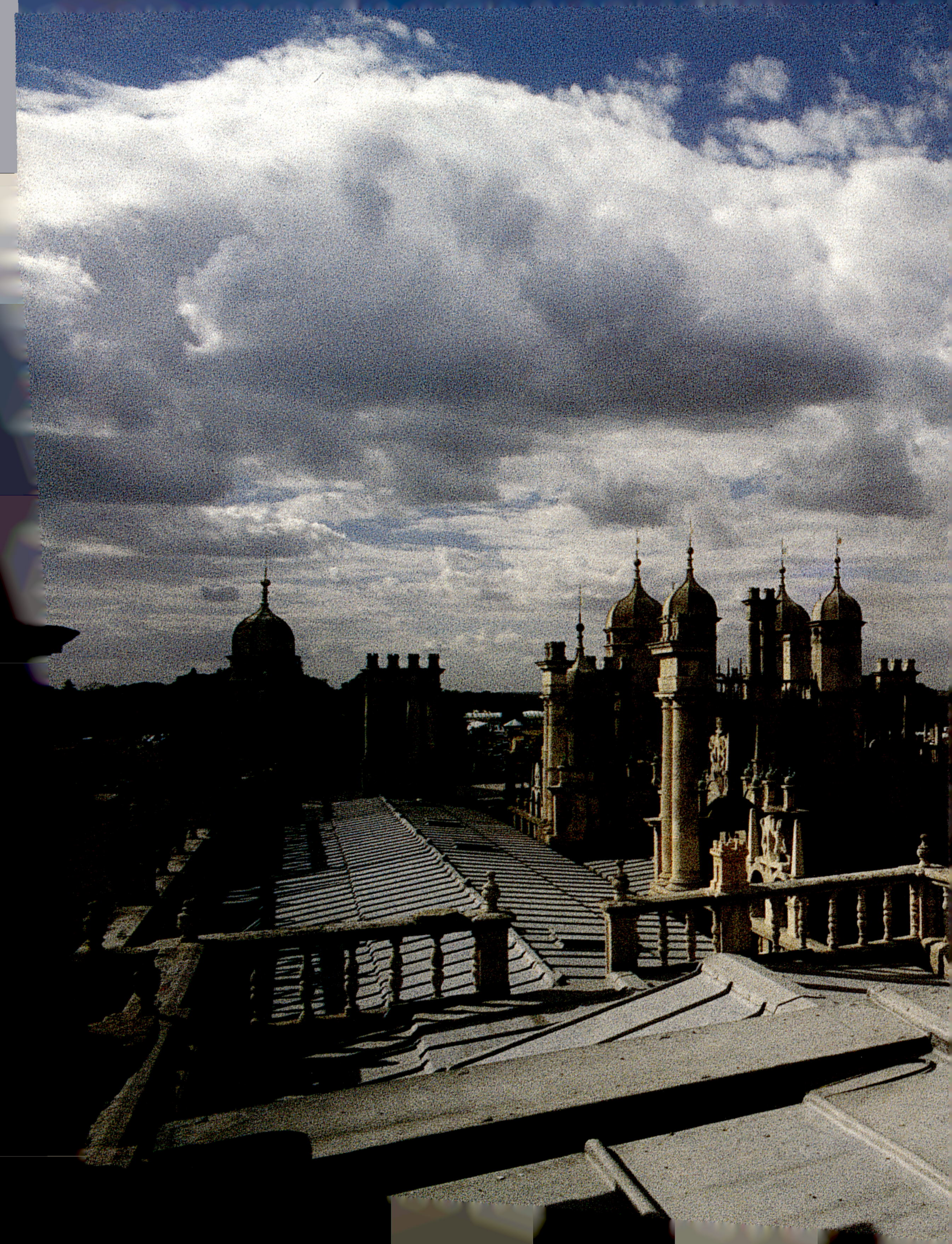

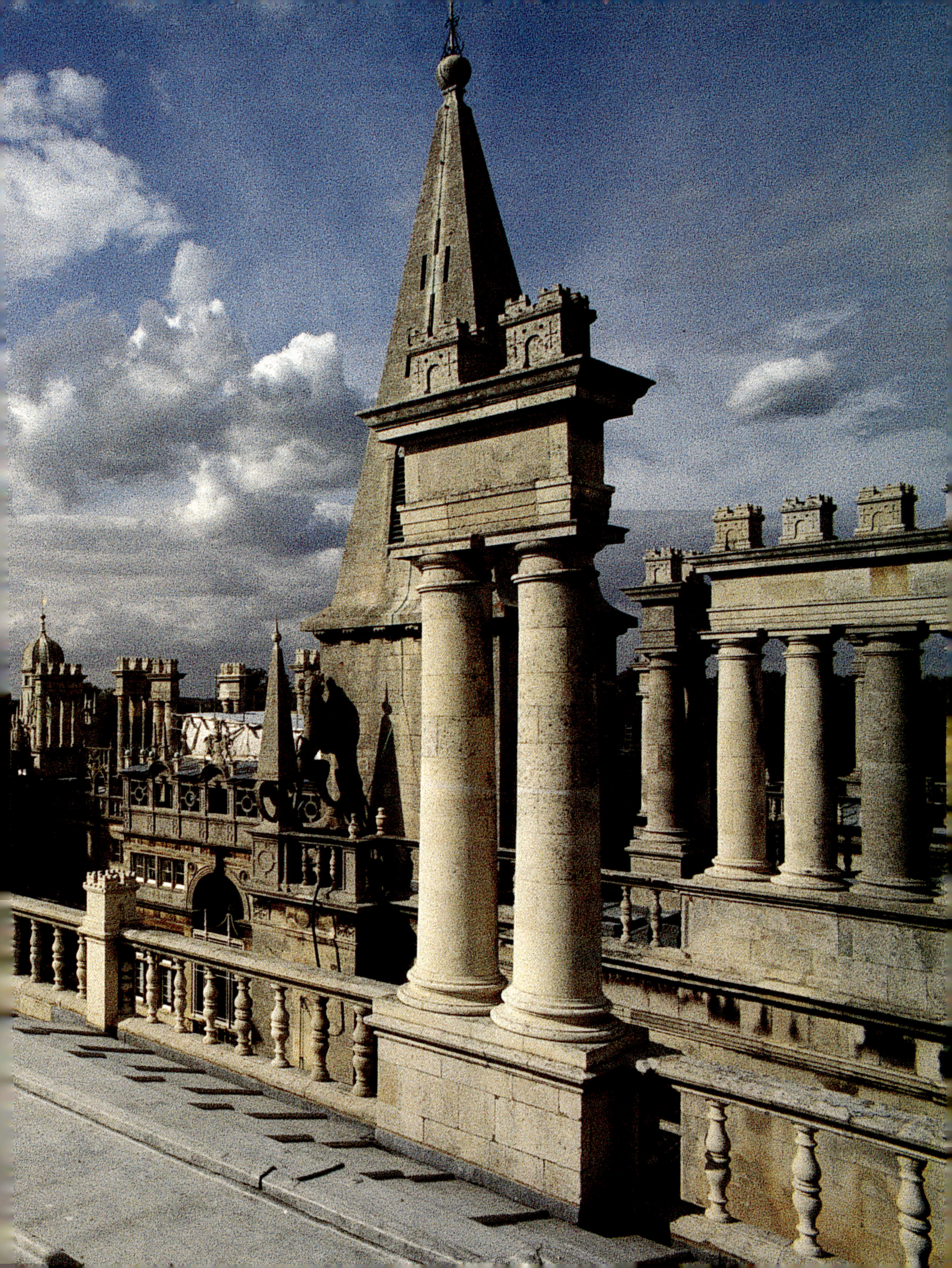

tours to Italy, buying paintings to complement the collection started by the 5th Earl. He also completed work on the state rooms, commissioning leading craftsmen and buying fine pieces of furniture. It was the 9th Earl who brought Lancelot 'Capability' Brown to Burghley. A Northumberland man, Brown had few contemporary rivals in the art of landscape architecture. He spent twenty-three years (1756–79) carrying out structural alterations to the house, as well as landscaping the park. Among many innovations he planted more trees and moved others – including mature ones – to form 'clumps': a feature which was one of his hallmarks. The famous 'Capability's Cutting' follows one of the drives to the house. He created the lake by linking old stew ponds with a small stream which later was also used for the trout hatcheries. He also designed the orangery, which is now a tea-room; the delightful pavilion by the lake; the three-arched Lion Bridge; and the stables – a block of twenty-four stalls and eighteen boxes in a three-sided castellated courtyard.

The southern boundary of the park was originally formed by the wall which now separates it from the golf course and which follows the line of Ermine Street, the old Roman road from London to York. (During the event, the steeplechase course and the Members' caravan park are situated in this area.) At the end of the 18th Century the 10th Earl extended the park to 1400 acres.

It was in recognition of the 10th Earl's charitable work that the title of Marquess was bestowed on the Burghley Cecils, in 1801, and to celebrate the honour he built the splendid 'bottle lodges', the main entrance gates. For many years, to avoid creditors, he had led a curious existence masquerading as a landscape

Page 10 Throughout the years, Burghley has nearly always been blessed with fine weather – as in these two pictures, which have an almost movie-set quality. *Pages 12/13* Distant view of marquees from the roof of Burghley House with its doric-columned chimneys and oriental-looking turrets. *Opposite* Capability Brown's Lion Bridge and pavilion. *Above* The Members' caravan park, which provides special amenities such as nightly barbecues, *below*.

15

painter in Shropshire, where he met his second wife, a winsome country girl called Sarah Hoggins. They eventually returned to Burghley, where their portrait by Sir Thomas Lawrence can be seen in the Billiard Room. Their romance is recounted in Tennyson's poem *The Lord of Burghley*.

Though from the earliest years, horses obviously played a day to day part in the life of Burghley, it was the 6th Earl who first established the family connection with equestrian sport, by founding Stamford racecourse in 1717. It later fell into disrepair but was revived in the 19th Century by the second Marquess, Brownlow Cecil, who bred a few successful horses at his stud in Newmarket – and won trophies that he himself had donated to Stamford Races.

The Burghley Hunt, formed by the 5th Marquess in the early 1900s, began as a pack of harriers – hence the green livery. During World War II the Hunt was dispersed, to be revived by the 6th Marquess when he returned to Burghley after inheriting the title in 1956. 'Lordy', as he was affectionately known, had previously been MFH with the East Sussex and the Old Berks, but chronic arthritis forced him to give up riding, and the Burghley Hunt was finally disbanded in 1967. The stables have stood empty ever since, apart from Pony Club camp and a few days during the European Championships in 1971 when they were home to Princess Anne's Doublet.

The 6th Marquess will always be remembered (as Lord Burghley) for his achievements as an athlete – which were memorably depicted

16

Opposite Brigadier James Grose and his assistants in the early 1960s: *l to r* Michelle Asa-Thomas, Sarah Glyn and Jill Neill. *Left* Lord Exeter presents Brigadier Grose with a gift on his retirement in 1975.

Right Bill Henson, who has been Director since 1987.

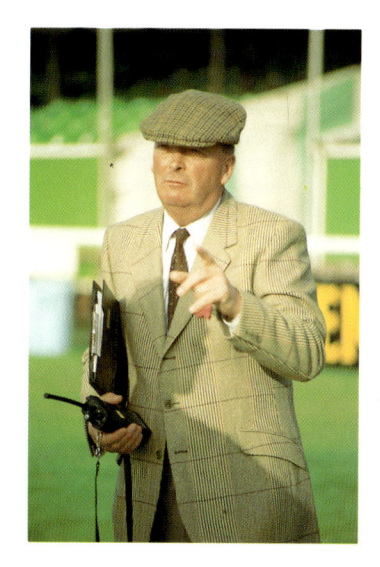

in the film *Chariots of Fire*. He won a gold medal in the 400-metre hurdles in the 1928 Olympic Games in Amsterdam and a silver medal in the 4×400 metres relay at Los Angeles in 1932.

In 1969 he set up the Burghley House Preservation Trust to safeguard the house and park for future generations. After his death in 1981 the title passed to his brother, Martin, who wanted to continue living on his ranch in Canada. The Trust therefore invited Lady Victoria Leatham, daughter of the 6th Marquess, and her husband Simon to take over as custodians of Burghley. A director of Sotheby's, Lady Victoria has applied her knowledge and skills to the formidable task of supervising the conservation and restoration of the contents. Some 600 paintings were in need of attention, as well as tapestries and furniture.

As President of the Horse Trials, Lady Victoria also plays an active part in the organisation and running of the event. It was in 1961 that her father, on hearing that the autumn three-day-event at Harewood could not be held because of an outbreak of foot and mouth disease in the north, invited the British Horse Society to transfer the event to his estate – and from the beginning he involved himself in the organisation with wholehearted enthusiasm; initially he also provided generous financial support.

The first Burghley Committee consisted of Lord Exeter (President), Sir Henry Tate (Vice-President), John Langton (Agent to the Burghley Estate), Giles Floyd, Brigadier James Grose (Director) and Bill Thomson (Course

Sir Henry Tate, Vice-President since the first event: *left* with Joe Wilcox, who was in charge of the arena parties from 1961 to 1975; *right* at the President's lunch, 1991.

Above, left 1961 The 'Harewood Hut', with *l to r* Sue Thomson, Leonard Snowden, Jan Aykroyd, Howard Aykroyd and Bill Thomson. *Below* 1991 The 'posh new palace' in Burghley Park, just off the Barnack Road. *Above right* Edna Stokes (now Lady Tate) on her retirement after twenty years as Horse Trials Secretary with *l to r* (front row) Bill and Sue Thomson, Lady Victoria Leatham, Margaret Purdy; (2nd row) Lana Wells, Liz Inman (hidden), Anne Stratton, Dick Saunders, Giles Floyd; (3rd row) Roy and Norma Bird, Michael Scott, Charles Stratton; (4th row) Caroline Burnaby-Atkins, Joan and Henry Nicoll; (back row) Bill Wells, Andrew Burnaby-Atkins, Simon Leatham.

Designer). Of these, Sir Henry is still Vice-President and Sir Giles and Bill Thomson are still committee members.

Brigadier Grose, who had recently retired from the Army, was highly respected for his organising ability, and he initiated systems which were adhered to until the advent of modern technology. Organising the voluntary help which has always been crucial to the success of the event was the responsibility of Sir Henry Tate. A former Master of the Cottesmore, he wrote to many local Hunt members asking them to be fence judges, course stewards, etc. He recalls that in the early days there was resistance among hunting people against horse trials because it was felt that this 'artificial' sport would lure folk away from hunting. 'It was not easy to recruit fence judges,' he says, 'but having done so you couldn't get rid of them – even when they were in their eighties!'

The Hunt helpers tradition continues, and specific areas of the cross-country course still retain the names of local Hunts: Burghley, Cottesmore, Fitzwilliam and Quorn.

The original Burghley 'office' was an ex-Army hut inherited from Harewood horse trials, and working conditions for the first few years were not exactly ideal. As the hut had windows on three sides, in summer it was like an oven and in winter it dripped with condensation generated by the one small Calor gas heater. In order to provide Brigadier Grose with his morning coffee the kettle had to be filled from the standpipe outside the stables; and as the hut had no guttering, on rainy days it meant a mad dash with umbrella at the ready, and coat on. The same applied when visiting the Elsan at the end of the Dutch barn. 'There were nettles inside and out. Swallows used to nest there, too,' recalls Lady Tate who, as Edna Stokes, was one of the first staff members. When an extension was added to the hut in

Above, left At the beginning of horse trials week, Elizabeth Inman, Trials Secretary, and Jacqueline Stevens, Membership Secretary, move from their permanent office to *right* the custom-built pavilion which is the focal point of activities during the event.

Overleaf View of Stamford across the River Welland.

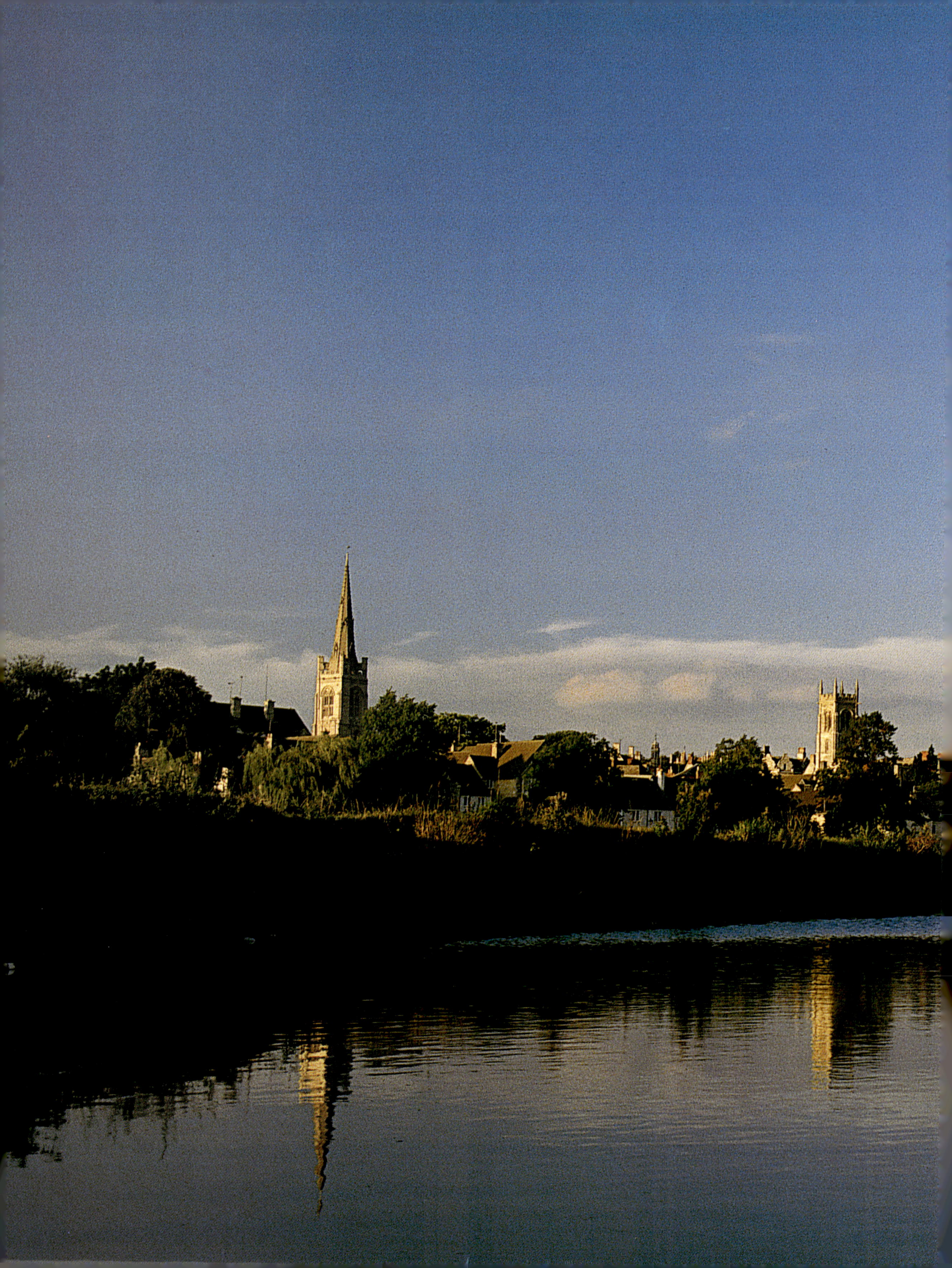

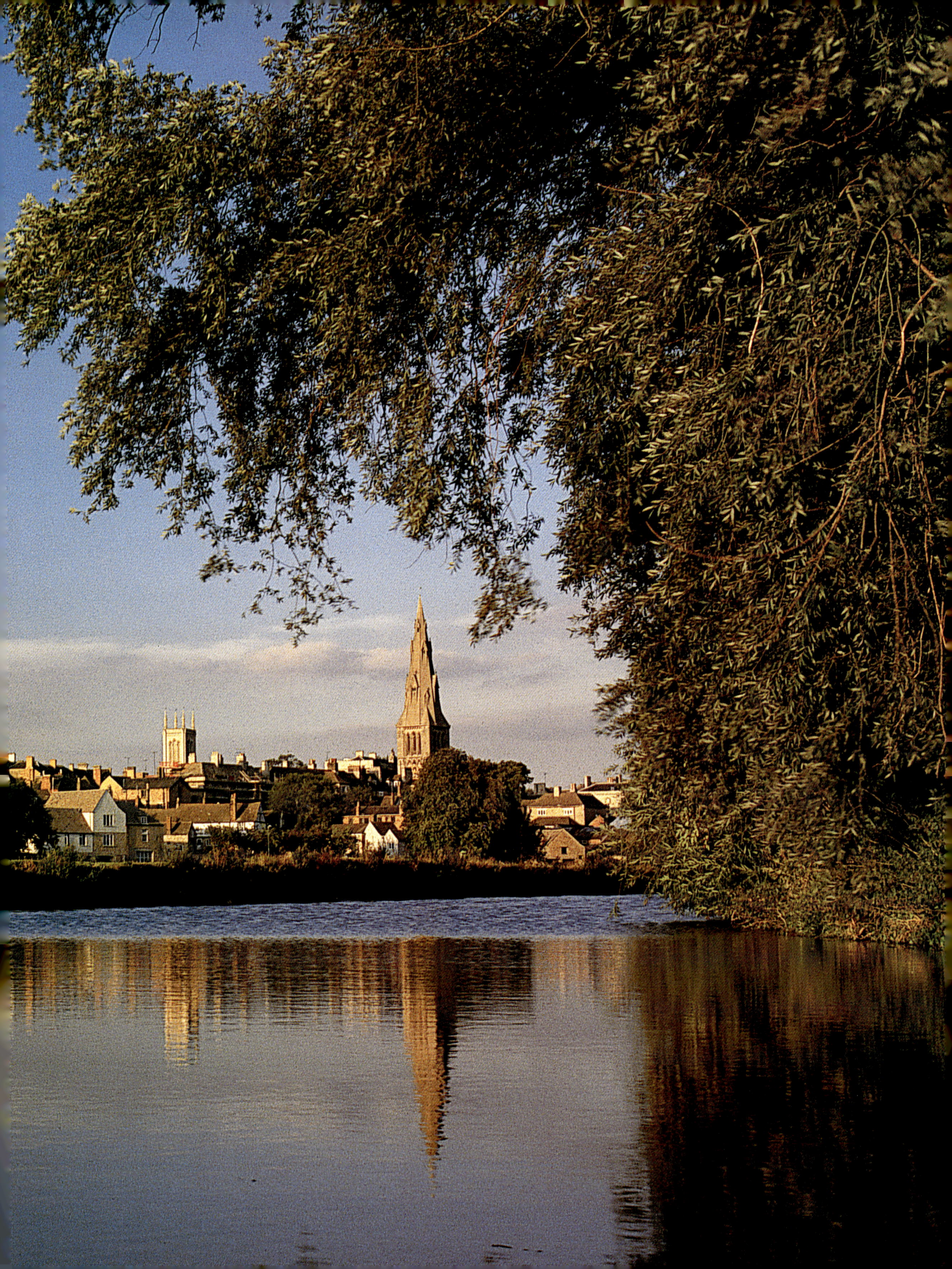

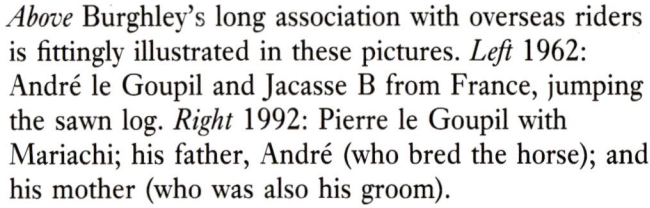

Above Burghley's long association with overseas riders is fittingly illustrated in these pictures. *Left* 1962: André le Goupil and Jacasse B from France, jumping the sawn log. *Right* 1992: Pierre le Goupil with Mariachi; his father, André (who bred the horse); and his mother (who was also his groom).

Below The Russians, winners of the European Team Championship in 1962, out cubhunting with the Cottesmore. *Opposite page* (Above) Indispensable volunteers: from St John Ambulance Brigade and a local Hunt. (Below) Scoreboards: 1966 and 1992.

1977 she remembers catching forty-three mice in the office. 'The posh new palace' was erected on the site of the original hut, and this is where Liz Inman and her team work today. During the week of the event they move to the elegant white-painted pavilion in its familiar spot by the scoreboard.

After fifteen years, during which he set the high standards for which Burghley is still renowned, Brigadier Grose retired. He was succeeded as Director by Major Andrew Burnaby-Atkins who, due to ill health, was only able to remain in office for two years. Charles Stratton, who had been closely associated with Burghley since its inception, then took over until Bill Henson became Director in 1987.

Without financial backing it would be impossible to contemplate running a major three-day event, and this was provided first by Bass then by Raleigh. For the past ten years the sponsors have been Remy Martin who in 1991 confirmed their support by renewing their contract for another four years.

As an autumn event, Burghley was able to establish itself from the beginning as a venue for international competitions. The European Championships were held here in 1962 and the first World Championships in 1966. Since then it has been host to the 1974 World Championships and five European as well as a European Junior and European Young Rider Championships.

In thirty years, what was once a 'local get-together' has become a world-famous sporting fixture. Statistics show that in 1962 during the European Championships 1775 cars were recorded over the three days. Averaging four people per car this would add up to around 8000 spectators. In 1992 nearly 160,000 people attended during the four days – 60,000 of them on cross-country day. (For the first five years the event was held on Wednesday, Thursday and Friday; in 1966 for the World Championships it was moved to Thursday, Friday and Saturday; then the increasing number of entries meant that two days had to be allowed for dressage, and Sunday was added.)

Attracting, controlling, accommodating and entertaining such large crowds over a four-day period is a complex undertaking which now occupies, year-round, a full-time office staff of three, the Director, and the course builders.

Where once a handful of volunteers sufficed, some 800 to 1000 are now called on. Among them are the local Round Table, who provide 200 members to man the cross-country crossing points; and the Lions Club some 30 members to write up the scoreboards in the sponsors' and press marquees and to act as check-point stewards on the roads and tracks. The Scouts organise the parking for disabled drivers; the Pony Club provide some 30 mounted runners to carry score sheets from the fence judges to the scorers; soldiers of the King's Troop RHA are in charge of the stables; mounted policemen of the Nottinghamshire Constabulary and staff from the Cottesmore, Fitzwilliam and the other local packs help with crowd-control, and RAF Cottesmore provide radio operators, for the cross-country; the Red Cross and St John Ambulance Brigade provide advice, comfort and reassurance, as well as medical services. To this list must be added well over 100 officials, from arena stewards to veterinary officers.

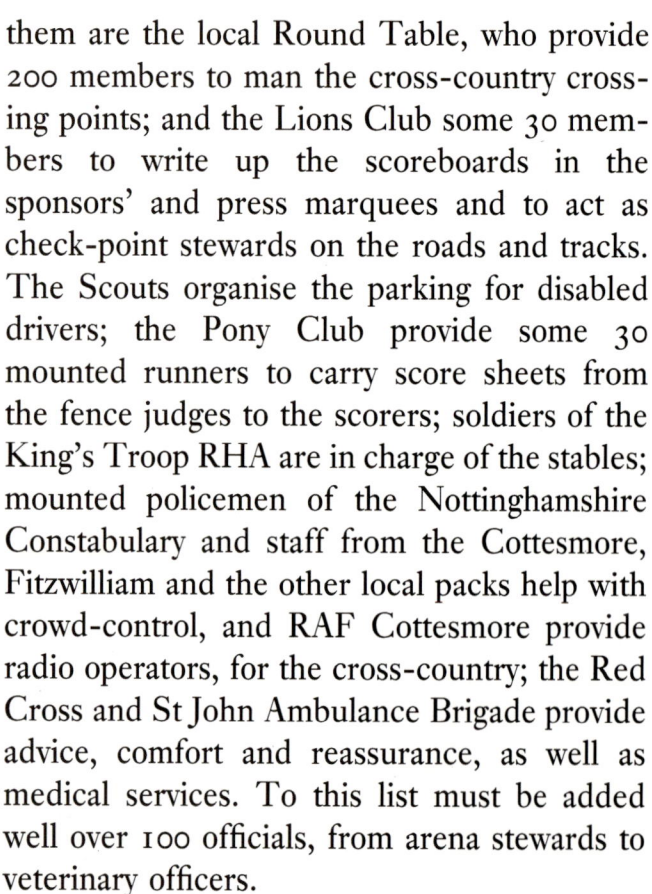

At the centre of local participation is the delightful town of Stamford, which lies on the ancient crossing of the River Welland, and has been a stopping-place for travellers on the Great North Road for over 900 years. Registered in 1967 as Britain's first Conservation Area, it has managed to escape the ravages of urban planning and is one of the few unspoiled towns left in England. In mediaeval times it was a prosperous wool market and an important centre of religious learning – hence its five churches: St Martin's, St Mary's, St Michael's, St George's and All Saints. In 1697 Celia Fiennes wrote: 'It is as fine a built town all of stone as may be seen.' Remarkably, her words are still applicable, for many of the handsome 16th and 17th Century buildings remain.

For event-goers probably the best-known building is the George Hotel, which dates back to the late 16th Century, when it served three dozen or so coaches a day on their way between London and York. In the old days it offered attractions such as cock-fighting, and during Stamford races a variety of sideshows. Foremost among these was Daniel Lambert, a man of colossal girth after whom one of the recurring Burghley fences is named.

The main road (A1) now bypasses the town but provides easy access to the horse trials: an advantage which could soon evaporate if it were not for careful planning by Michael Scott,

24

Opposite 'The Media': *left* in 1964 and *right* in 1991. *Above* Horse trials guests dining at The George.

Below (left) Portrait of Daniel Lambert, and his gravestone in the churchyard of St Martin's. *Right* The 1991 winner of the annual Stamford window-dressing competition sponsored by Remy Martin.

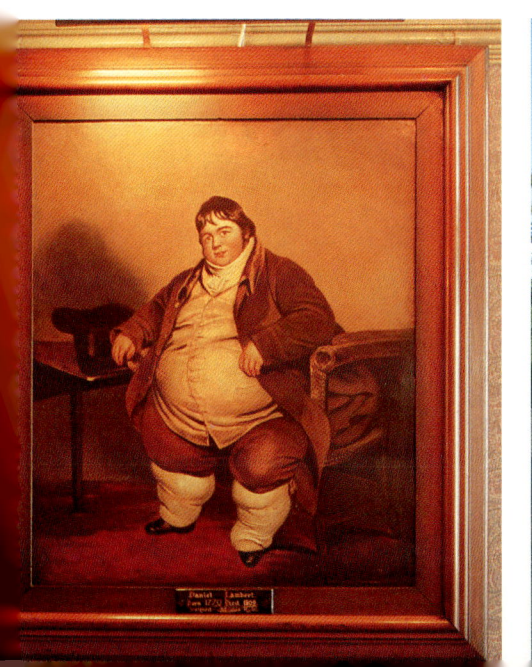

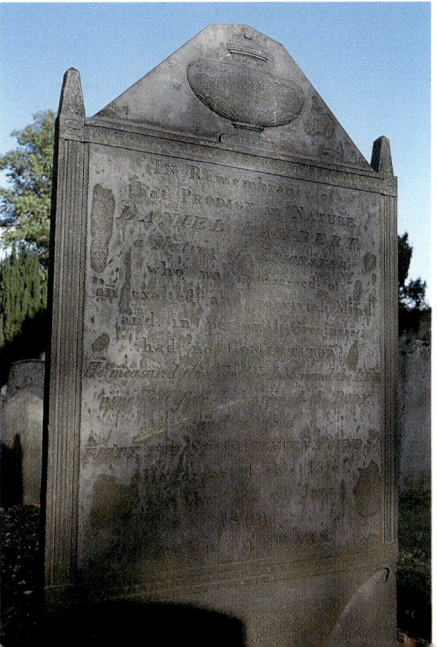

Left Traffic controller, waving his magic wand.
Above Mounted police of the Nottinghamshire Constabulary.

Opposite Spectators: 'then' (1962) and 'now' (1992).
Overleaf Burghley House in the afternoon sun.

Agent for the Burghley Estate, and the Director, in close consultation with the Peterborough police and the car parking company who are responsible for all the signposting. On cross-country day many thousands of cars have to be shepherded into place, and over the years the necessity of finding more and more space for them has resulted in the relocation of part of the cross-country course.

Like Badminton, Burghley is a 4-star competition (the FEI's highest level of three-day event), but the cross-country courses of each have always presented a different type of challenge, and the original course-designers – Bill Thomson at Burghley and Frank Weldon at Badminton – had notably different concepts, conditioned by factors such as the terrain and the time of year. For example, although Badminton's fences appear more imposing, the very undulating terrain of Burghley demanded a greater emphasis on balance and fitness. Nowadays, following changes of course-designers at both events – Mark Phillips at Burghley, Hugh Thomas at Badminton – the courses have changed in character: though in keeping with Bill Thomson's ideals, Burghley is still more encouraging for the less experienced horse.

Over the past five years, a gradual programme of improvement has resulted in the cross-country terrain becoming much easier on the horses. Ditches and furrows between the fields and in and out of the woods have been filled in, and small banks and unlevel areas that crossed the course have been removed. The ridge and furrow which was so much a feature of the Burghley course – and which was tiring and unbalancing for the horses – has been levelled, with the turf lifted off and replaced afterwards. The steeplechase course was levelled in the mid 1980s.

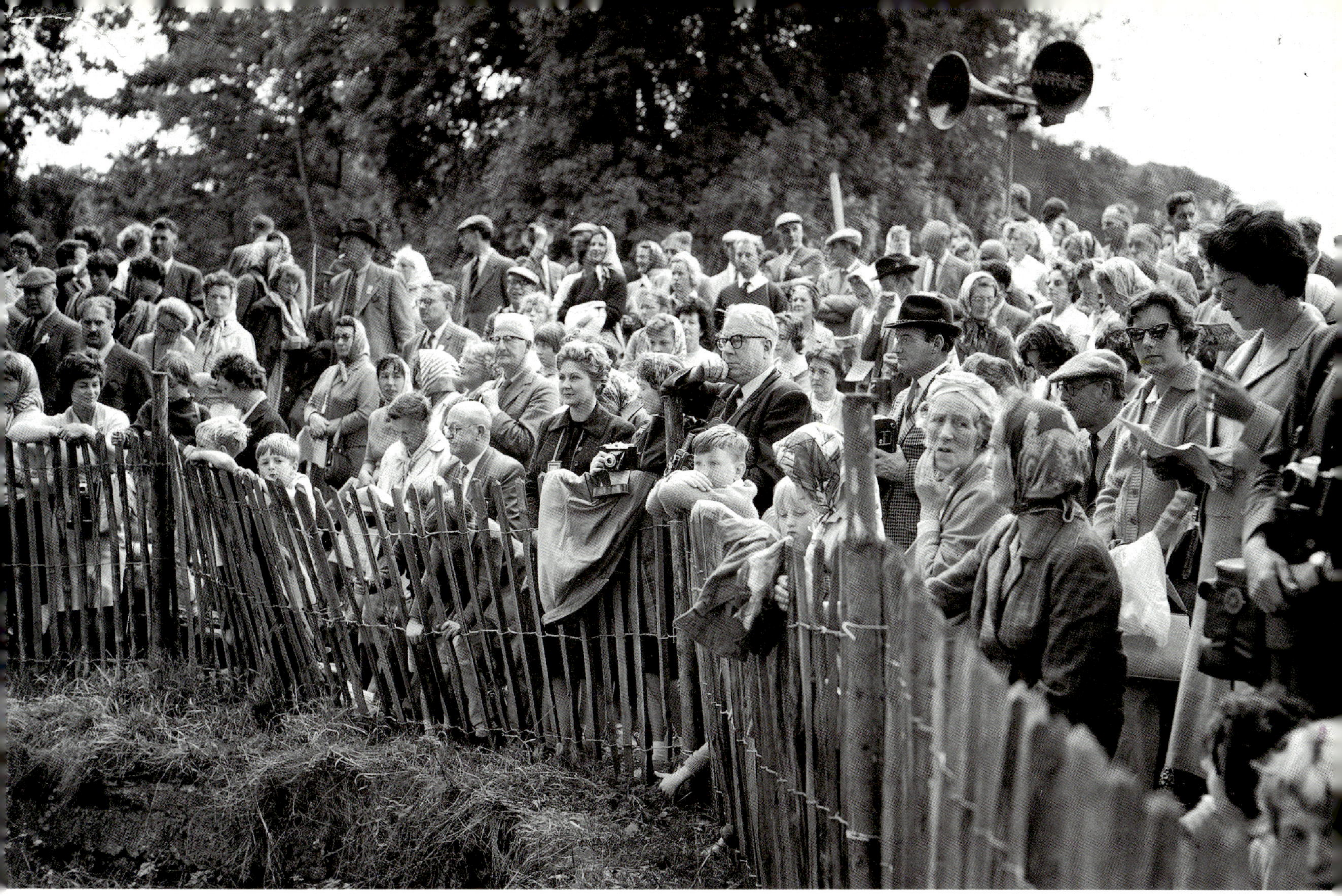

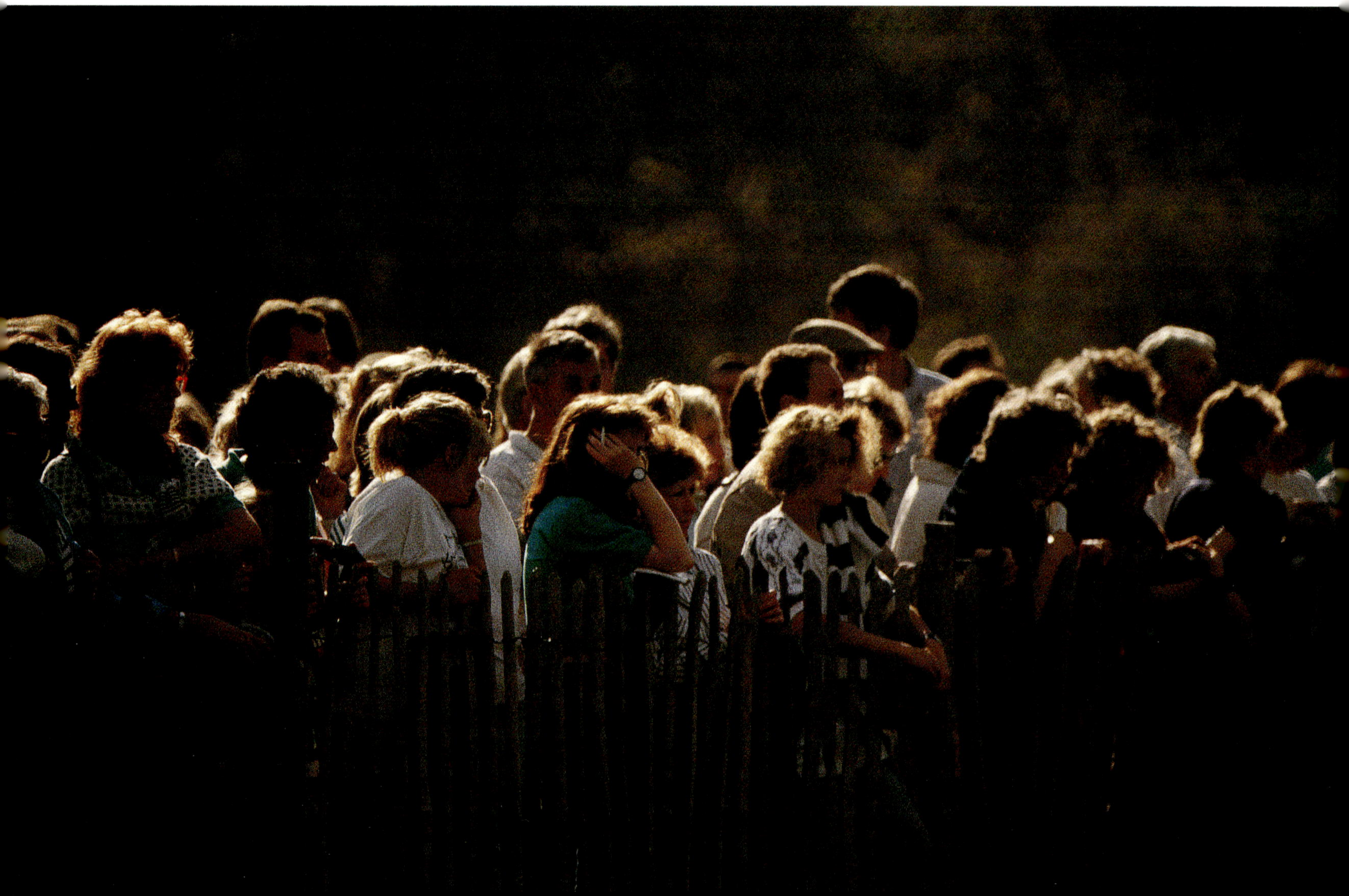

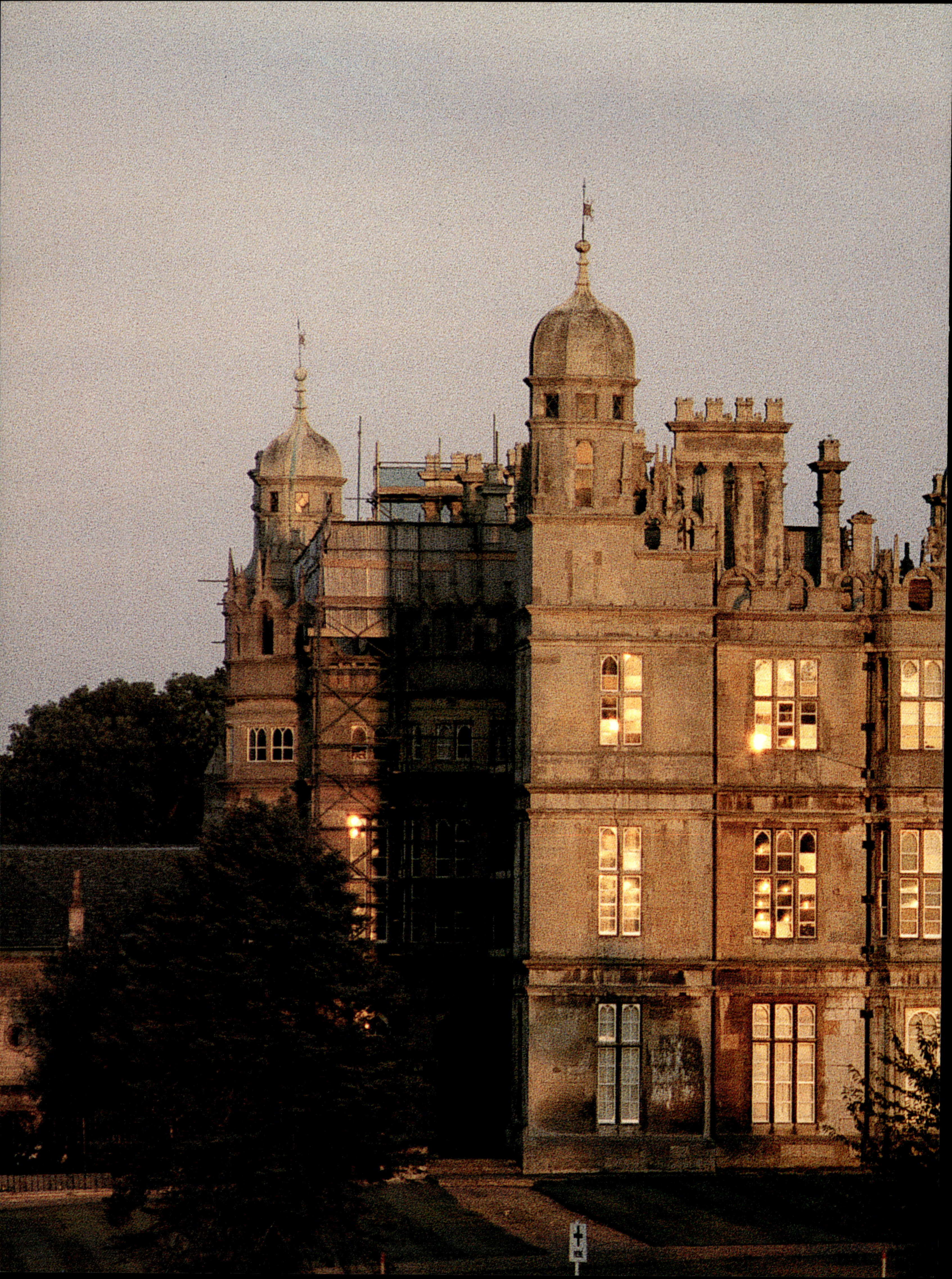

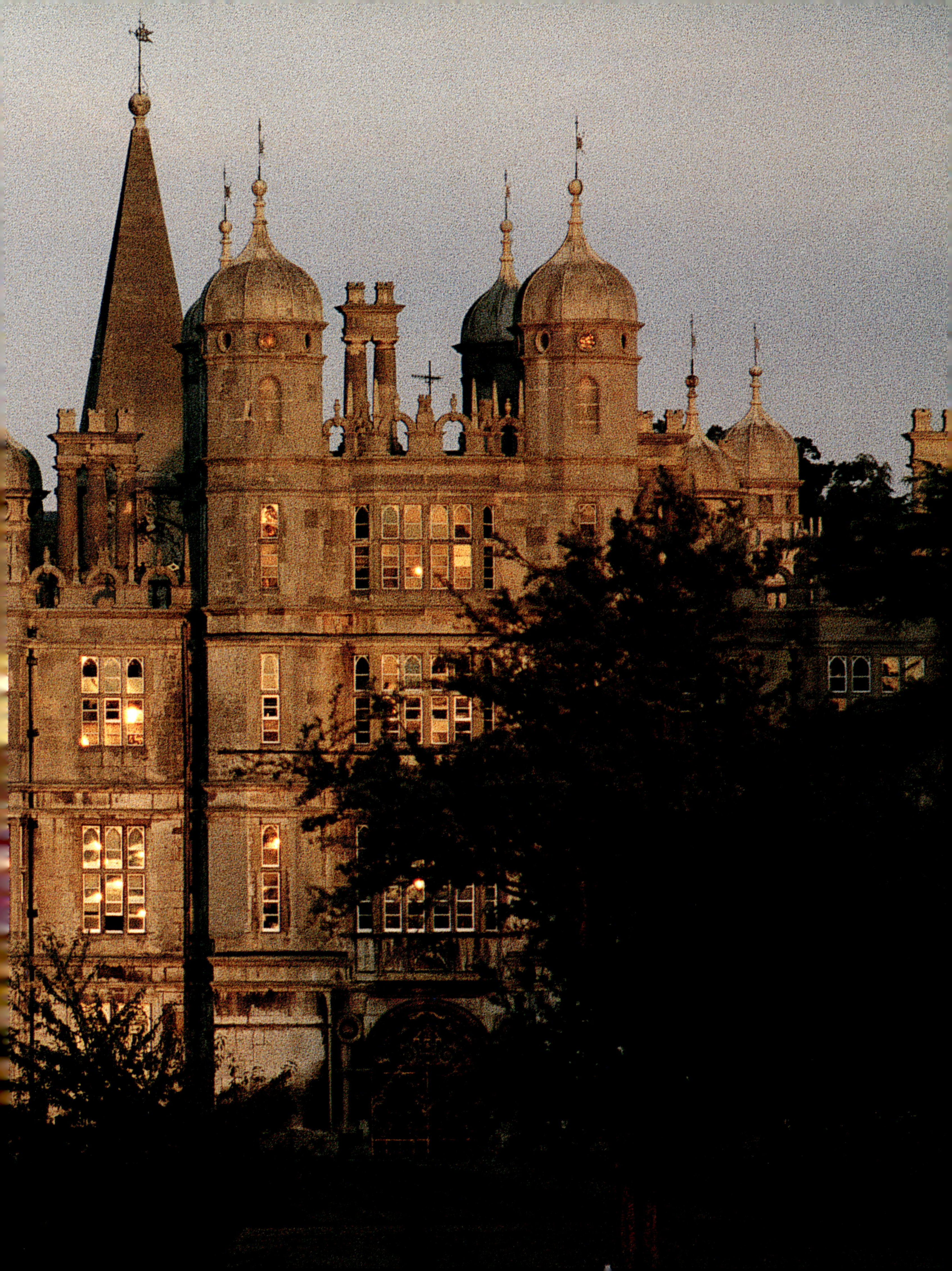

Preparations

(Left) Work on building the stands begins in July.
Below Mowing the centre line in the dressage arena.

Left Laying silt on the cross-country course.

Right 17,000 metres of string are used for cordoning off the cross-country course.
Below Course-builder preparing a cross-country fence.

Right The florists provide flowers for the official marquees, arena and stands, as well as the cross-country fences.

Long-serving helpers: *left* Noel Pegge, who has been Weighing Steward from the beginning. *Above* John Stevens, who for some thirty years graced the public address system as commentator.

Opposite page Lol Weaver (left) and Dennis Colton, who have presided over many an arena since the early 1960s.

For the past twelve years the course-building has been under the supervision of Philip Herbert, the Clerk of the Course, who describes himself as 'chief gaffer', working closely with Mark Phillips and a hand-picked team of craftsmen.

The design, construction and maintenance of a major three-day event course is never-ending, and as soon as one year's event is over, preparation begins for the next. Temporary obstacles, such as the Arena Fence, Remy Cognac Casks and Dog Kennel, are removed, as are fences which the designer has discarded from his plan for the following year. This gives the ground and the grass in various areas time to recover. During the summer, the grass is constantly cut with a gang-mower to encourage thick growth.

Burghley's light-reddish soil is over limestone, so it is free-draining. To combat hard going, hundreds of tons of silt are laid over the whole course in a 6-foot-wide track. Afterwards, the silt is spread out over the surrounding area. In unduly dry weather, the course is irrigated with water from the lake.

On cross-country day, ten men with 4-wheel drive vehicles, three tractors, and two fork-lifts are dispersed around the course to carry out any necessary fence repairs. They are equipped with spare materials for every obstacle on the course. Though it is rare for a fence to be broken, when repairs are needed the relevant team has to act with great speed. Philip Herbert points out that in the early days a top rail could be picked up by one man and carried on his shoulder, and post holes were dug with a spade. Nowadays, the timber is three times the size, and two men couldn't begin to pick up a top rail, so all handling and digging are mechanised and posts are hammered into the ground by a tractor-driven post-driver.

During the past decade, cross-country fences have become much more complex, offering more alternatives, which means a lot more work for the builders. Formerly, fence materials were obtained from the estate, but timber of the required present-day proportions is no longer available and has to be brought in from outside.

Fences which appear consistently, in one form or another, and of which the names are familiar to Burghley devotees, all have interesting origins. As already mentioned, *Capability's Cutting* is one of Lancelot Brown's avenues leading to the South Gate; the *Trout Hatcheries*, created by the 3rd Marquess in the 19th Century, were in use until shortly before the horse trials were inaugurated in 1961; the Maltings was originally an oast house; *Chabonel Spinney* was named after a butler interested in trees; the *Dairy Farm* once housed a herd of dairy cows; *Waterloo Plain* commemorates Wellington's great victory over the French. (Most large estates had woods named 'Waterloo' or 'Trafalgar'; in Lincolnshire and Derbyshire it was traditional to have a 'Waterloo' wood, and the cluster of trees by Waterloo Plain is known as 'Waterloo Spinney.') The *Leaf Pit* was the site of the 18th-Century New Inn, which was excavated and used for the dumping of leaves.

Spectators who know their way around Burghley Park may wonder why there is no fence into the lake, as at Badminton. Liz Inman has an explanation for this: 'Bill Thomson always wanted to build a fence where the causeway is now, west of the Lion Bridge. Lord Exeter was against it because he thought that it might encourage spectators to stand on the bridge to watch, thus causing traffic hold-ups. Also, as the lake doesn't have a naturally solid bottom it would have been a very expensive project. Philip Herbert once had the idea of making a crossing to an island – but it would have presented course-walking problems!'

All the land used during the event (some 500 acres) is agricultural: mostly rented by local farmers for grazing cattle and sheep. The deer park is divided into two by a fence, and two weeks before the event the deer are moved over to the half not being used for the horse trials. As the fence stretches right across the course it has to be removed before the event and replaced afterwards.

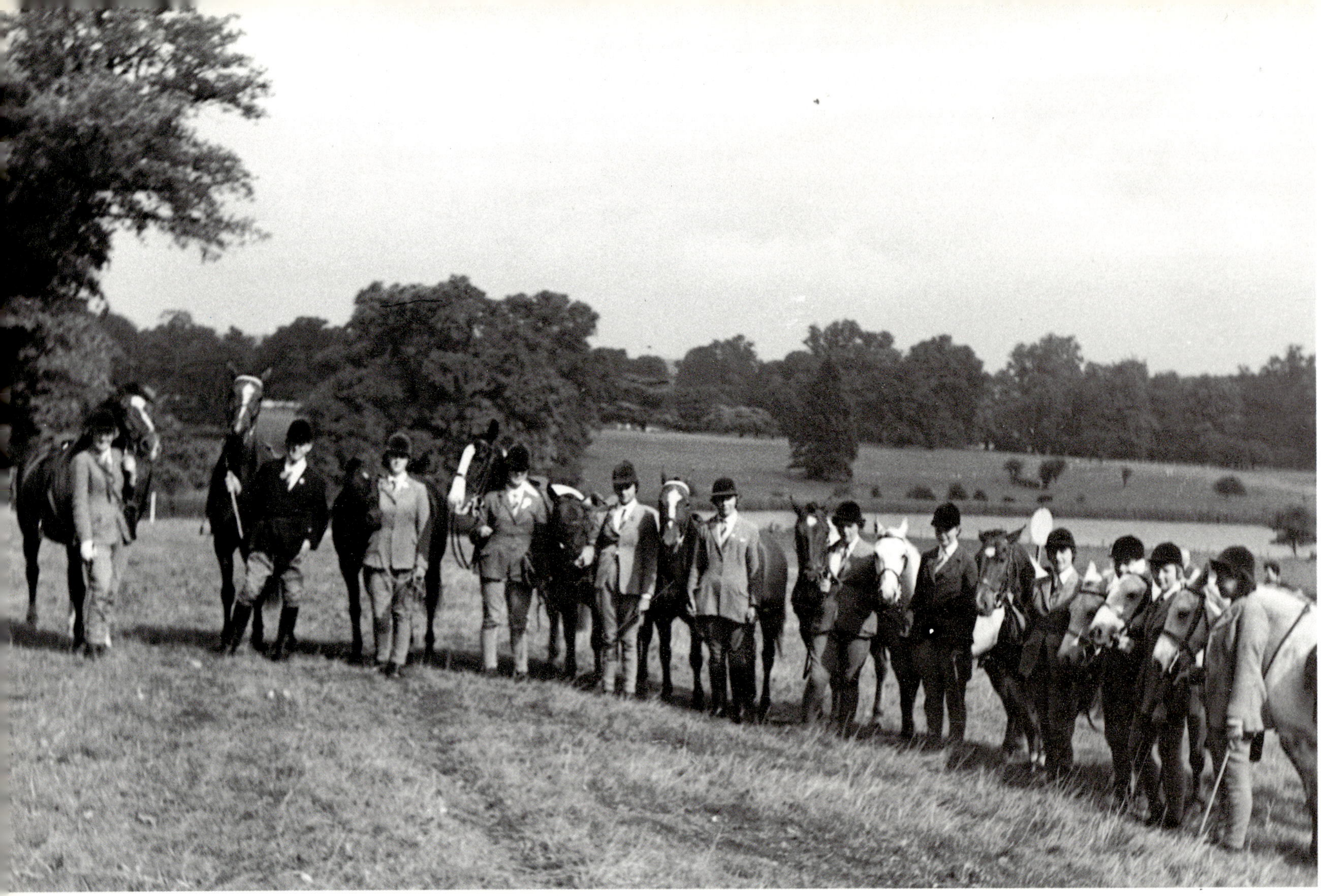

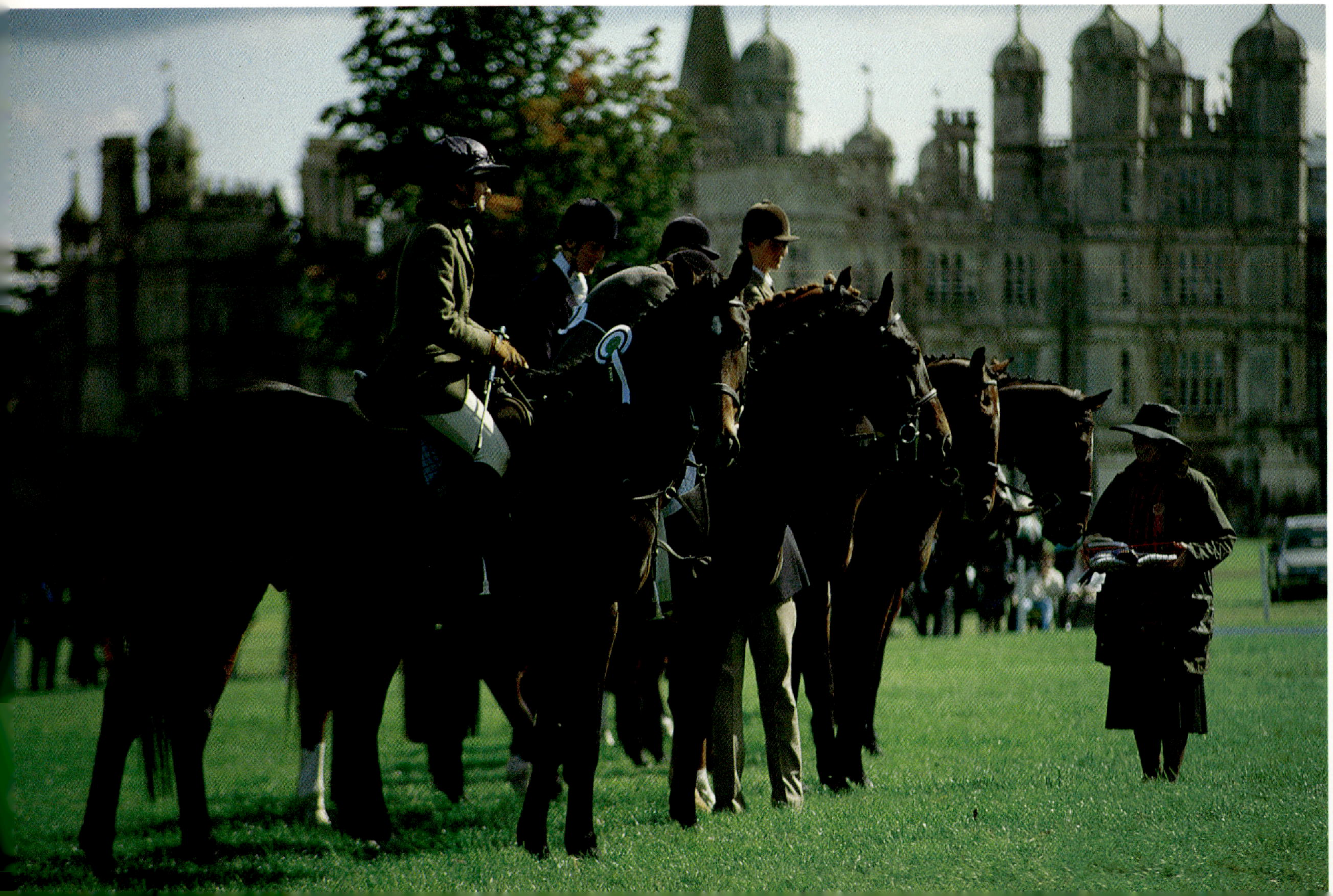

During horse trials week, other attractions are provided to entertain spectators – one of the most important being the Pony Club Team Jumping Competition which dates back to 1963 and in which some 35 to 40 teams take part. The Working Hunter class, which used to be a feature of Burghley, has been replaced by the Young Event Horse class. Inaugurated in 1987 and sponsored by Pet Plan, this important competition is aimed at producing future international three-day event winners.

Every year, different attractions are provided in the main arena – among them stallion, heavy horse and native pony parades, dressage displays, the Hermès Concours d'Elégance, and military bands.

Increasingly popular are the trade stands, which have been an essential part of the scene since the first event. Representatives of names listed in the 1961 programme – Devon Clothing, Garrard, F. R. Gray (China), Herbert Johnson, Midland Bank, G. C. Smith Coachworks and Sturgess Land-Rover – were to be found in 1992, enjoying their traditional champagne breakfast in the members' marquee on the Friday morning. For the past twelve years the number of trade stands (just over 200) has remained more or less the same.

Always mindful of maintaining spectators' interest, Bill Henson has introduced several

The Pony Club has been involved with Burghley since the very beginning: *opposite* (above) 1962 style, as mounted runners; and in the Team Jumping Competition (*top of this page*), showing the winners' line-up, 1992. *Opposite, left*. Prize-winners in the Burghley Young Event Horse of the Year competition, launched in 1987. *Above* The judges. *Right* The Burghley Cake, presented each year to the winner of the Three-Day Event. *Overleaf* View from the roof.

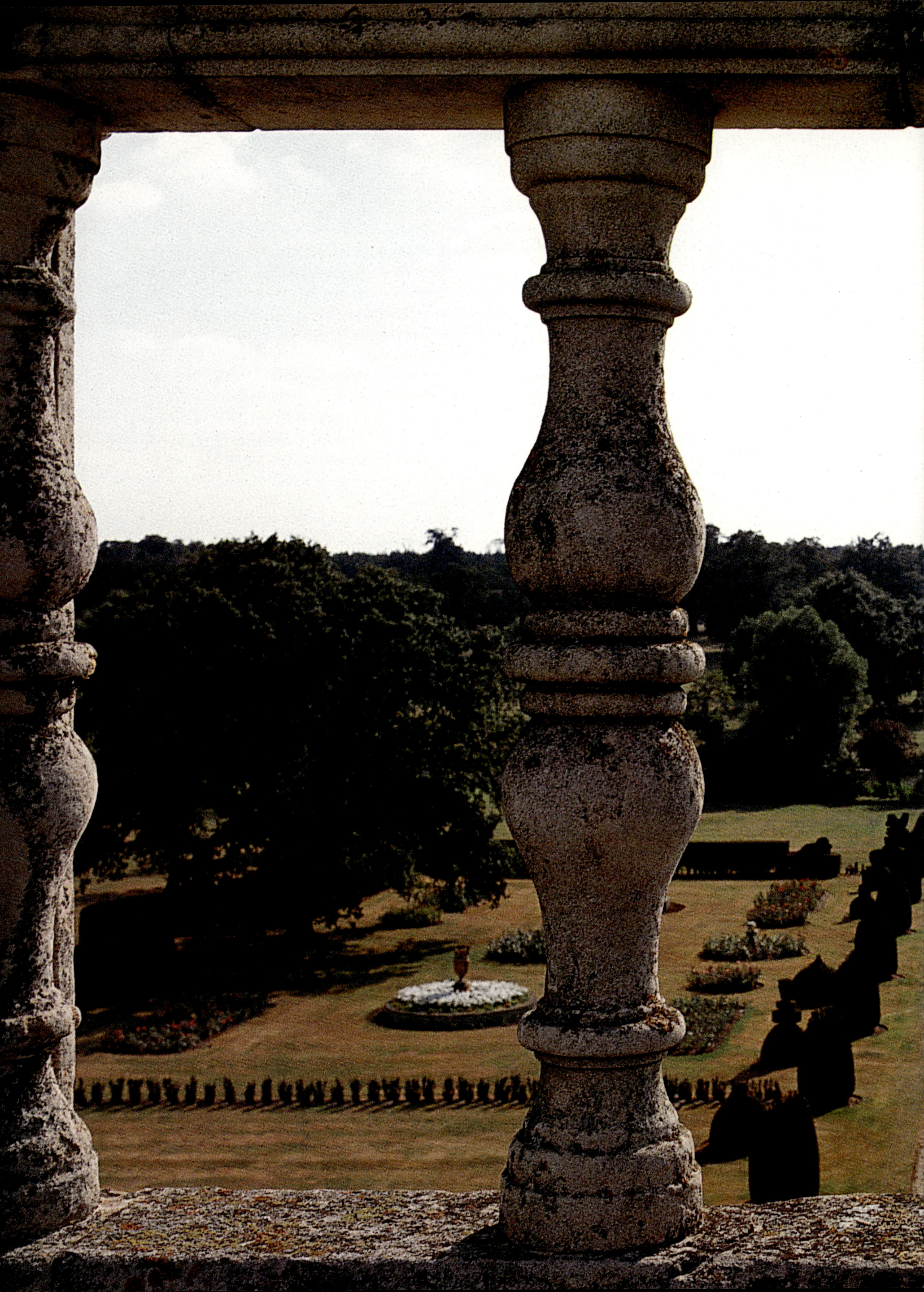

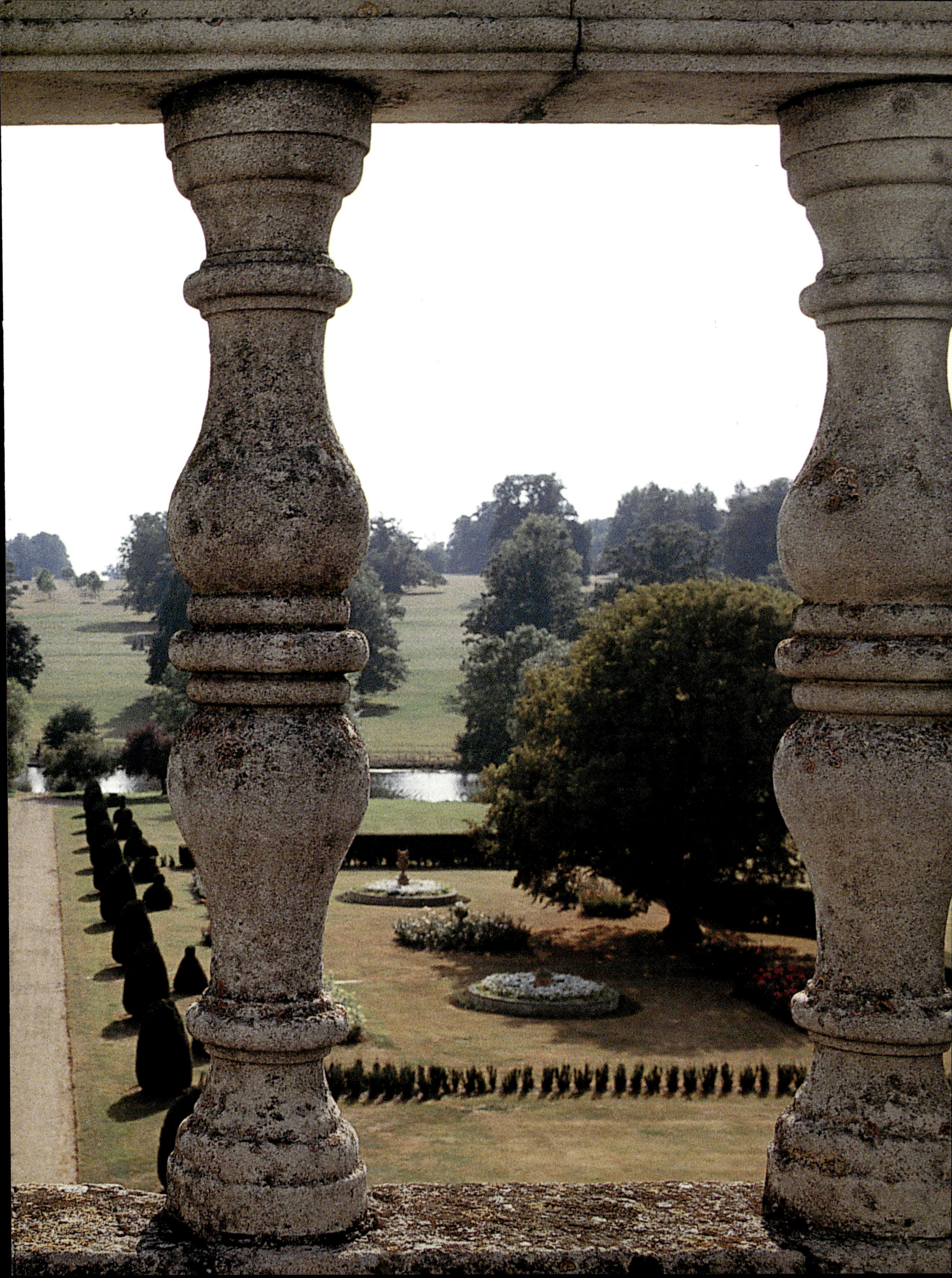

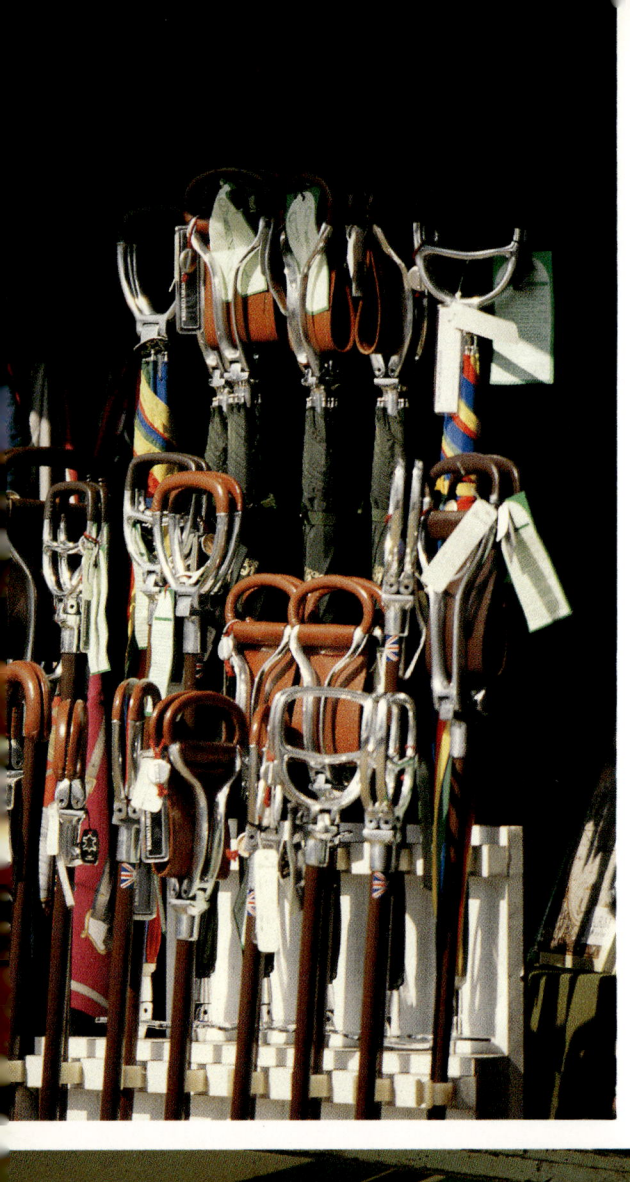

The tradestands offer a fascinating array of products. Among the most popular are the bulbs grown in nearby Spalding.

Opposite The silver wine-cooler, one of the treasures of Burghley House, which is used during the pre-trials cocktail party.

new ideas, such as head-set commentaries for dressage, show jumping and cross-country; the siting of a cross-country fence in the main arena; and the huge closed-circuit TV movie screen. Each year he provides a report summarising the event, and in November the committee meet to comment on it and to discuss new ideas. Though always ready to encourage suitable innovations, Lady Victoria, the committee, and the sponsors are anxious to maintain the traditions and high standards for which the event is internationally famous.

For all of us who are involved – competitors, officials, office staff, voluntary workers – and for many of the thousands of spectators who come here each year, Burghley has a special magic. As well as evoking much of that magic, the photographs on the following pages provide a day-by-day record of one of the world's greatest sporting events.

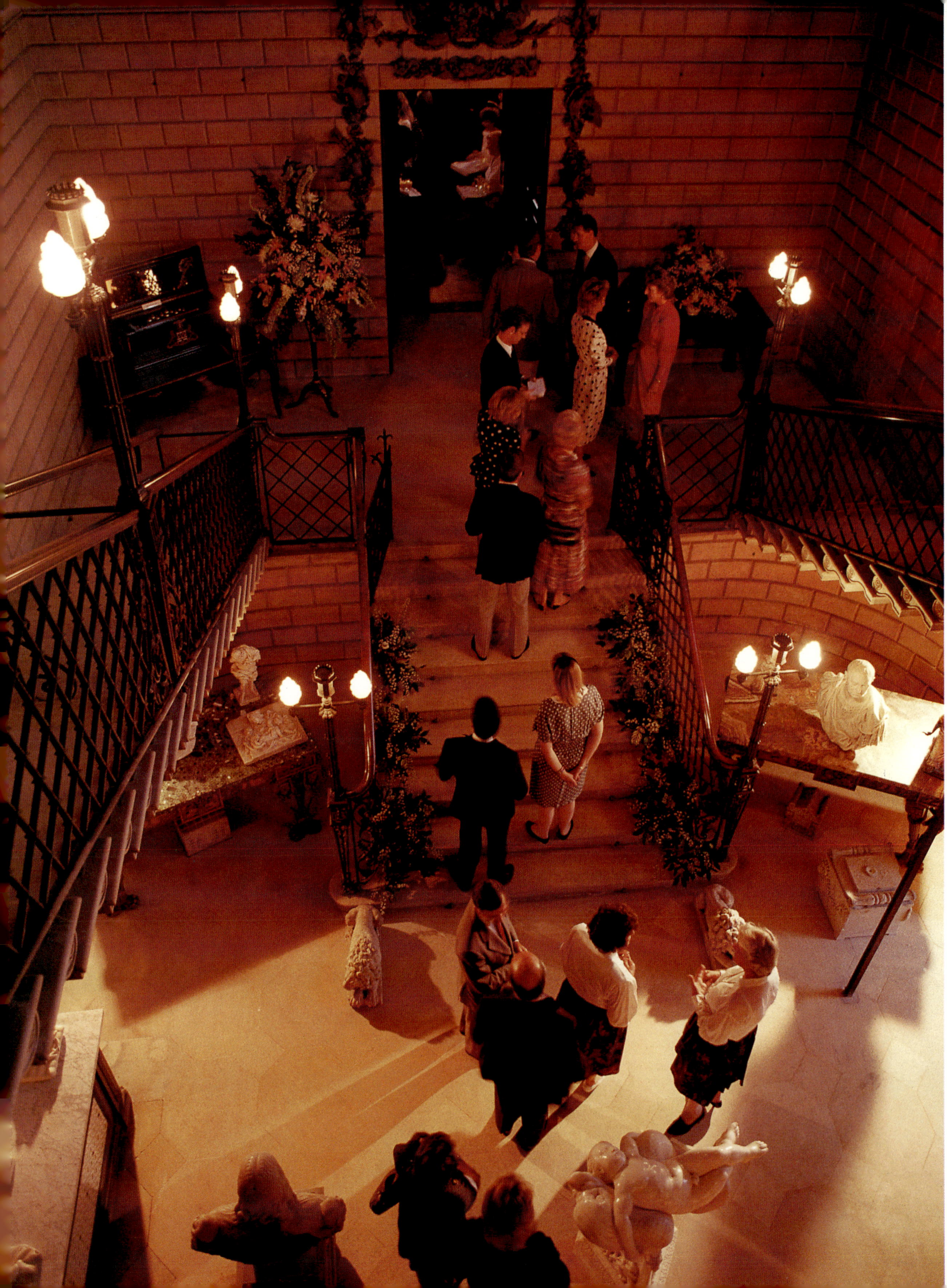

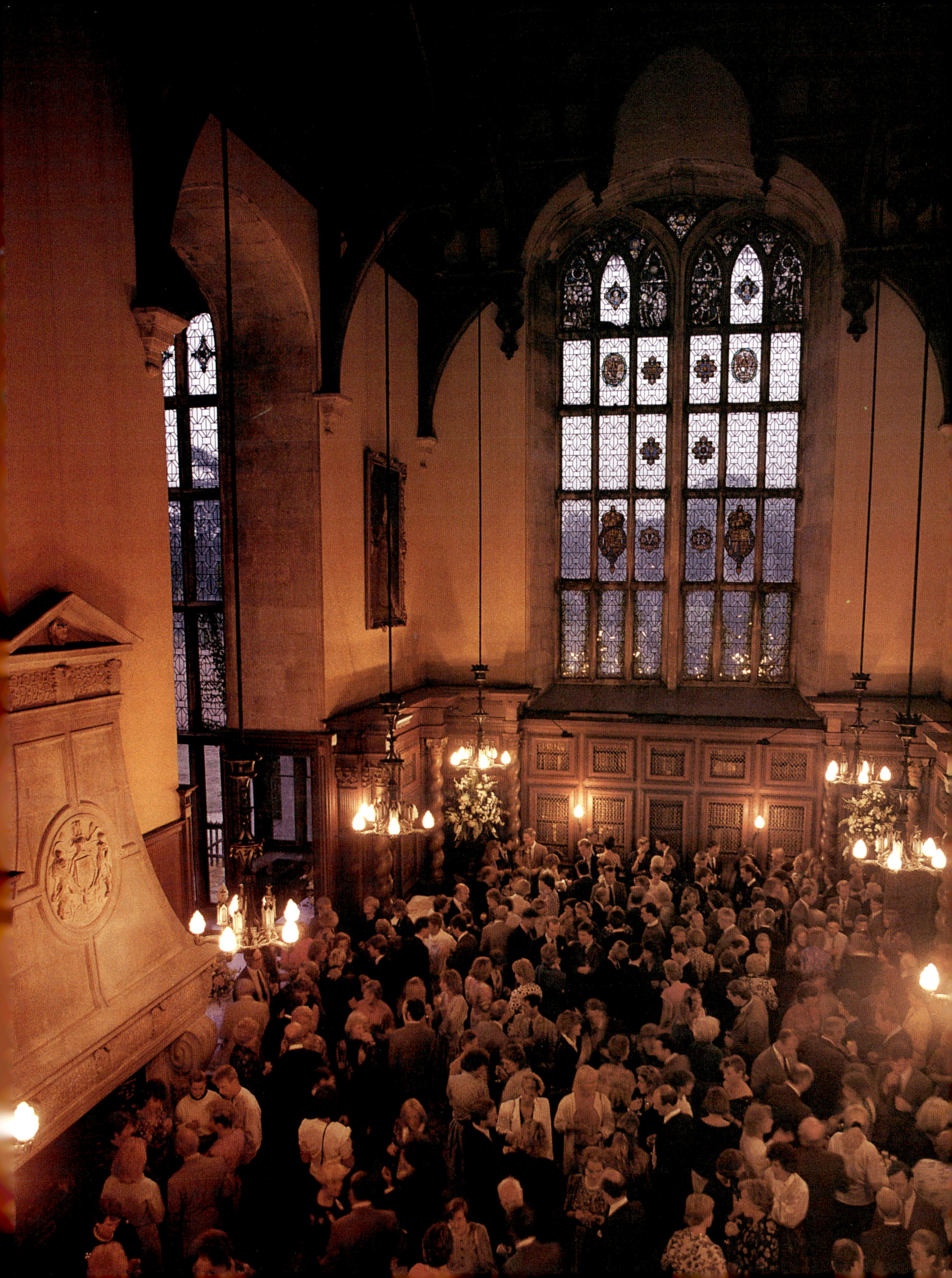

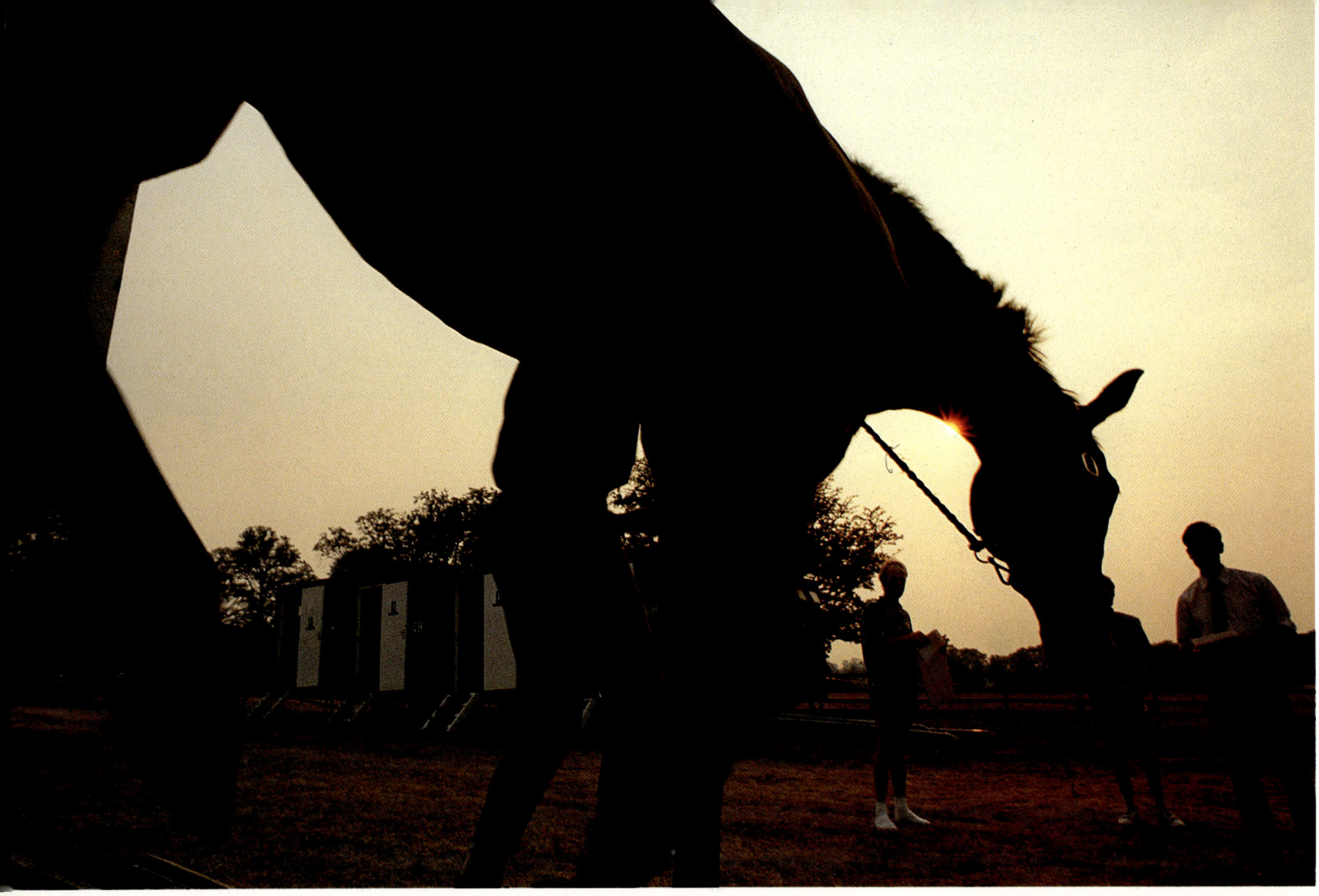

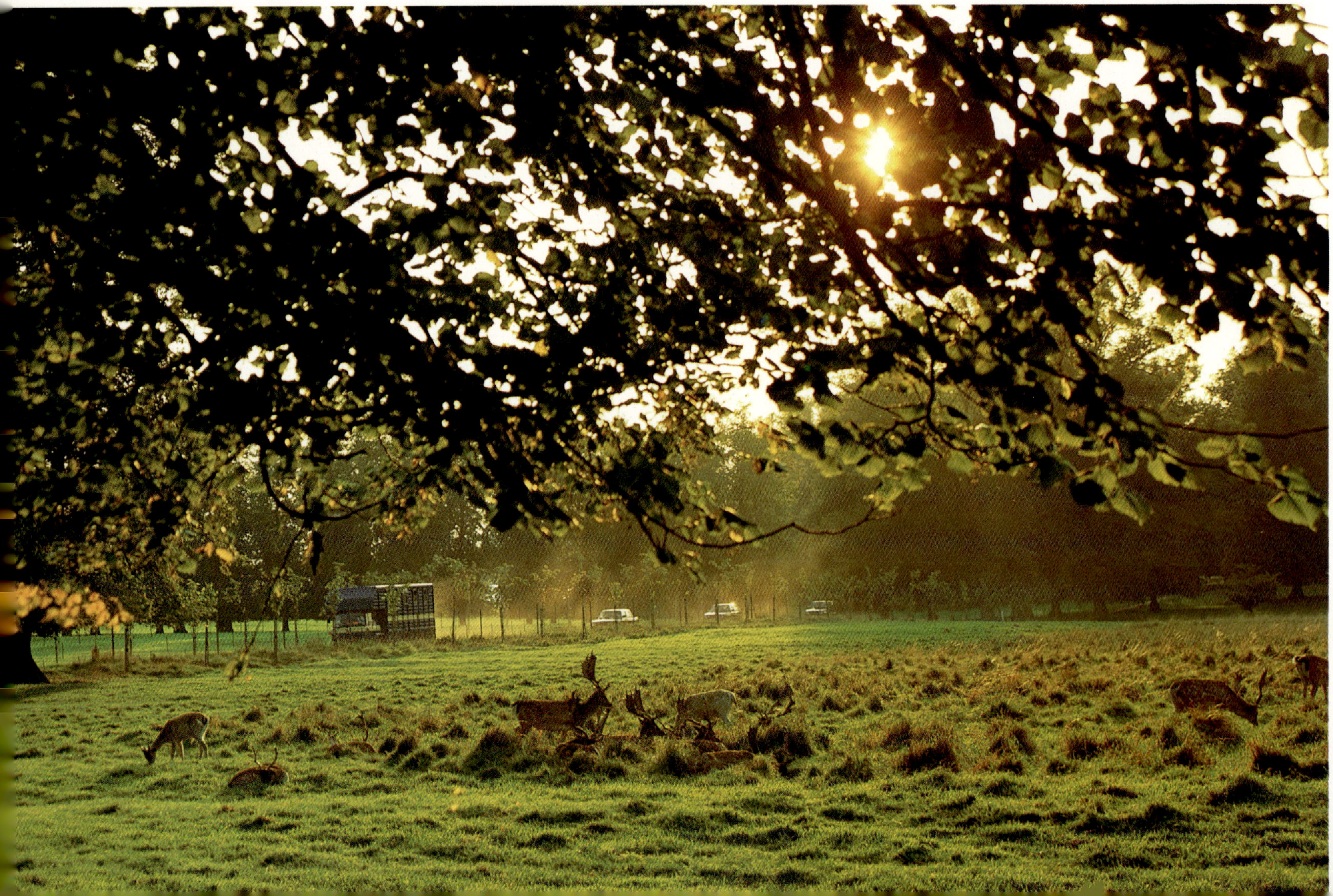

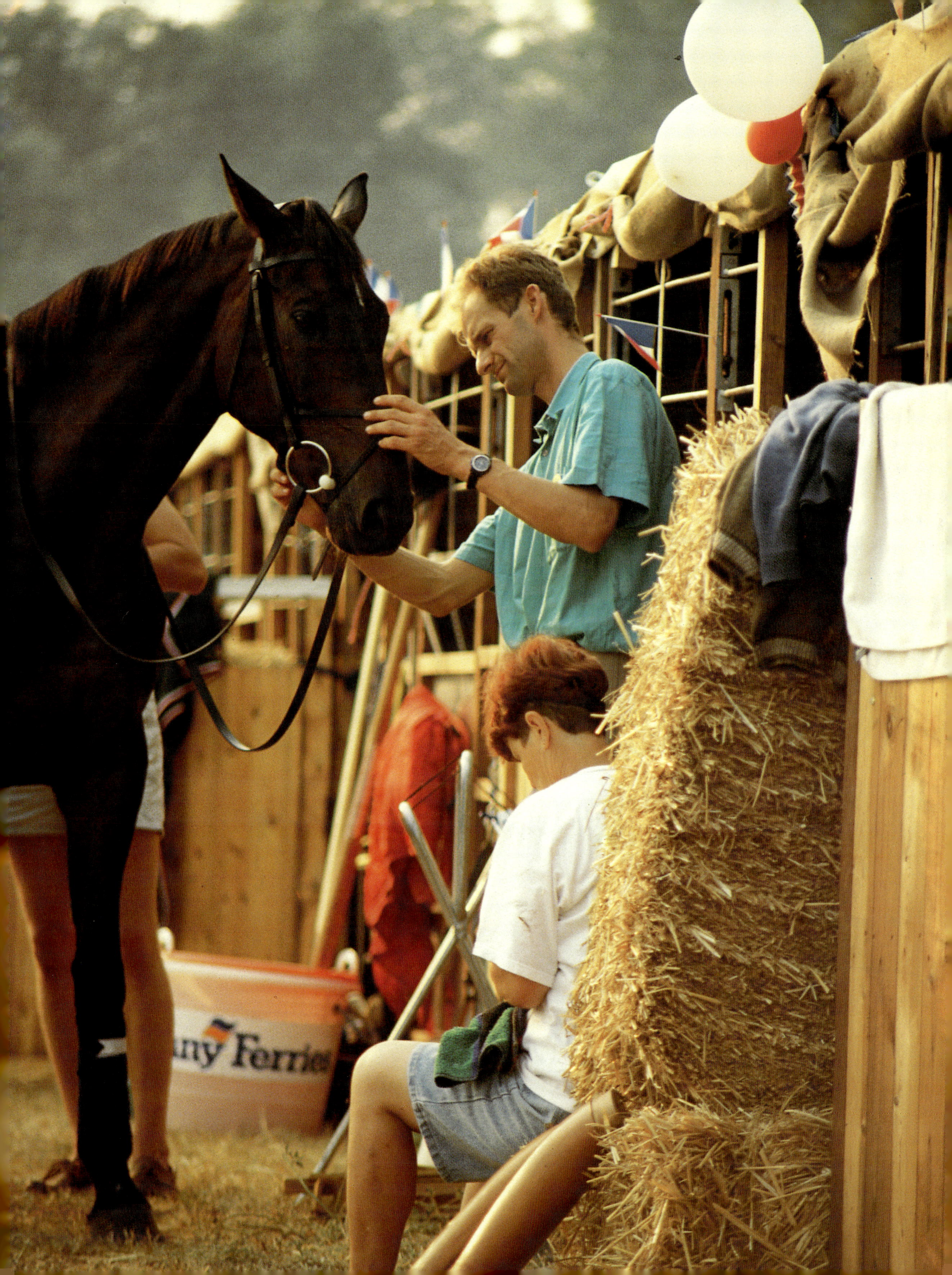
any Ferries

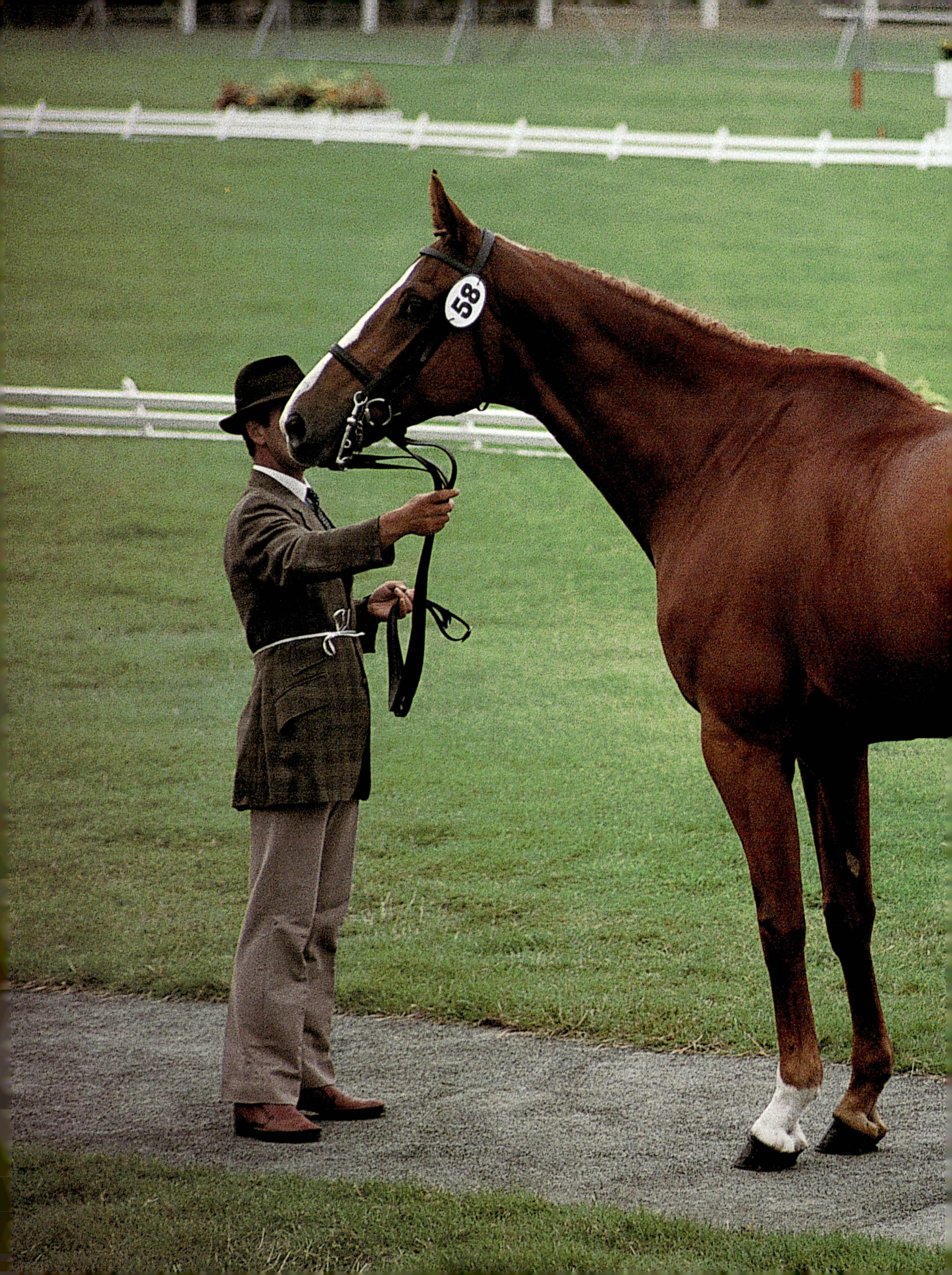
58

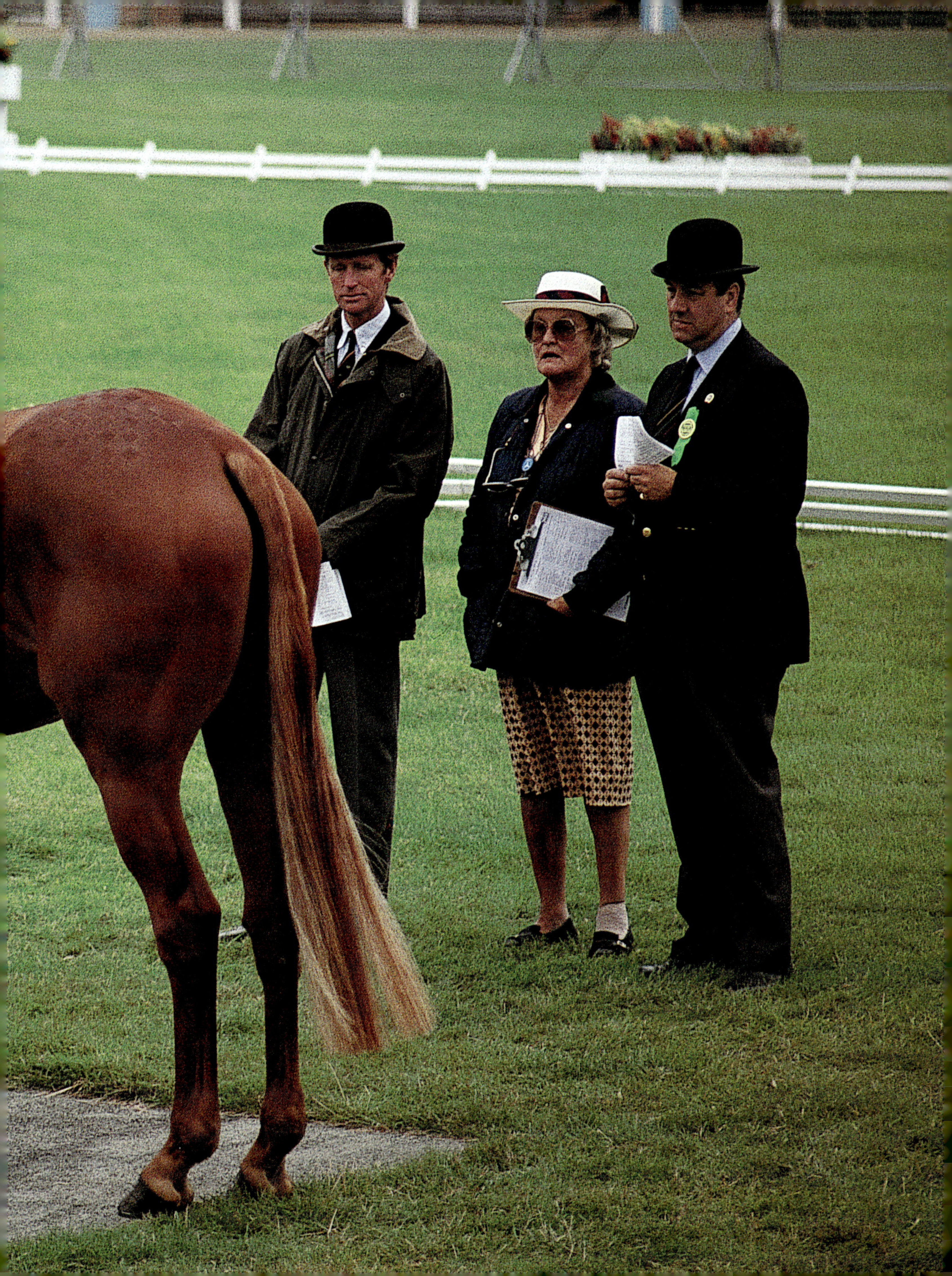

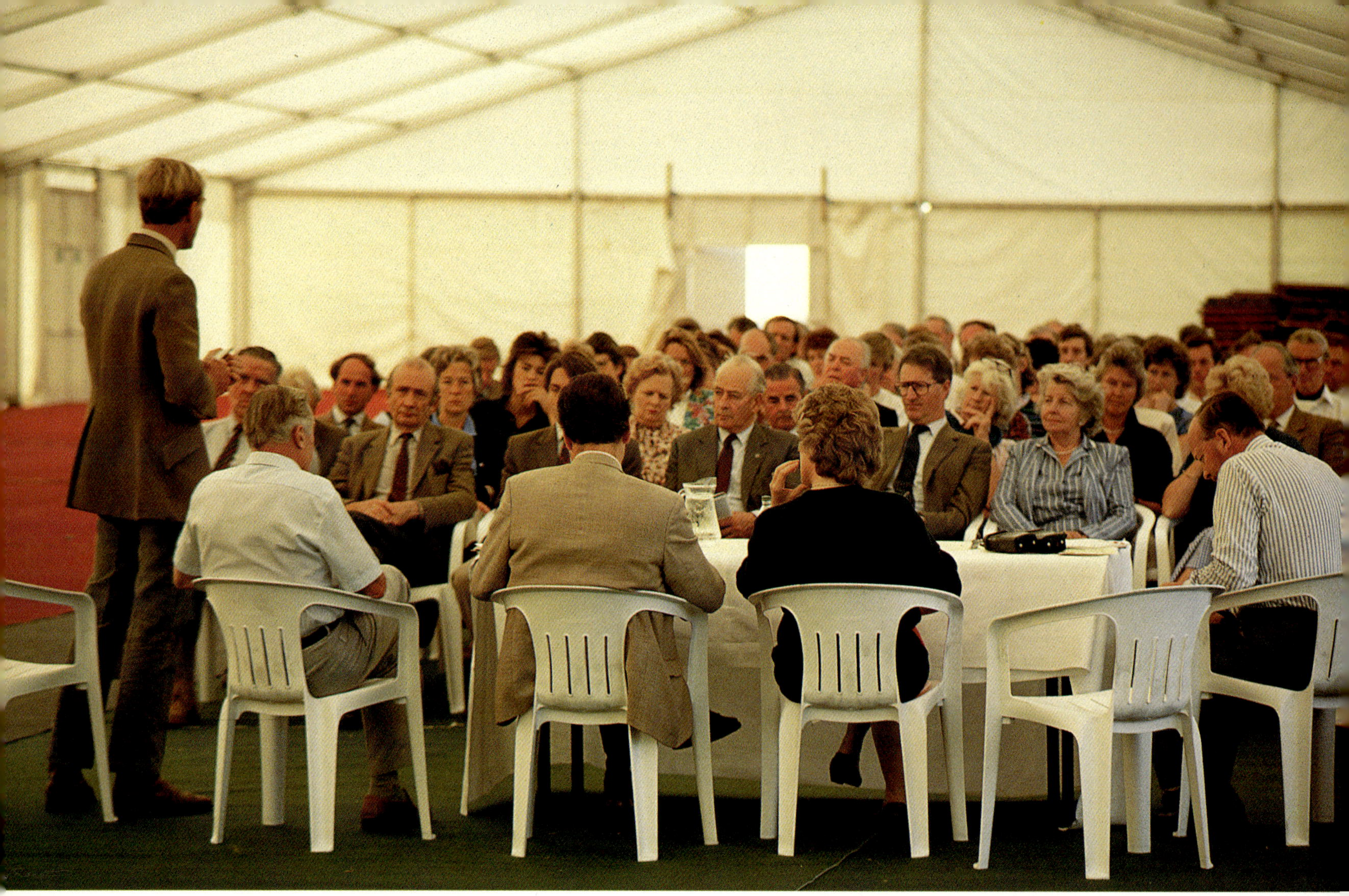

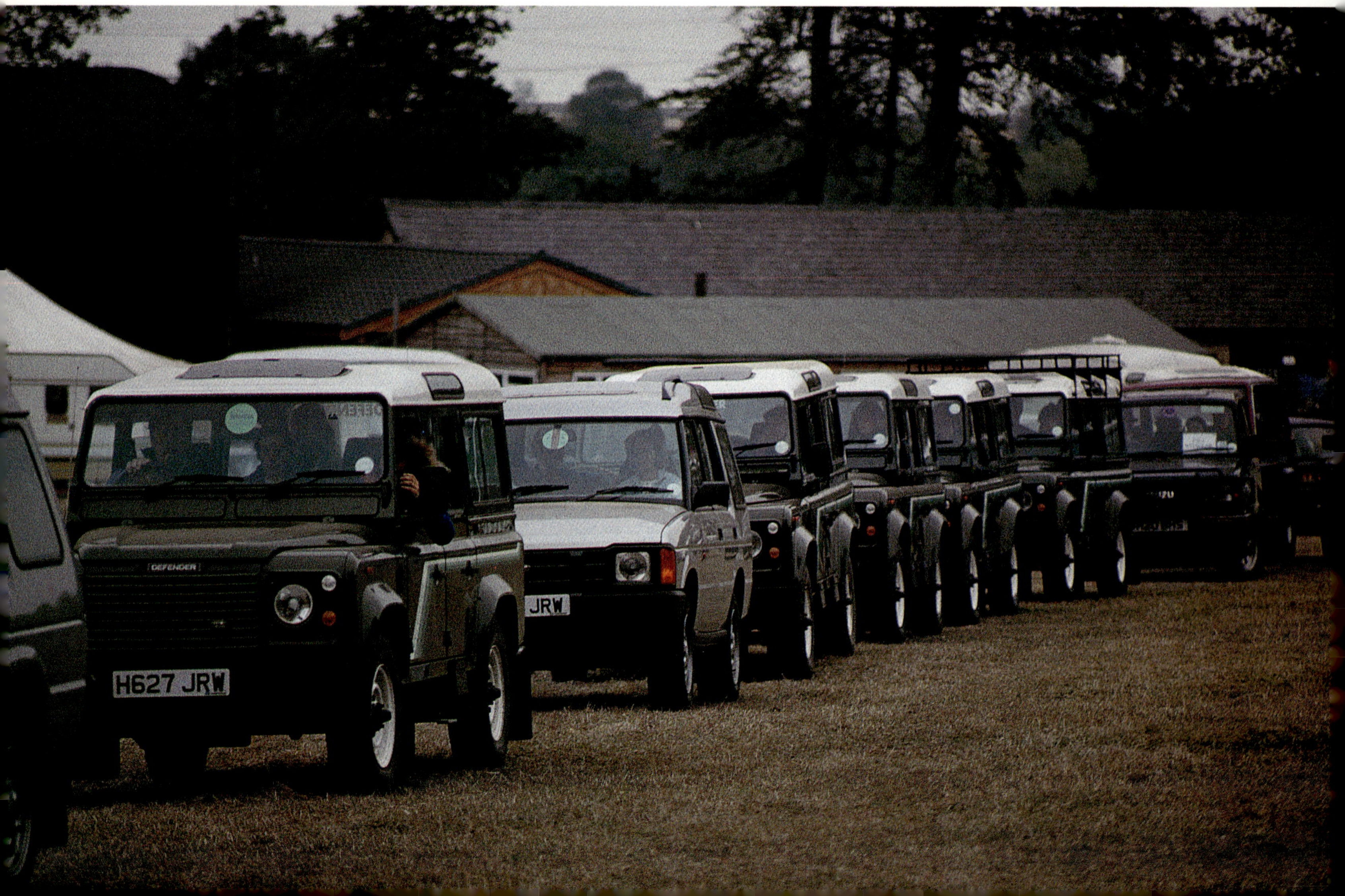
DEFENDER
H627 JRW
JRW

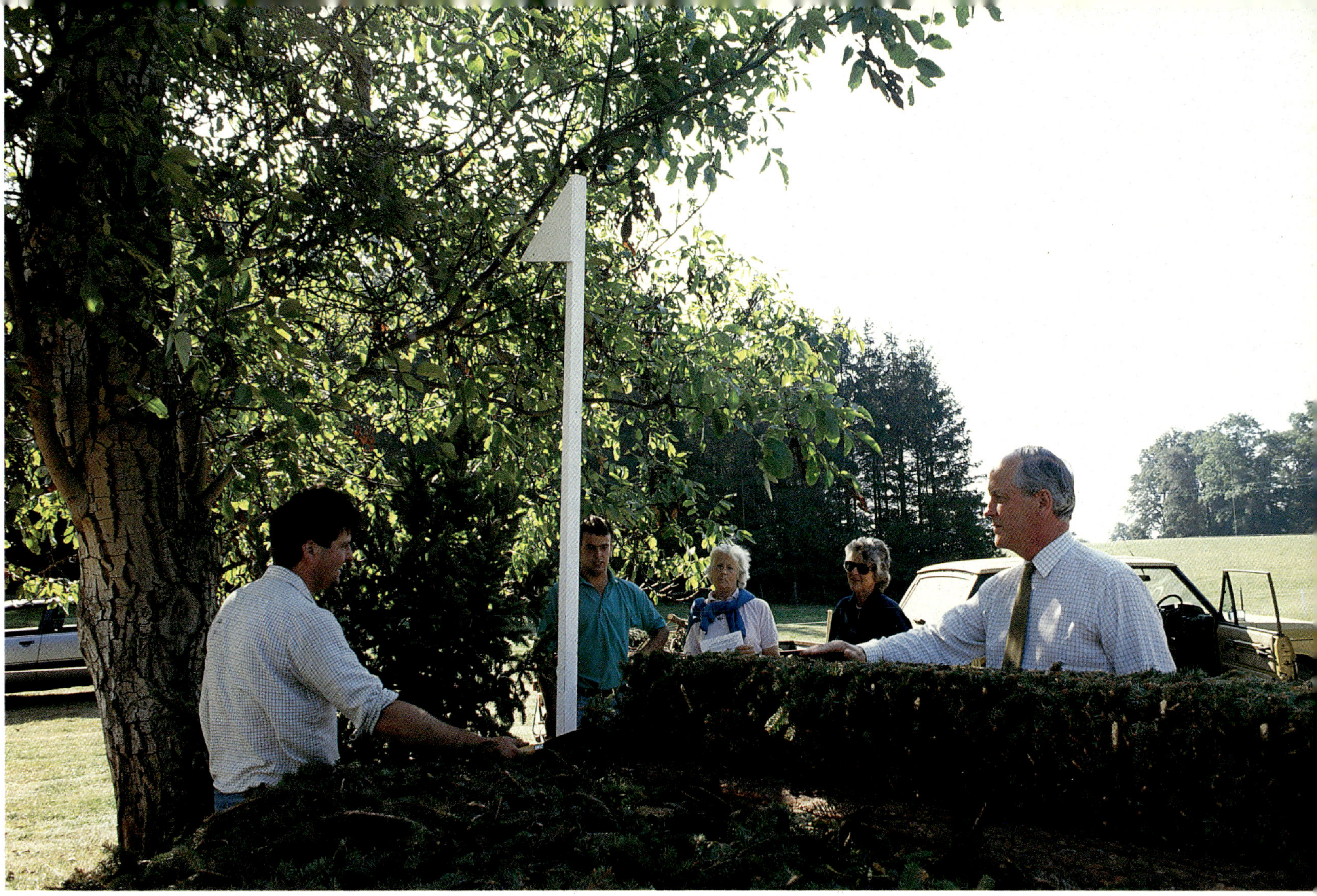

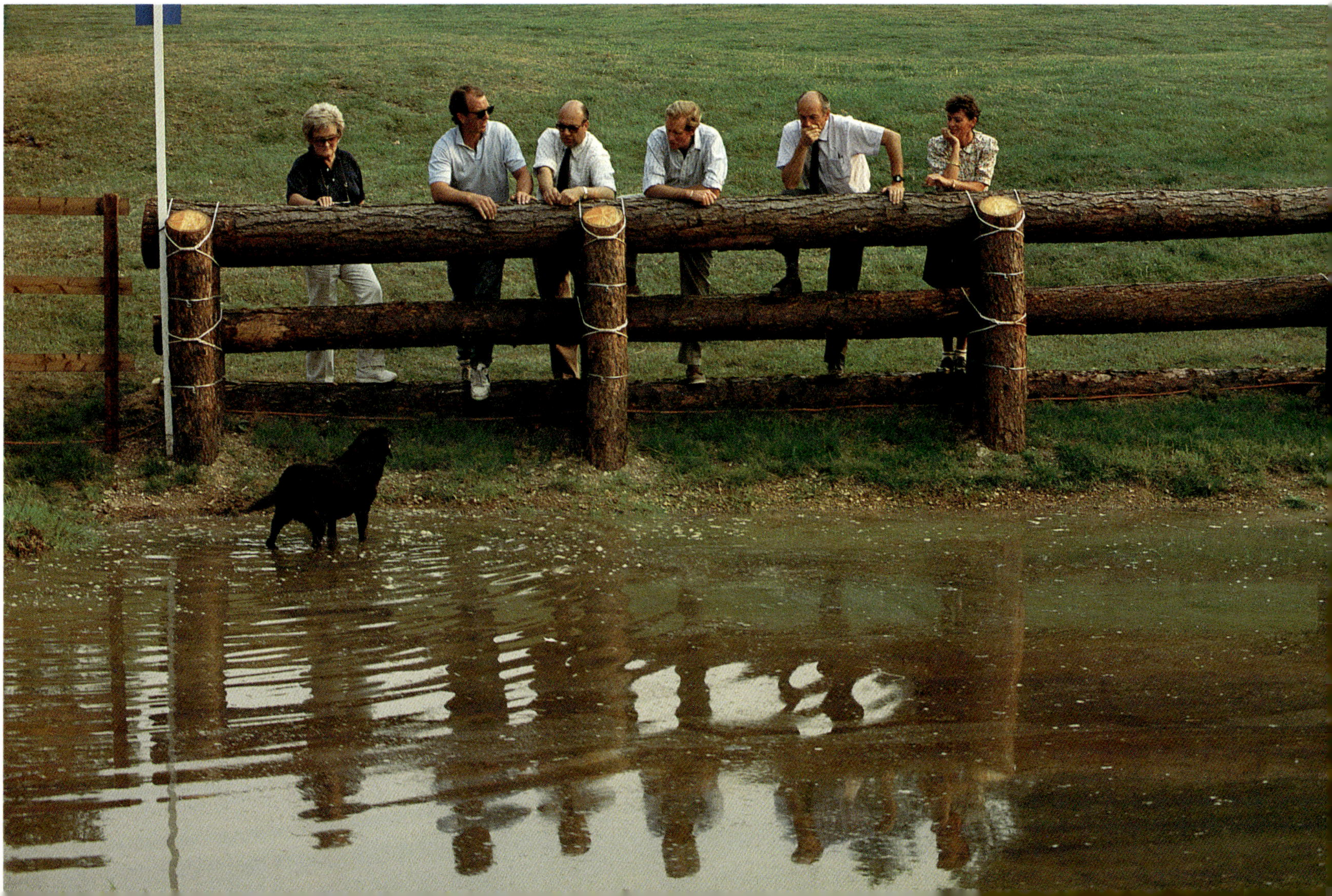

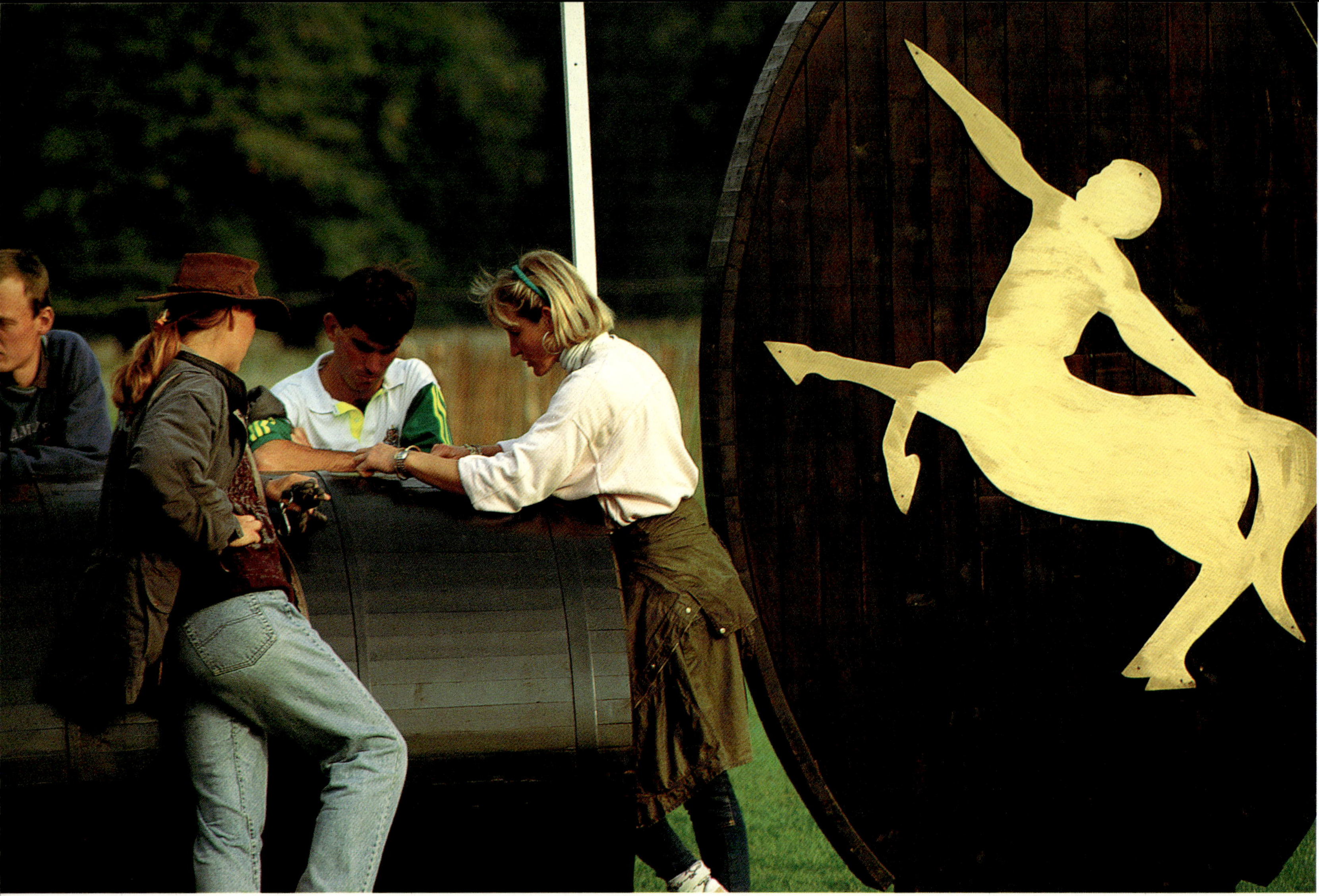

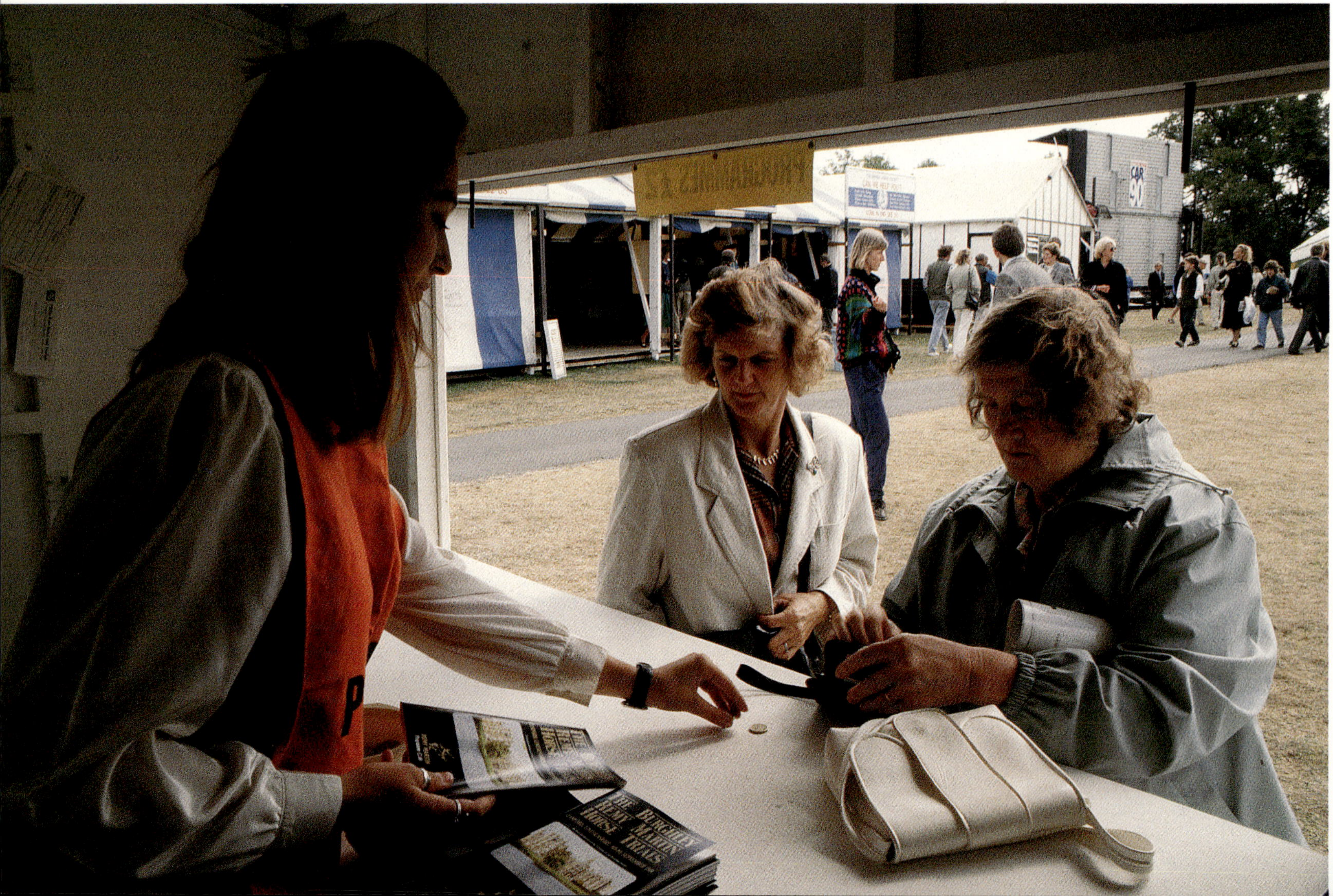

THE BURGHLEY
REMY MARTIN
HORSE TRIALS

49

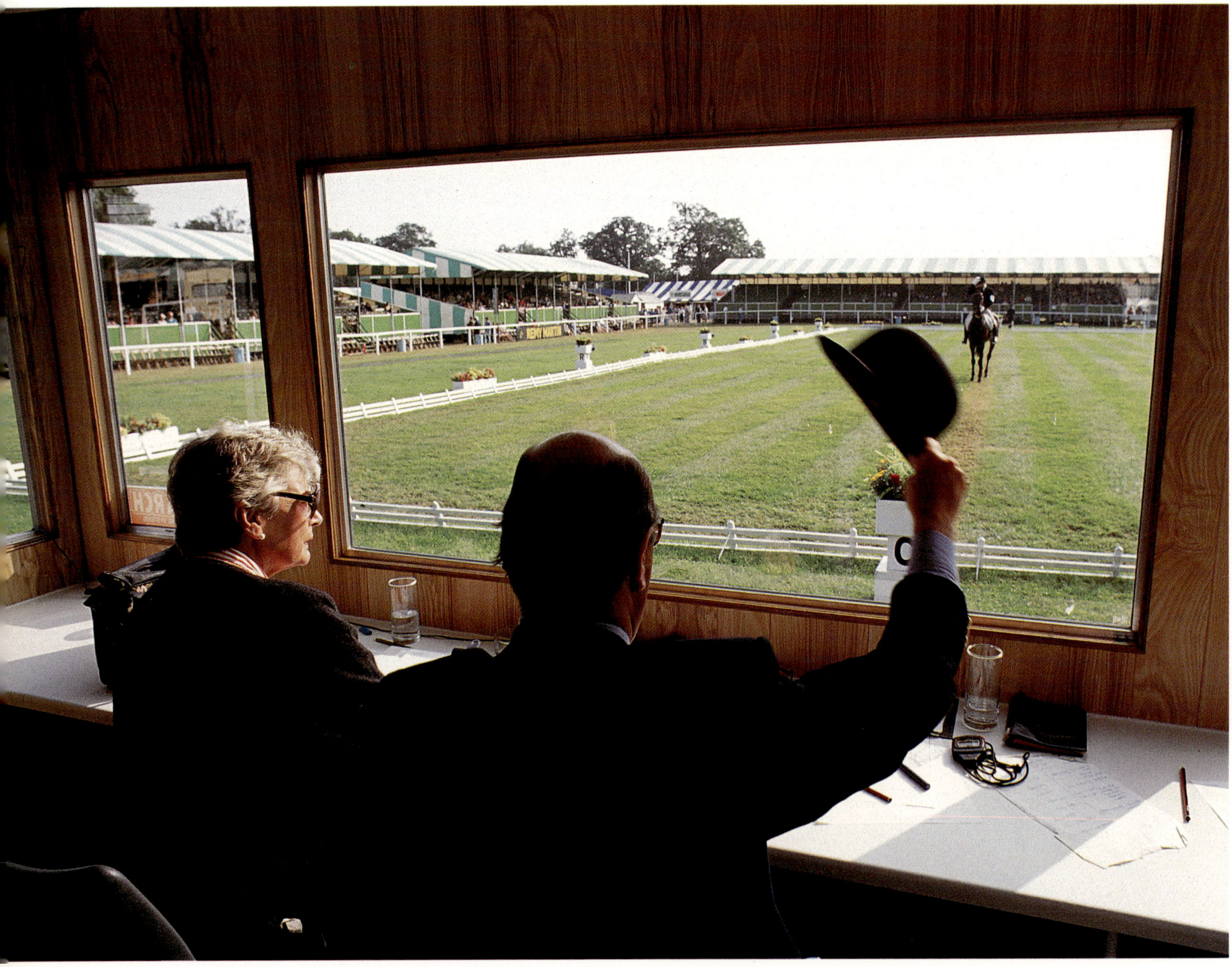

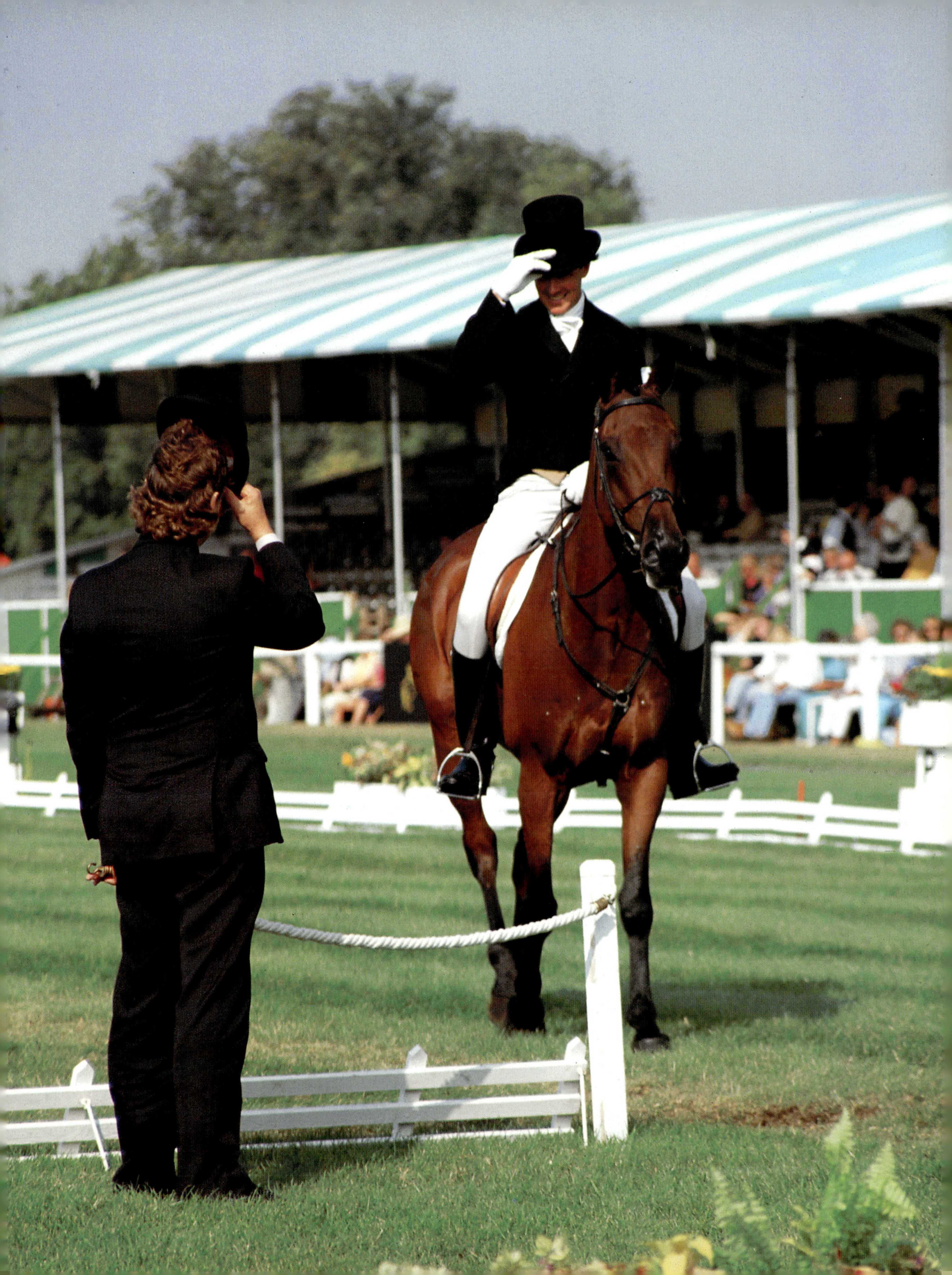

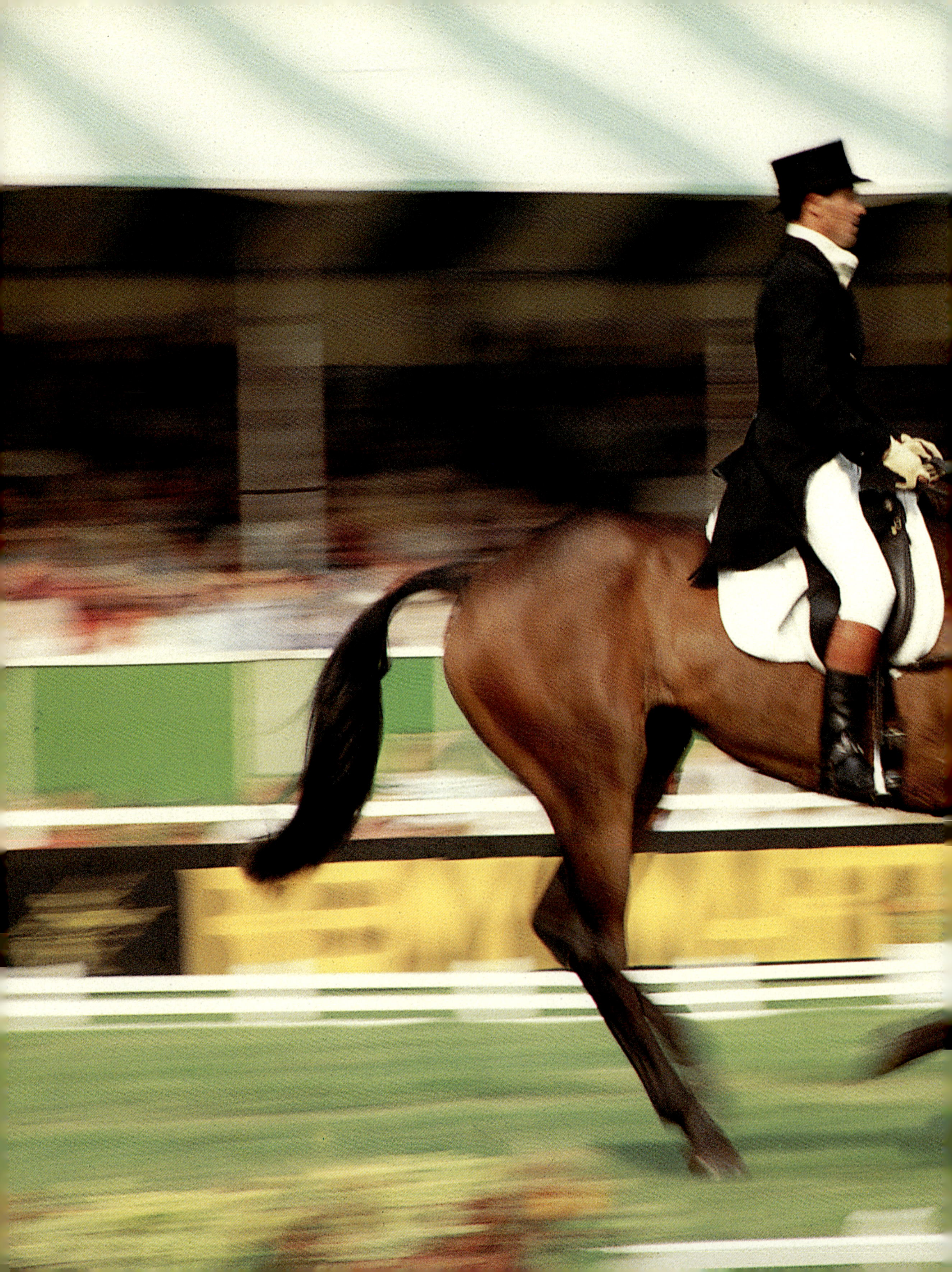

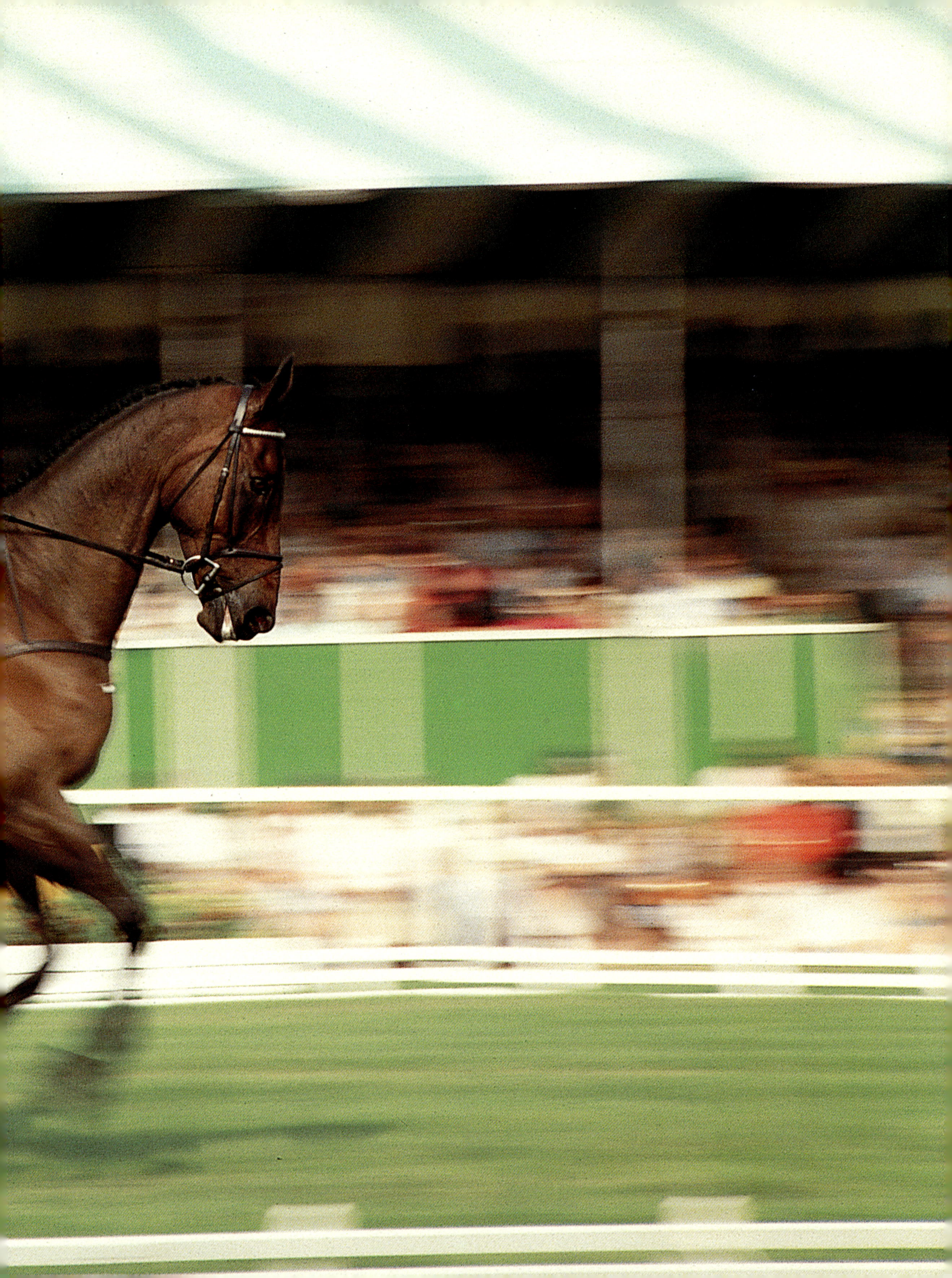

106
WELTON GREYLAG
Rider: Mark Todd (NZL)

KOREA

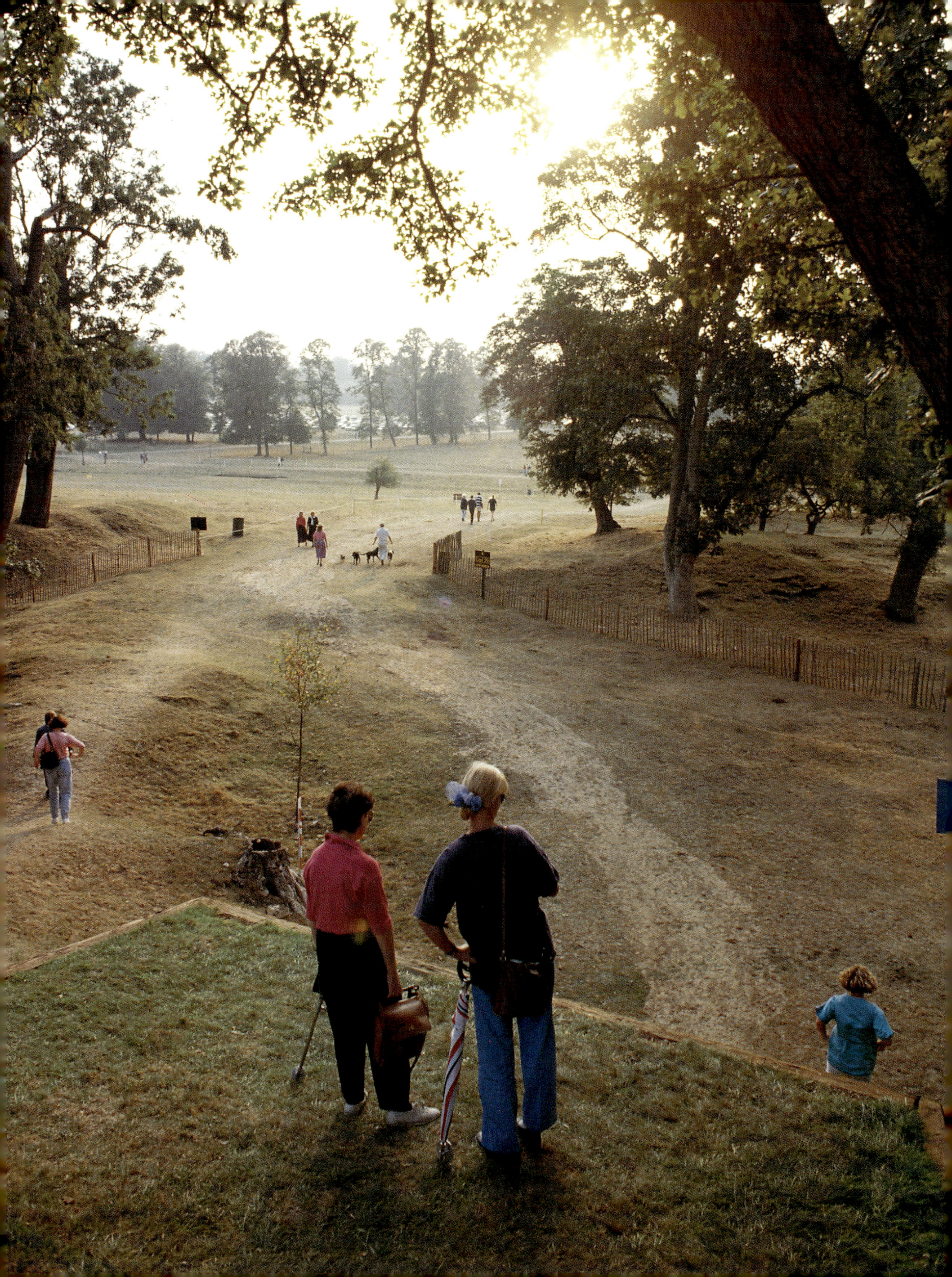

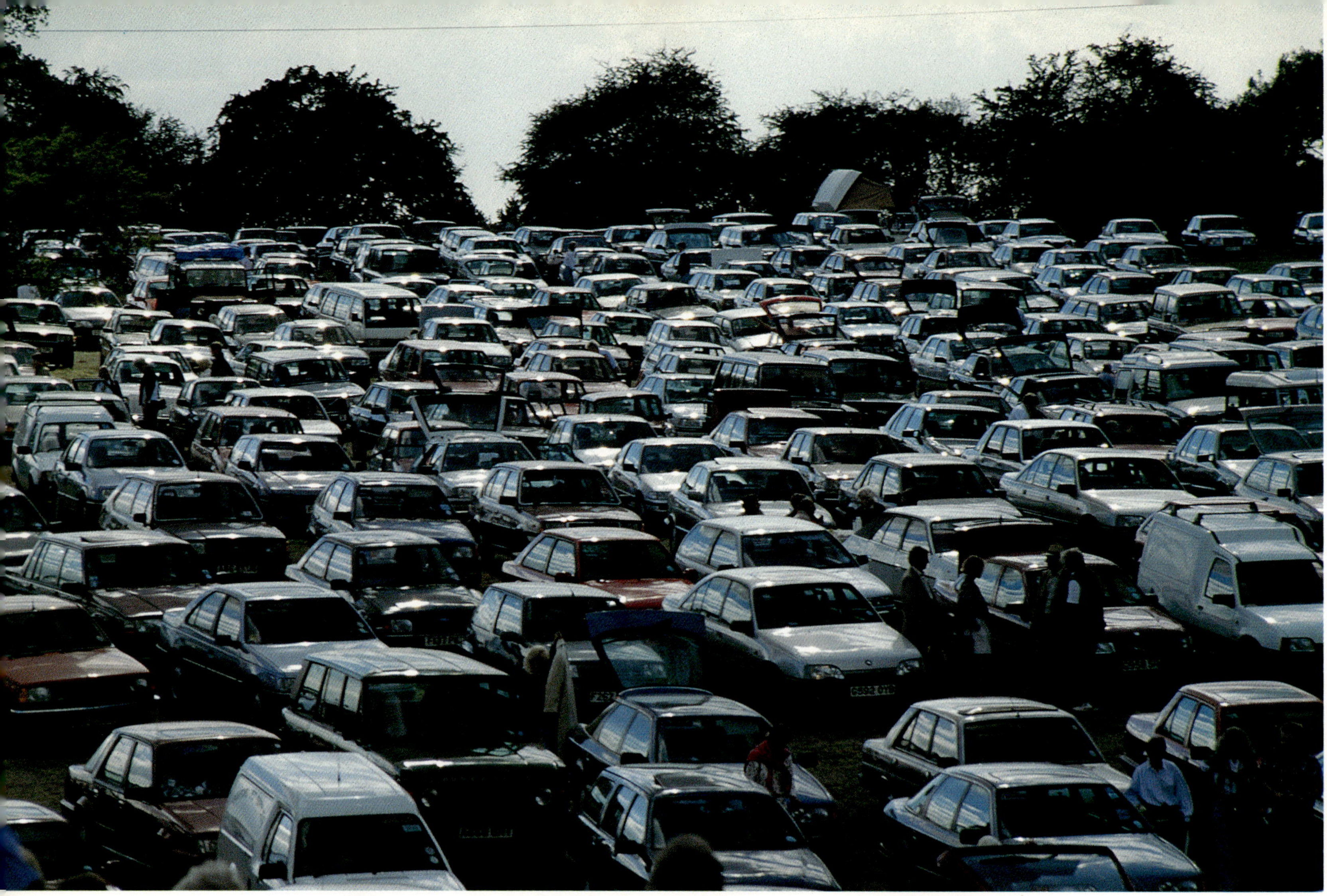

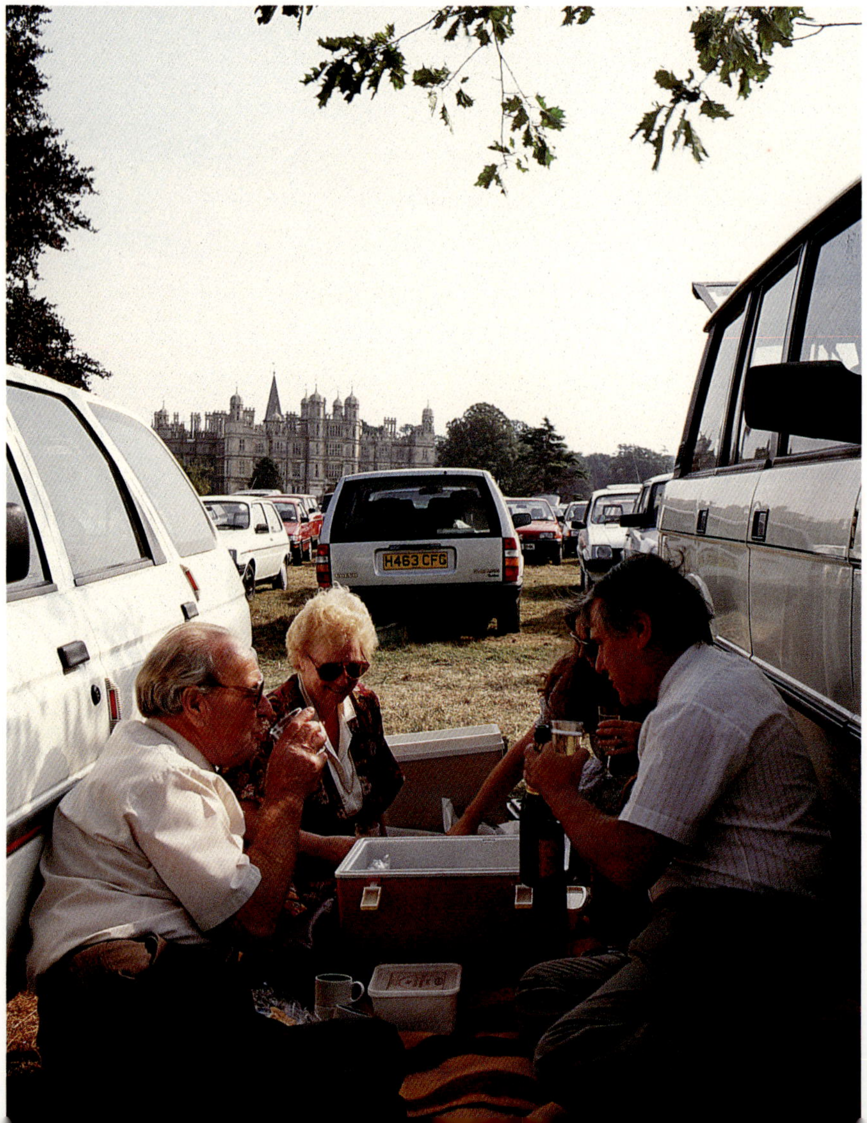
H463 CFG

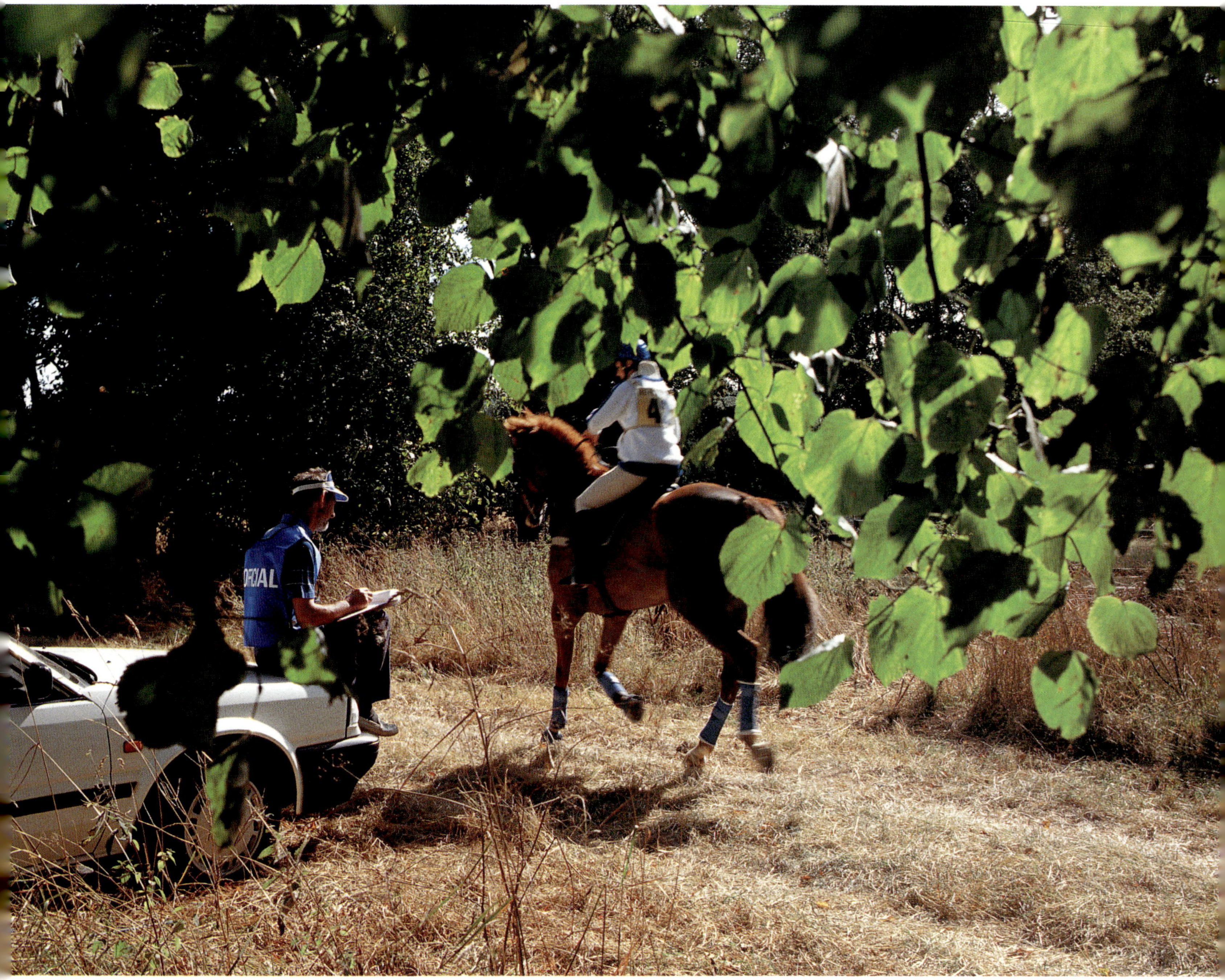

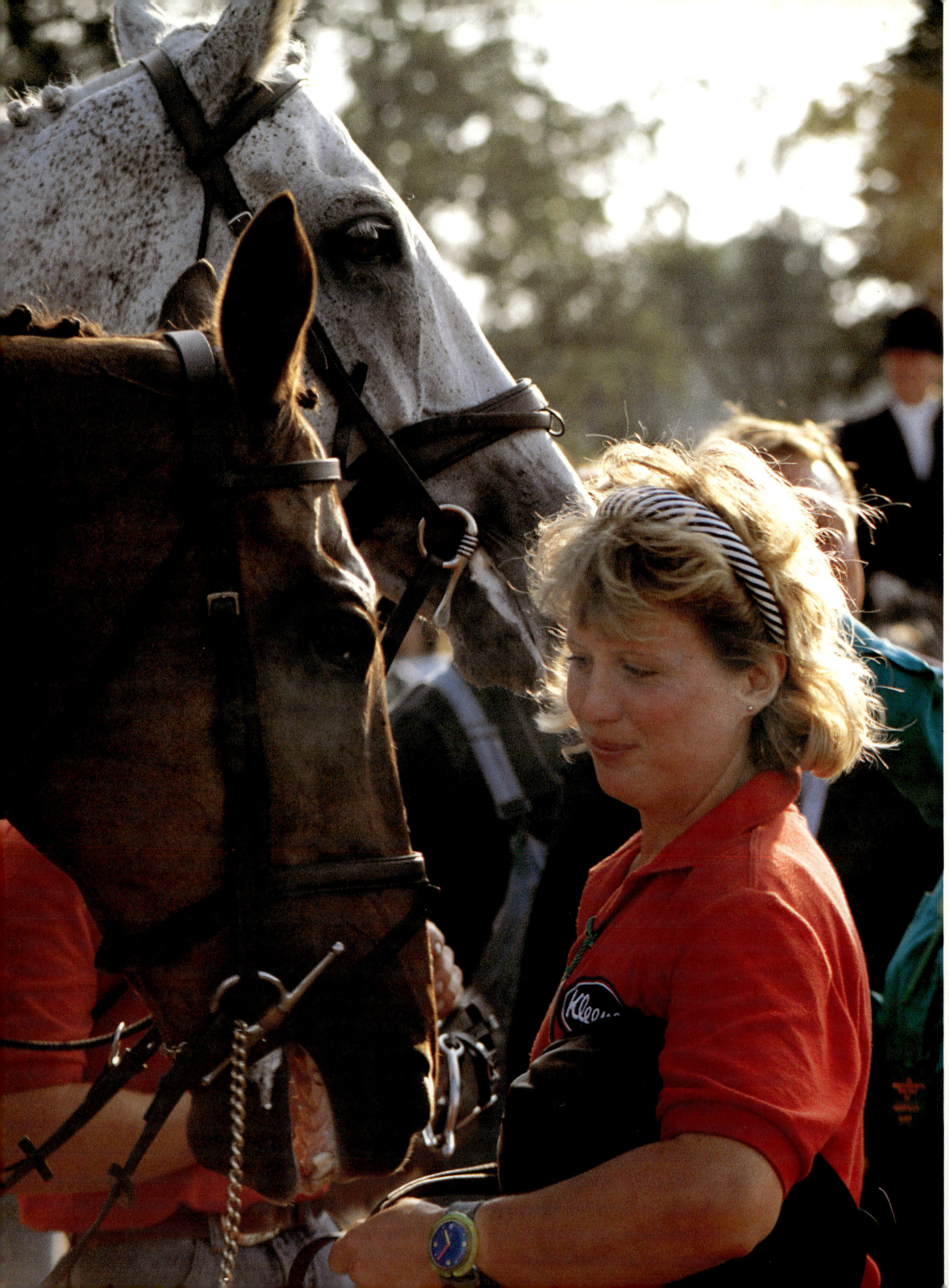

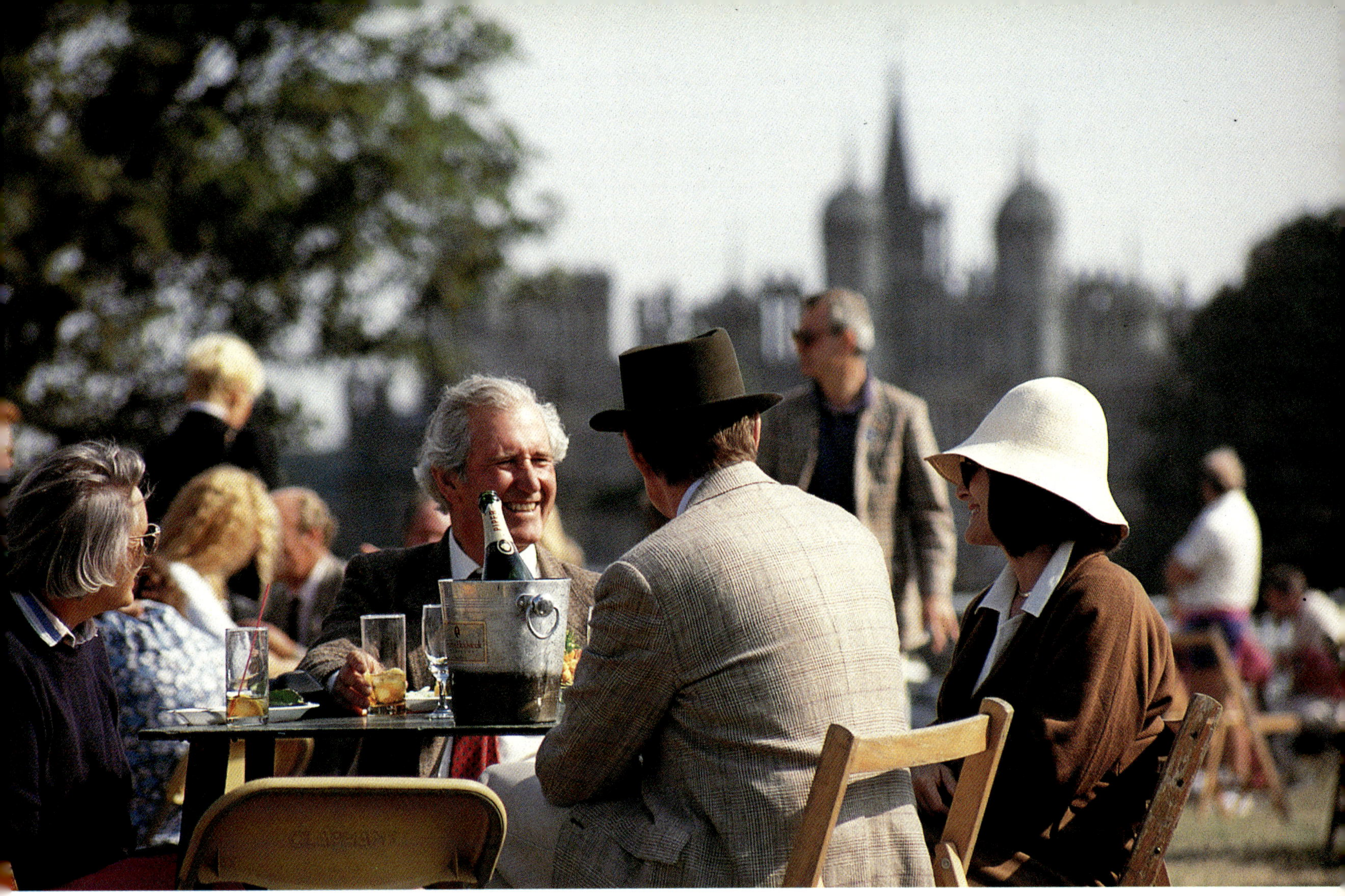

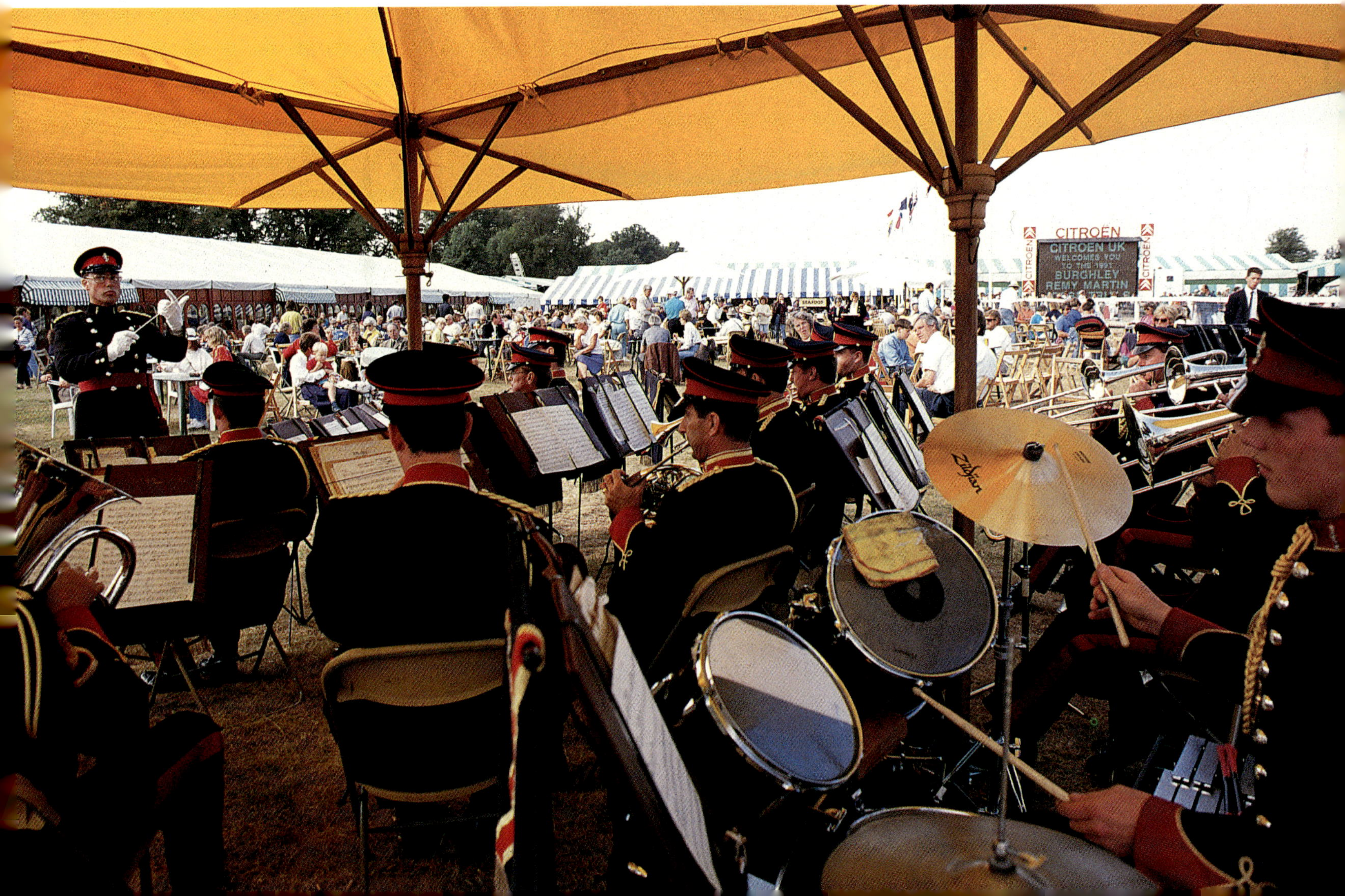
CITROEN
CITROEN UK
WELCOMES YOU
BURGHLEY
REMY MARTIN

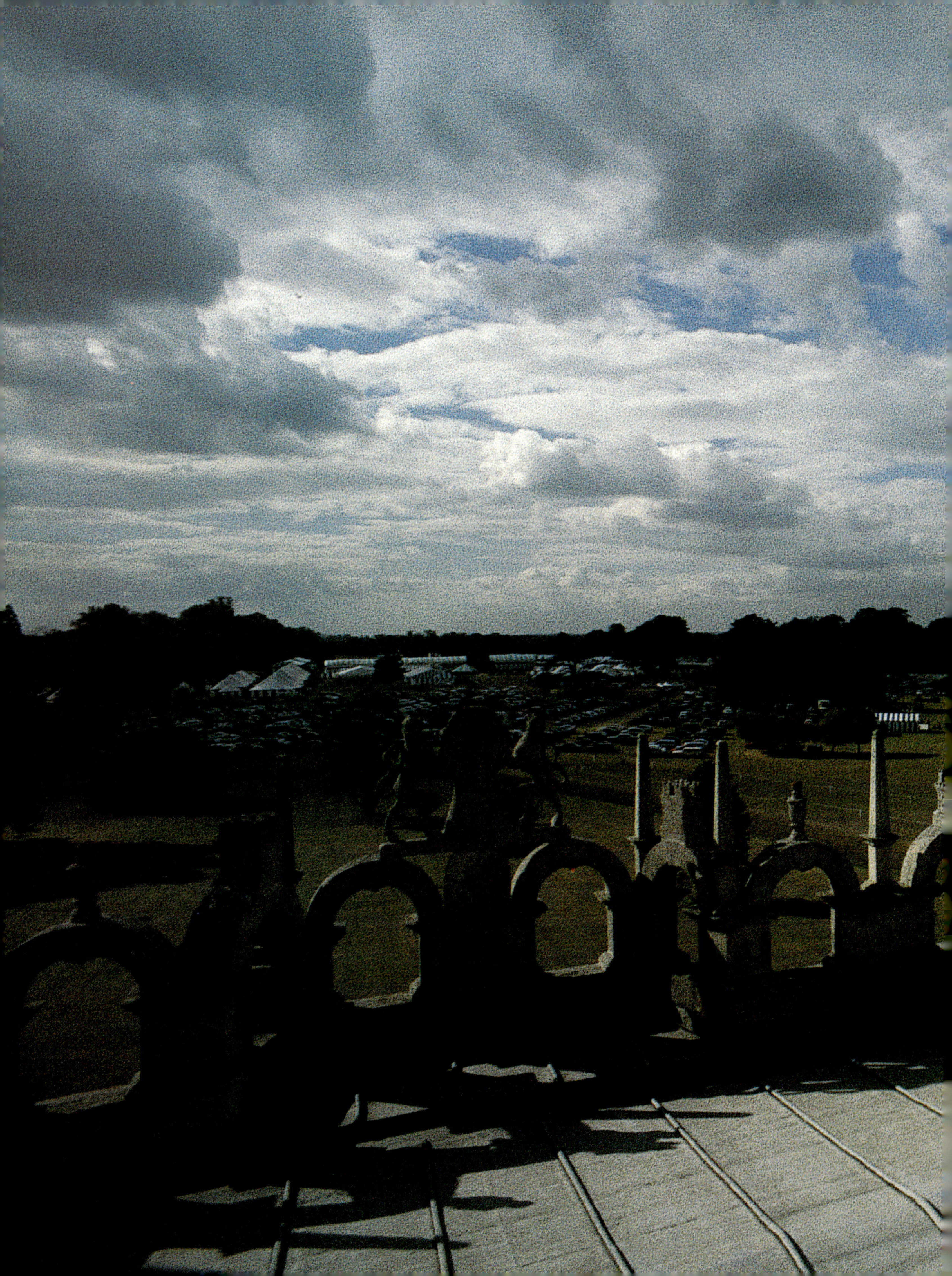

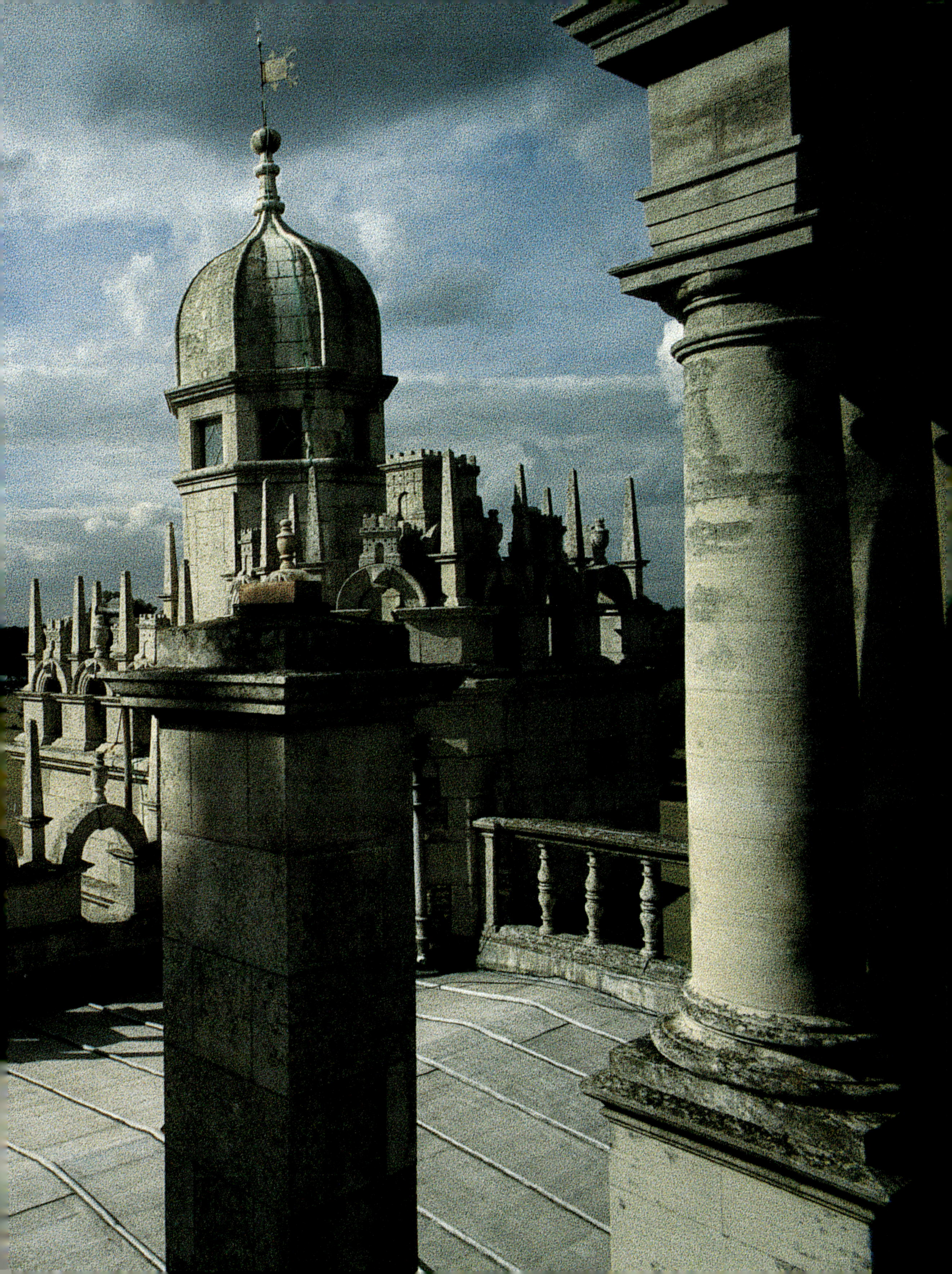

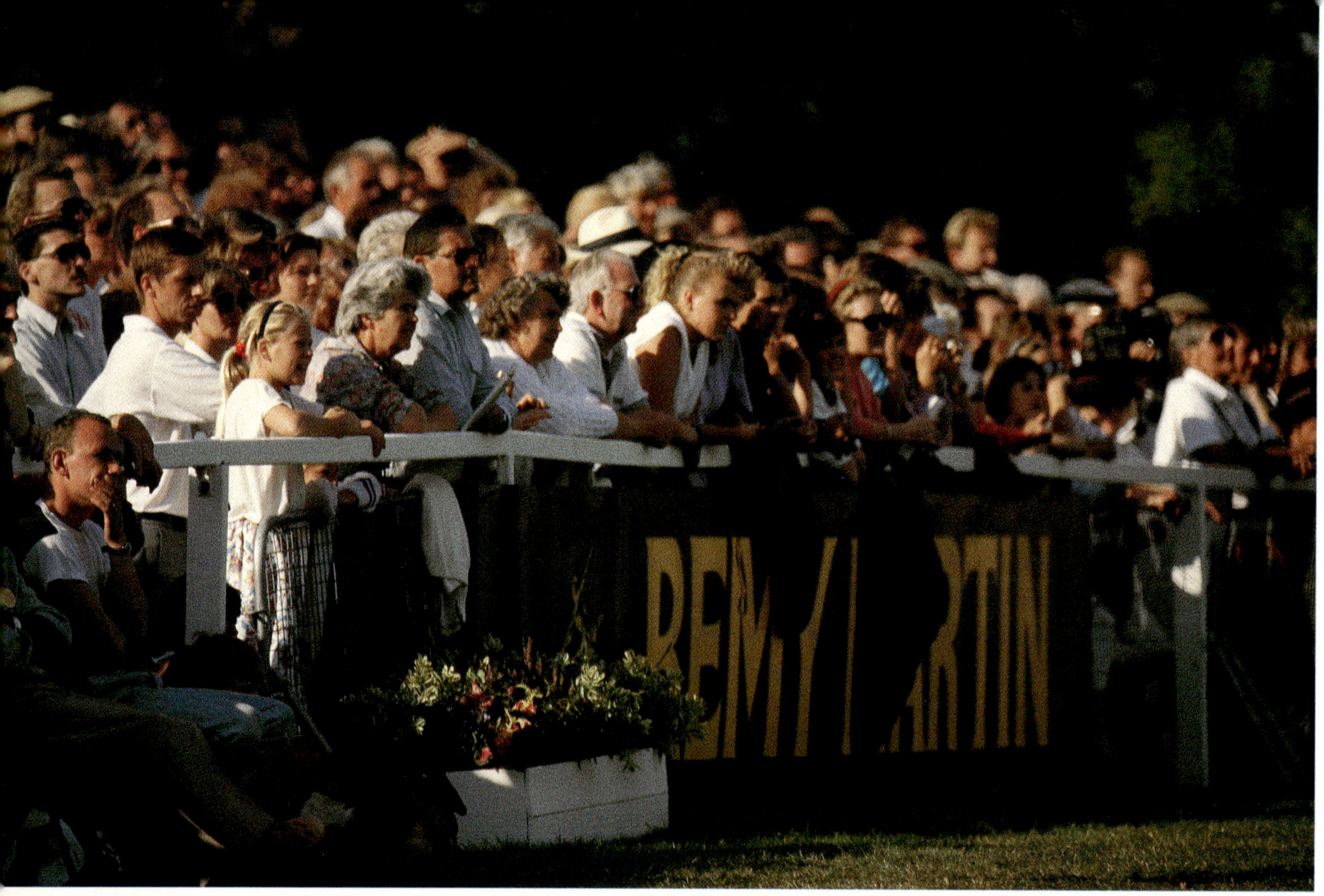
REMY

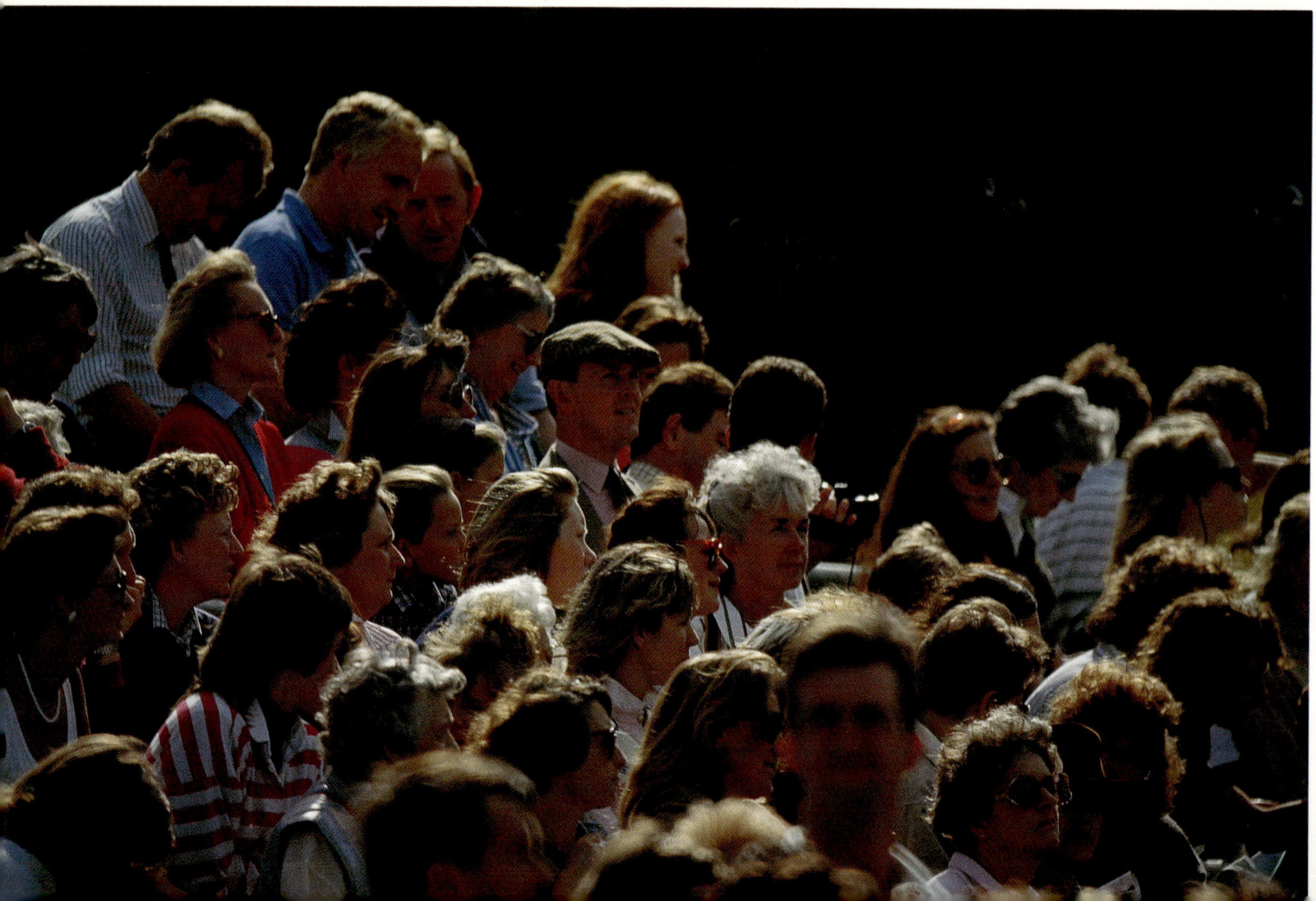

SINCLAIR TRAILERS
C & C
THE BURGHLEY REMY MARTIN HORSE TRIALS

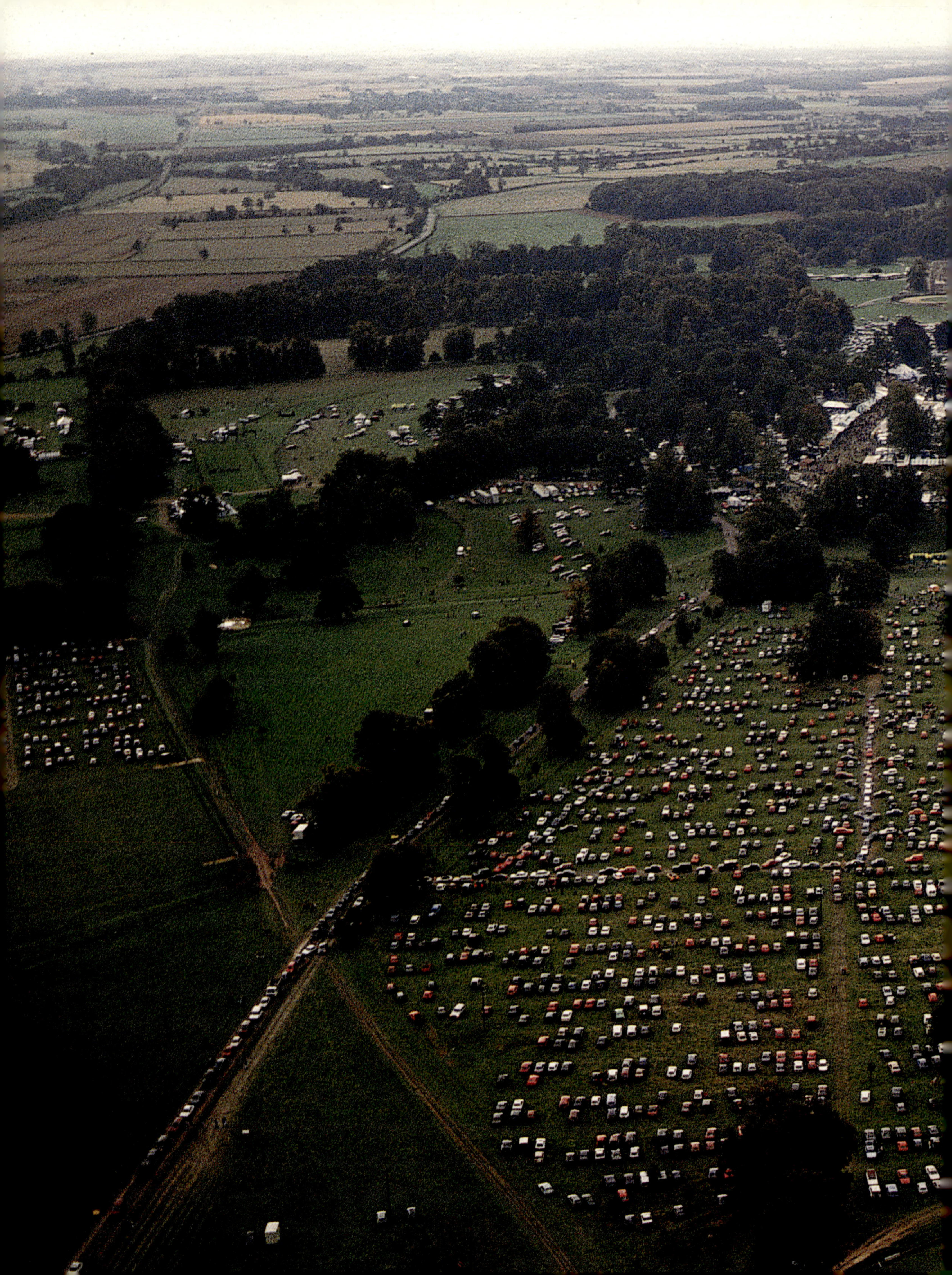

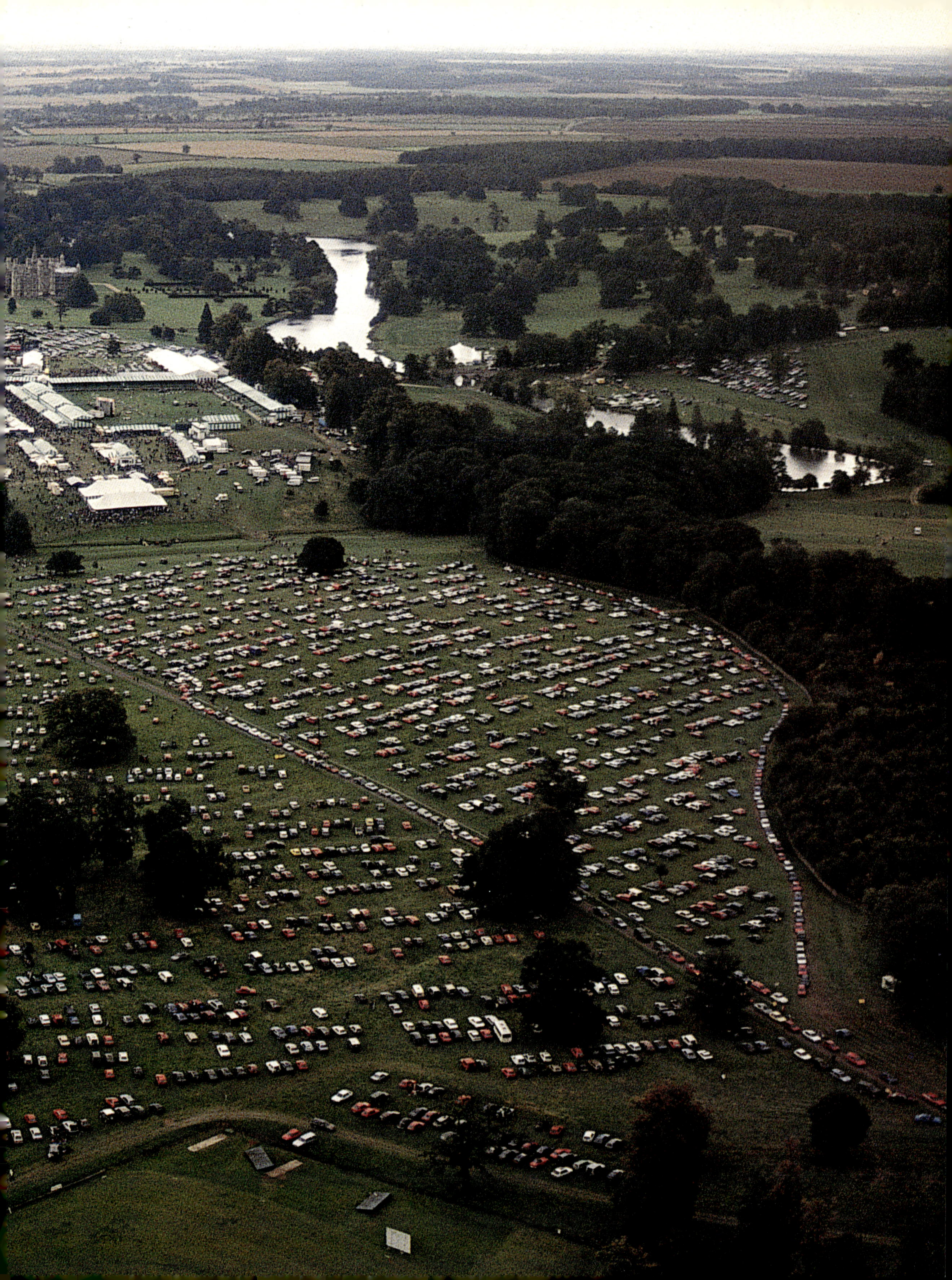

REMY MARTIN
AVENUE B
AVENUE A
SECRETARY
SCOREBOARD
TELEPHONE
FIRST AID
TOILETS
The Daily Telegraph

THE BURGHLEY REMY MA[RTIN]
HORSE TRIALS

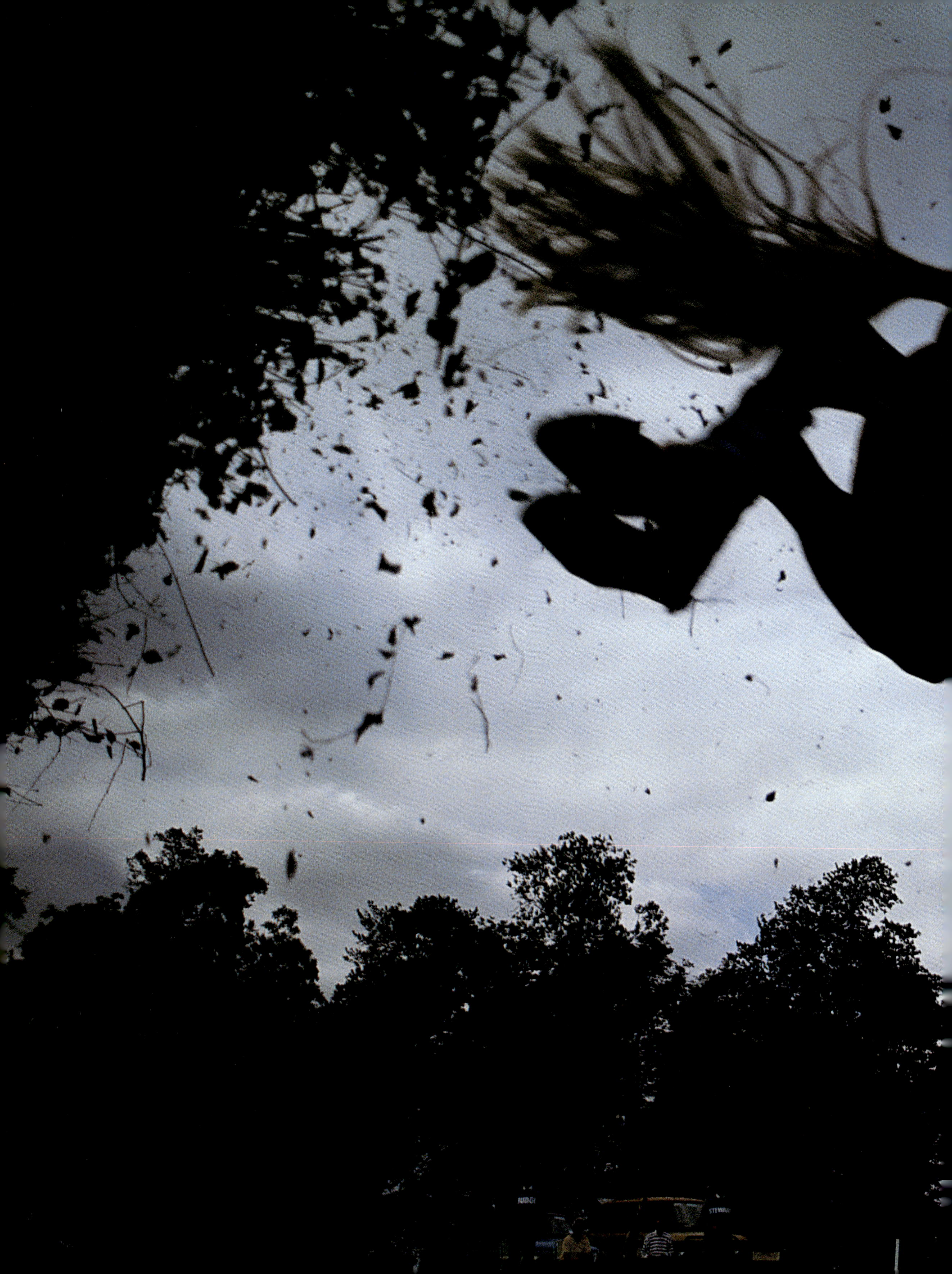

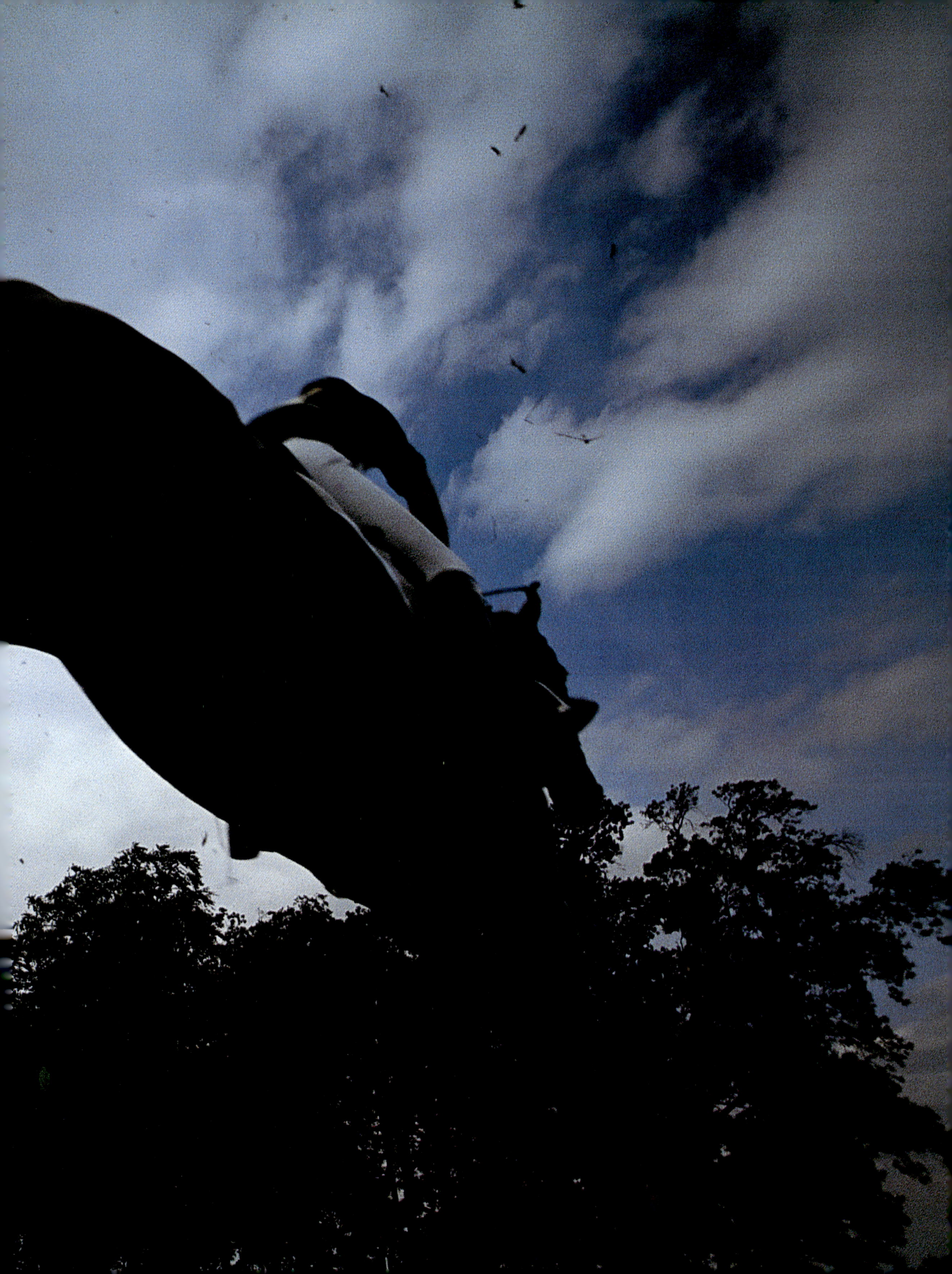

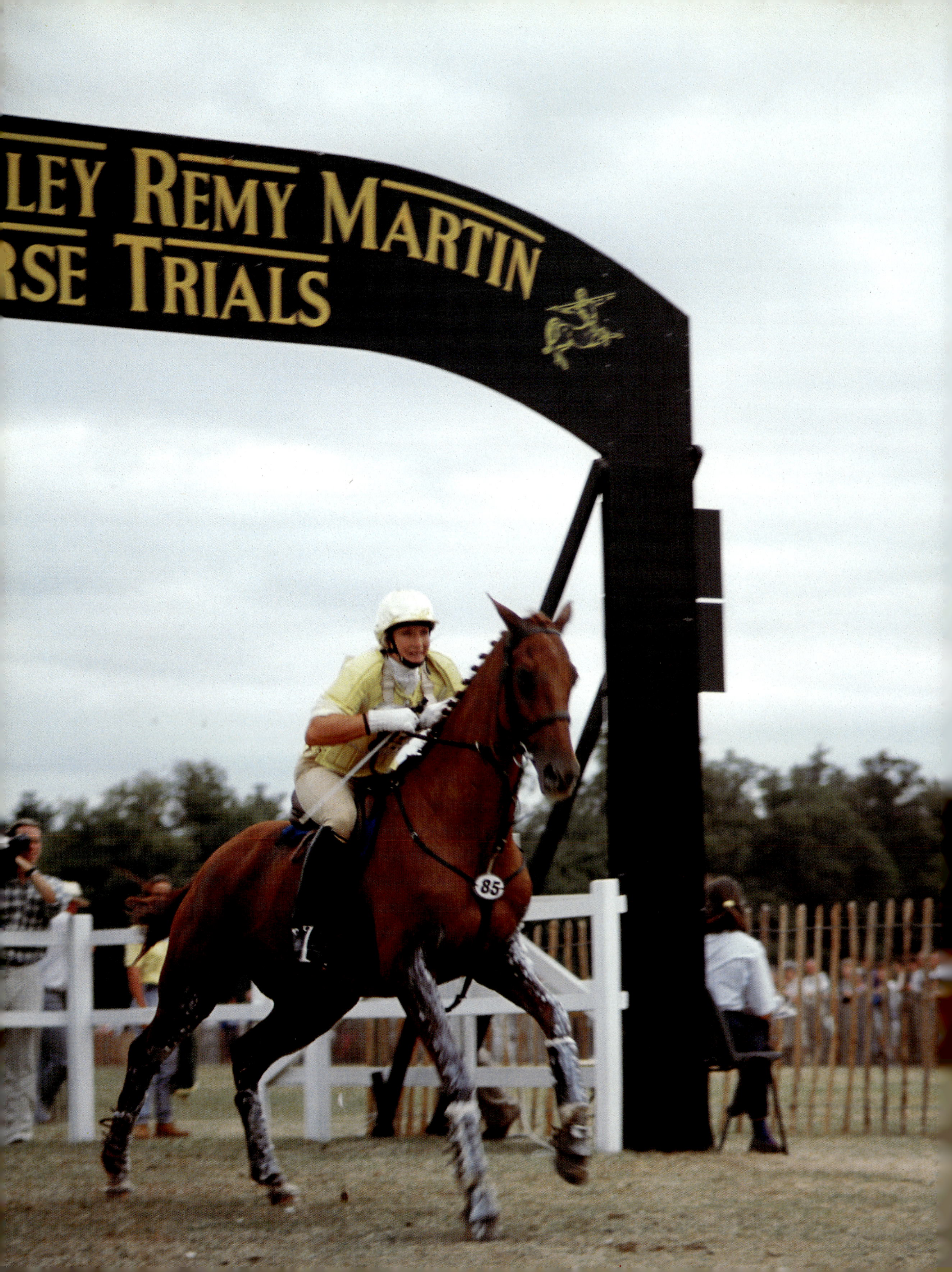
LEY REMY MARTIN
RSE TRIALS
85

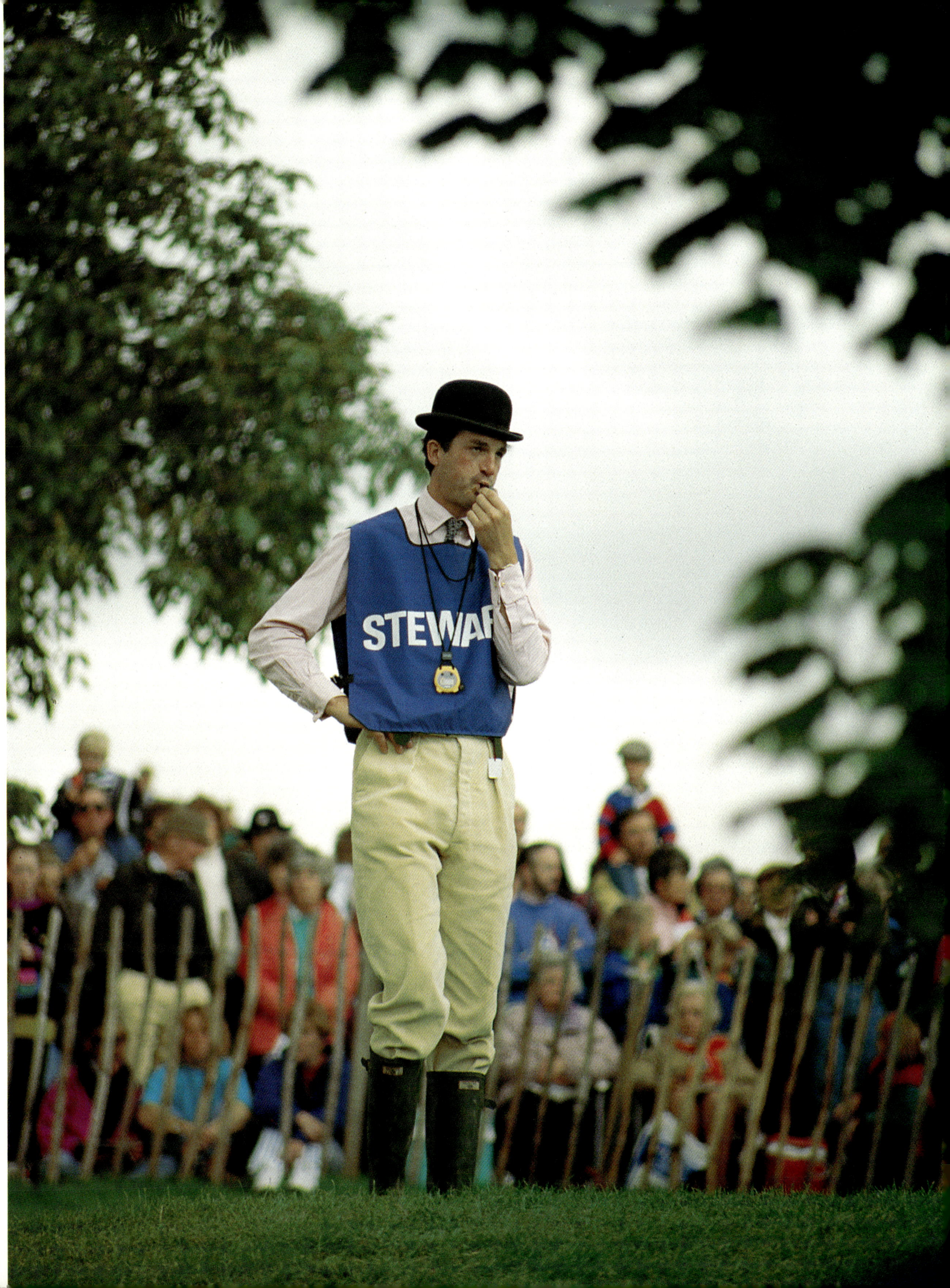
STEWAR

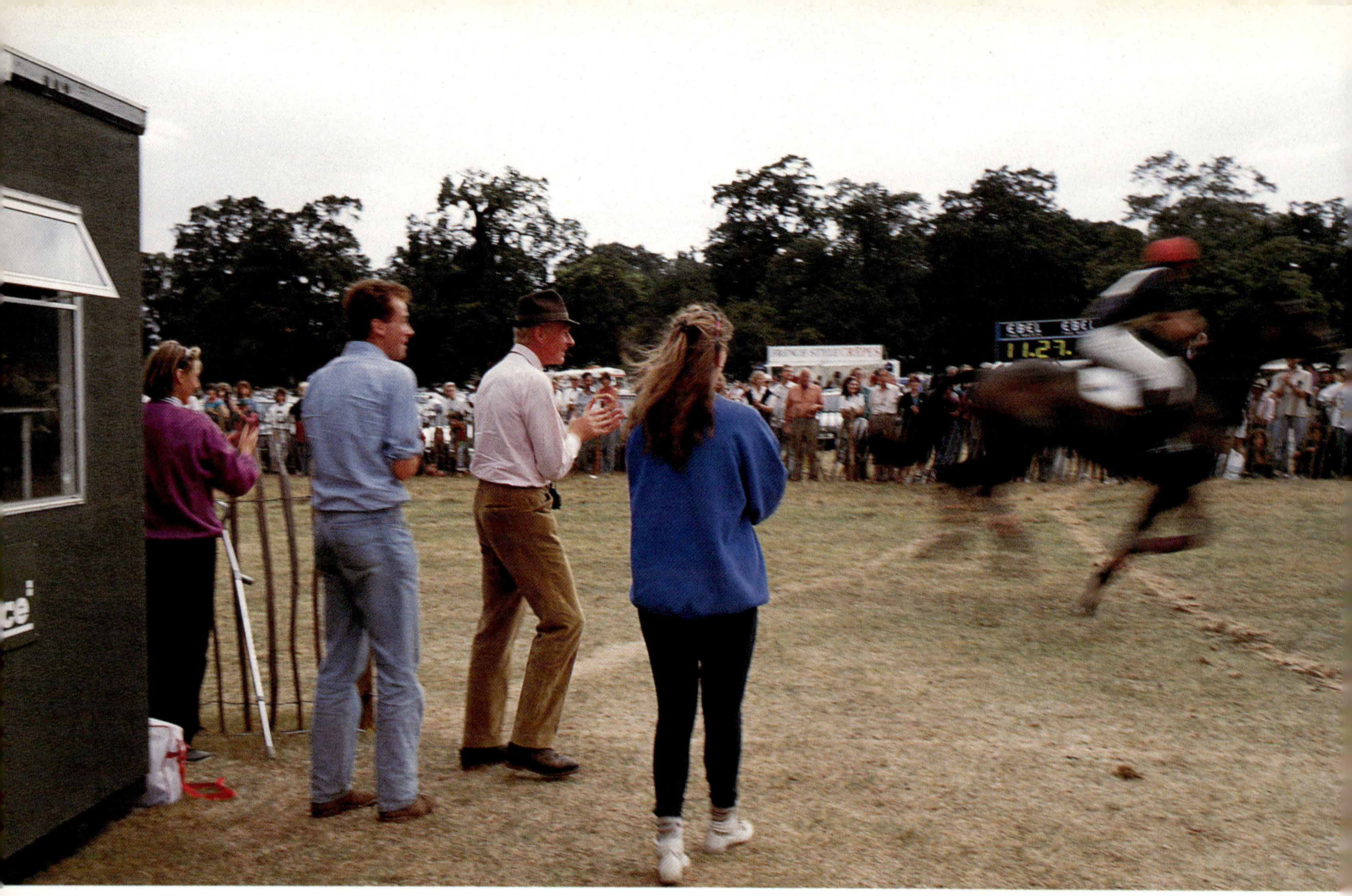
EBEL EBEL
11.27.

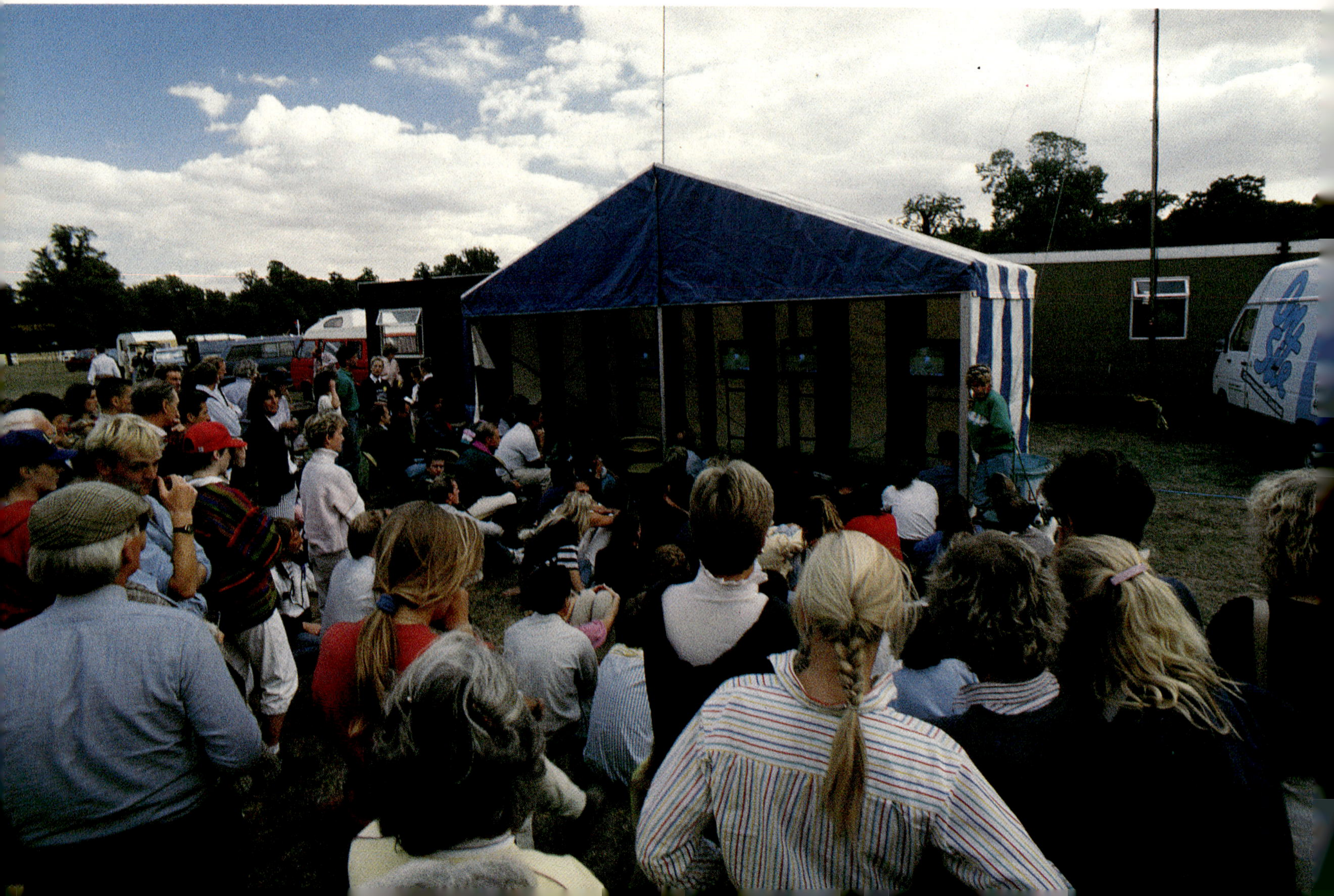

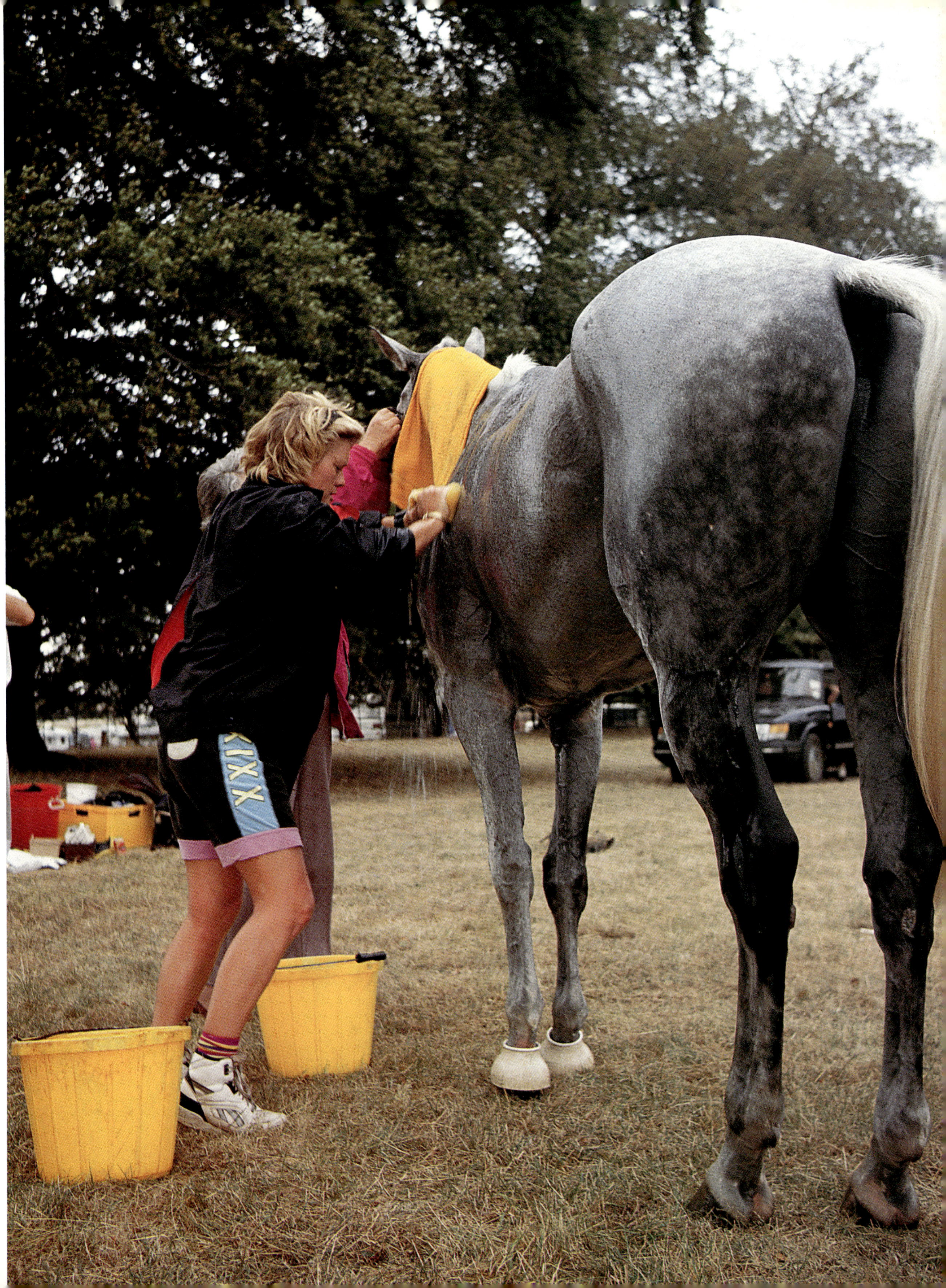

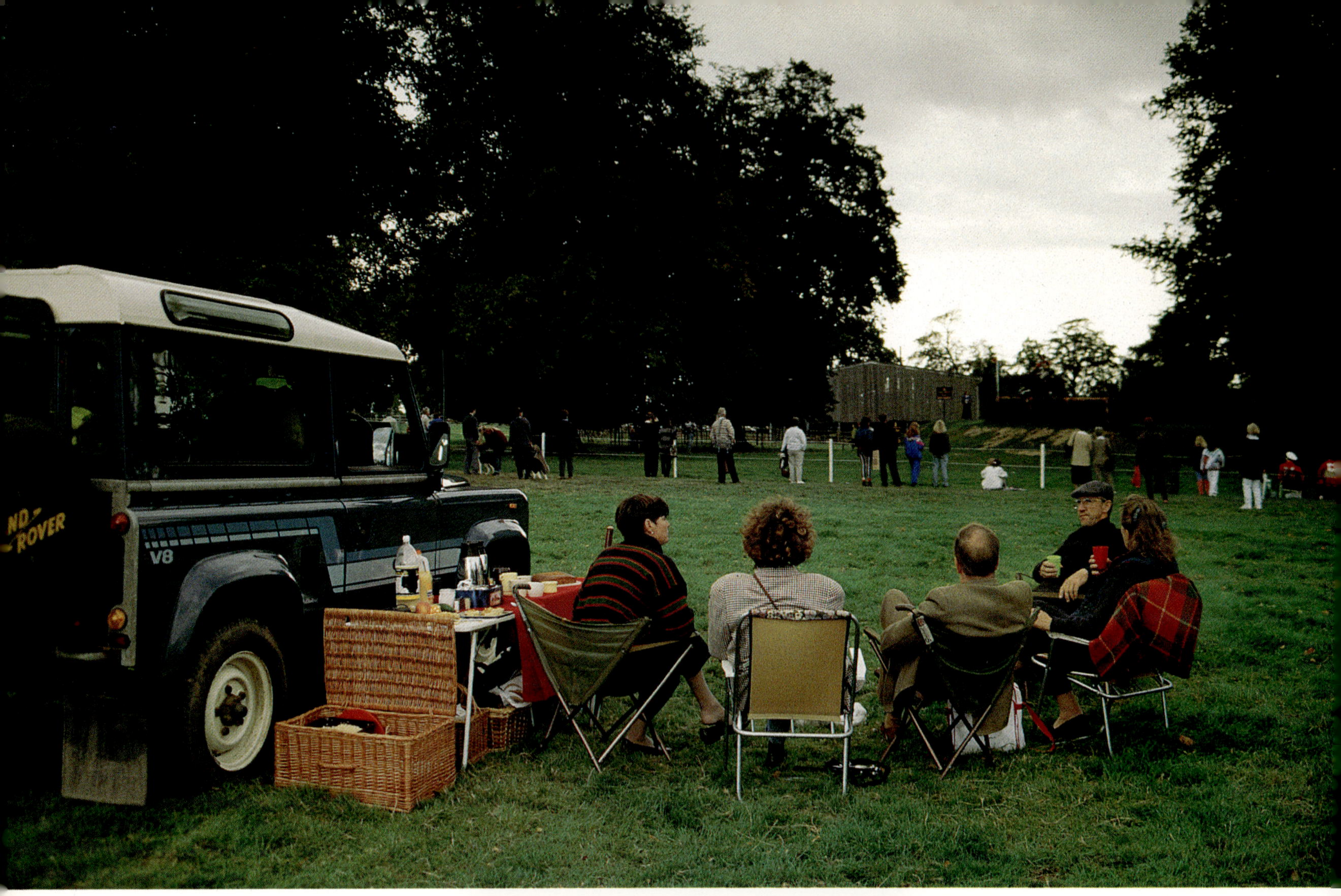
ND ROVER
V8

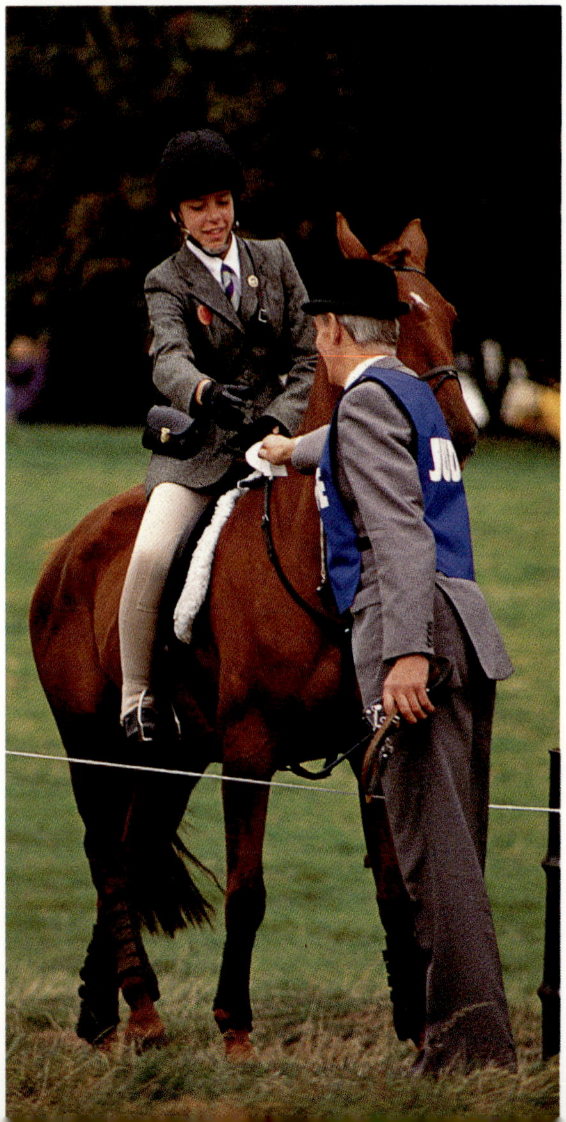

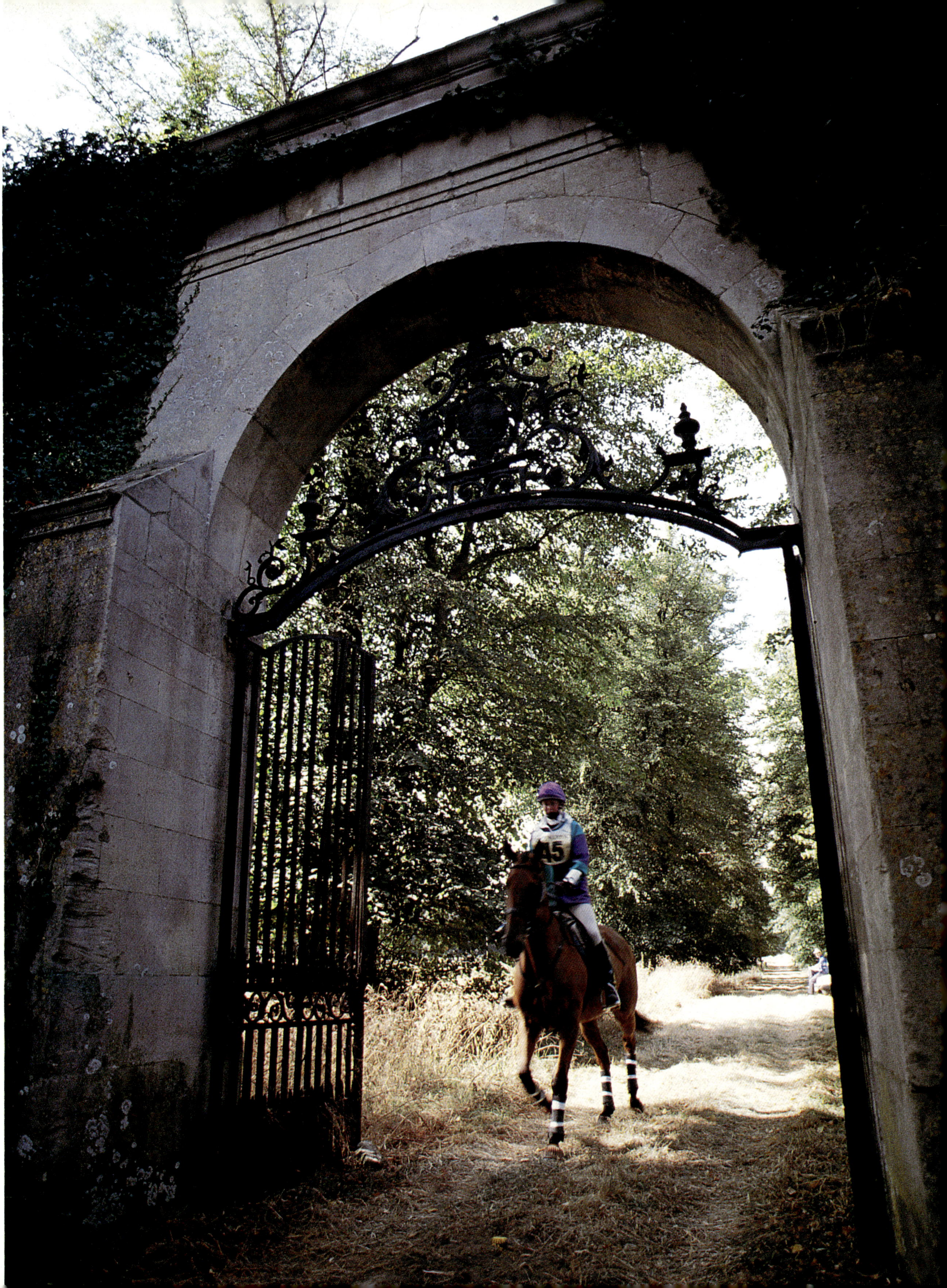
45

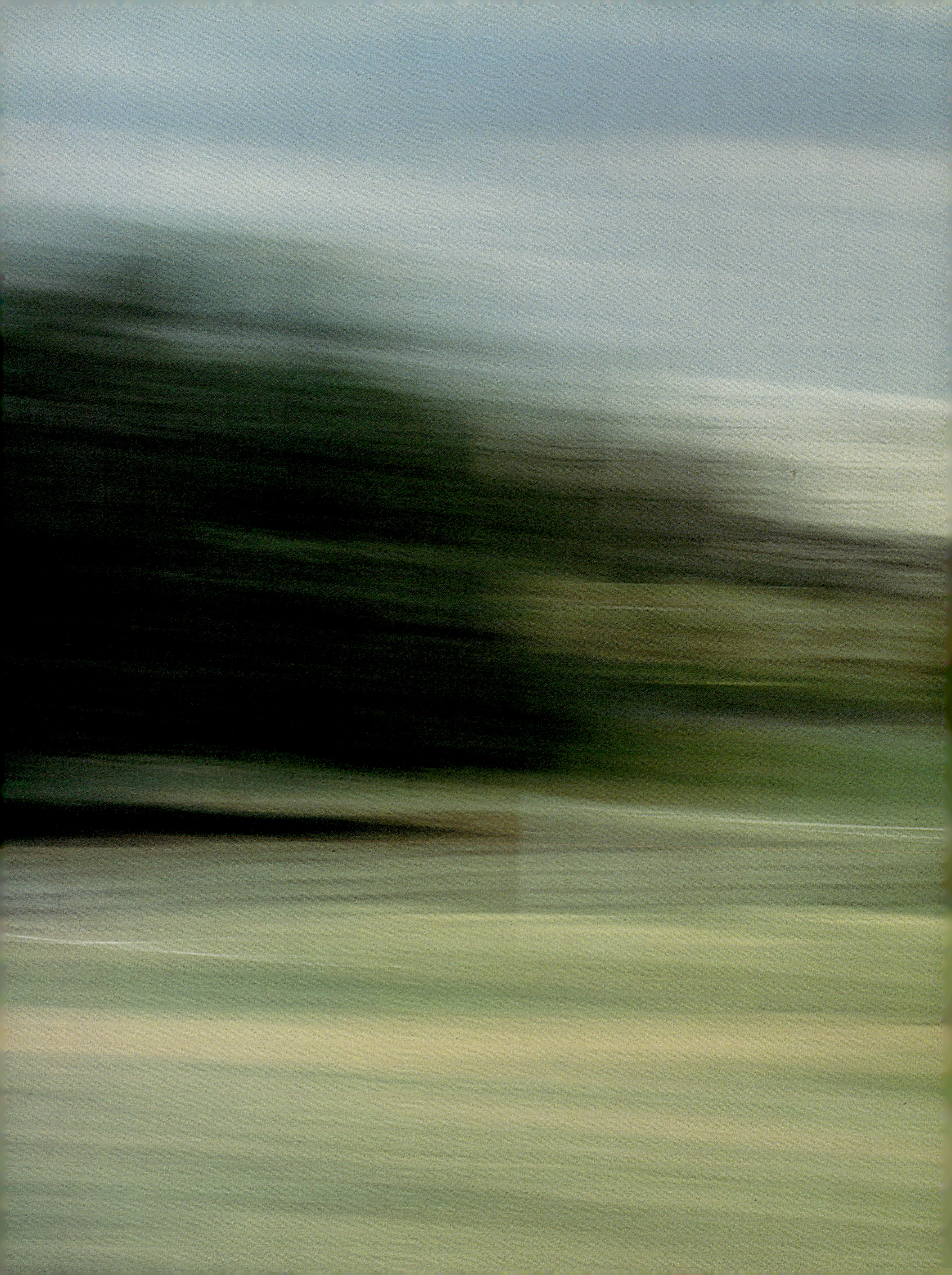

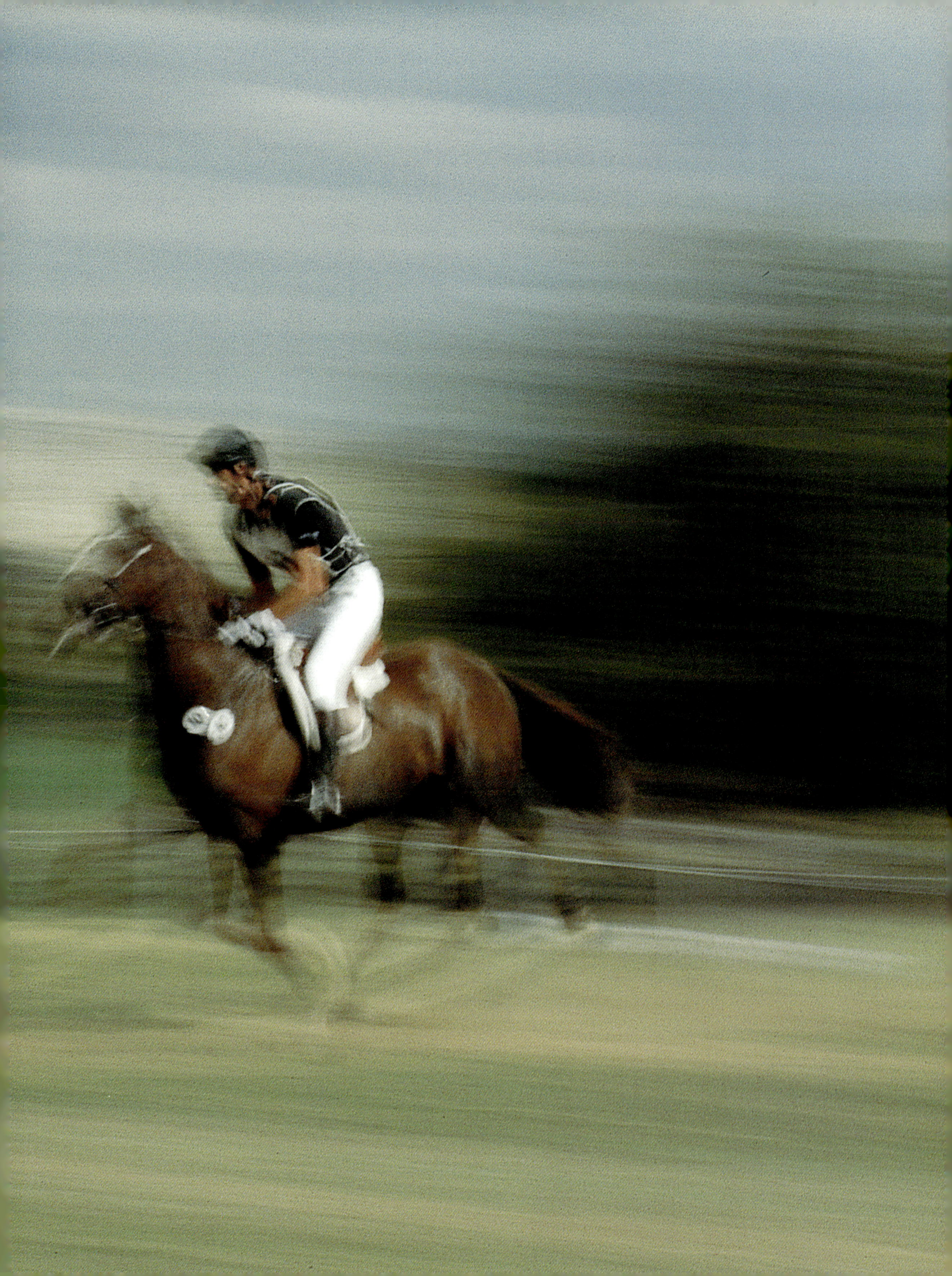

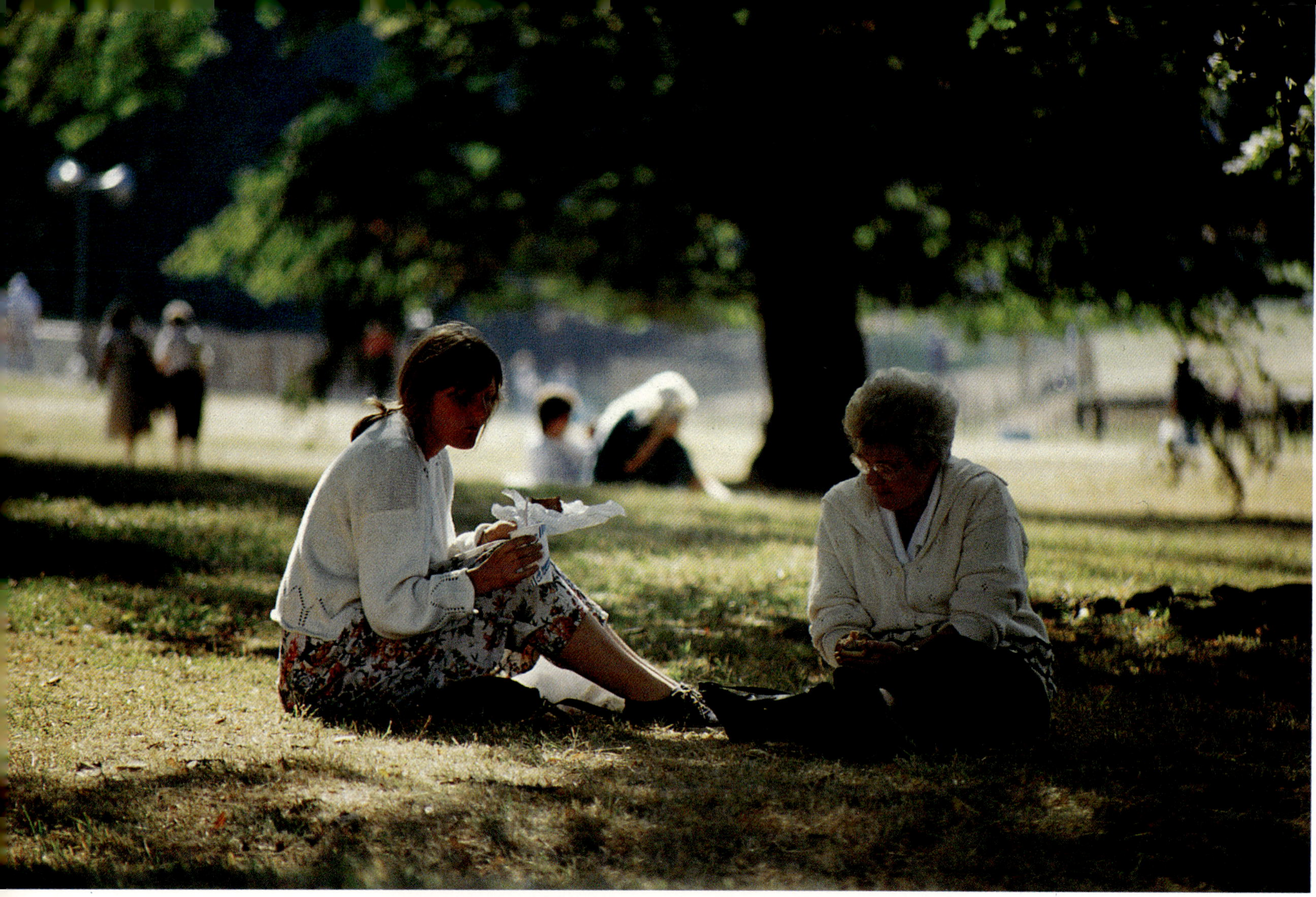

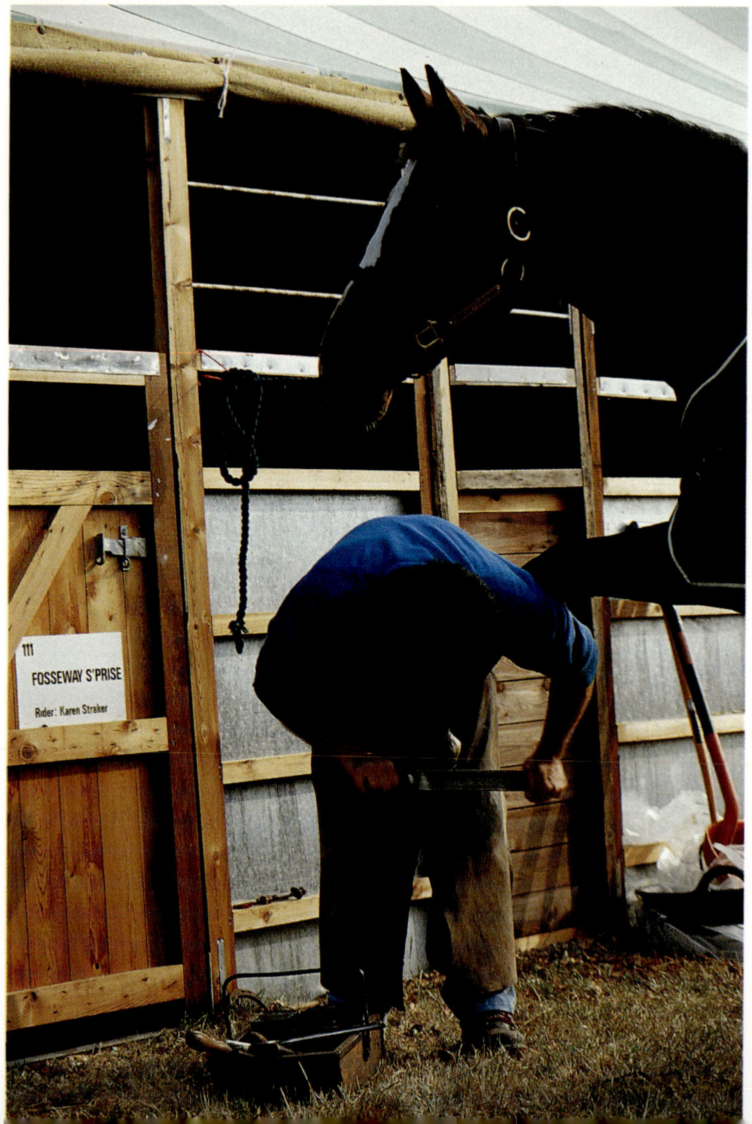
111
FOSSEWAY S'PRISE
Rider: Karen Straker

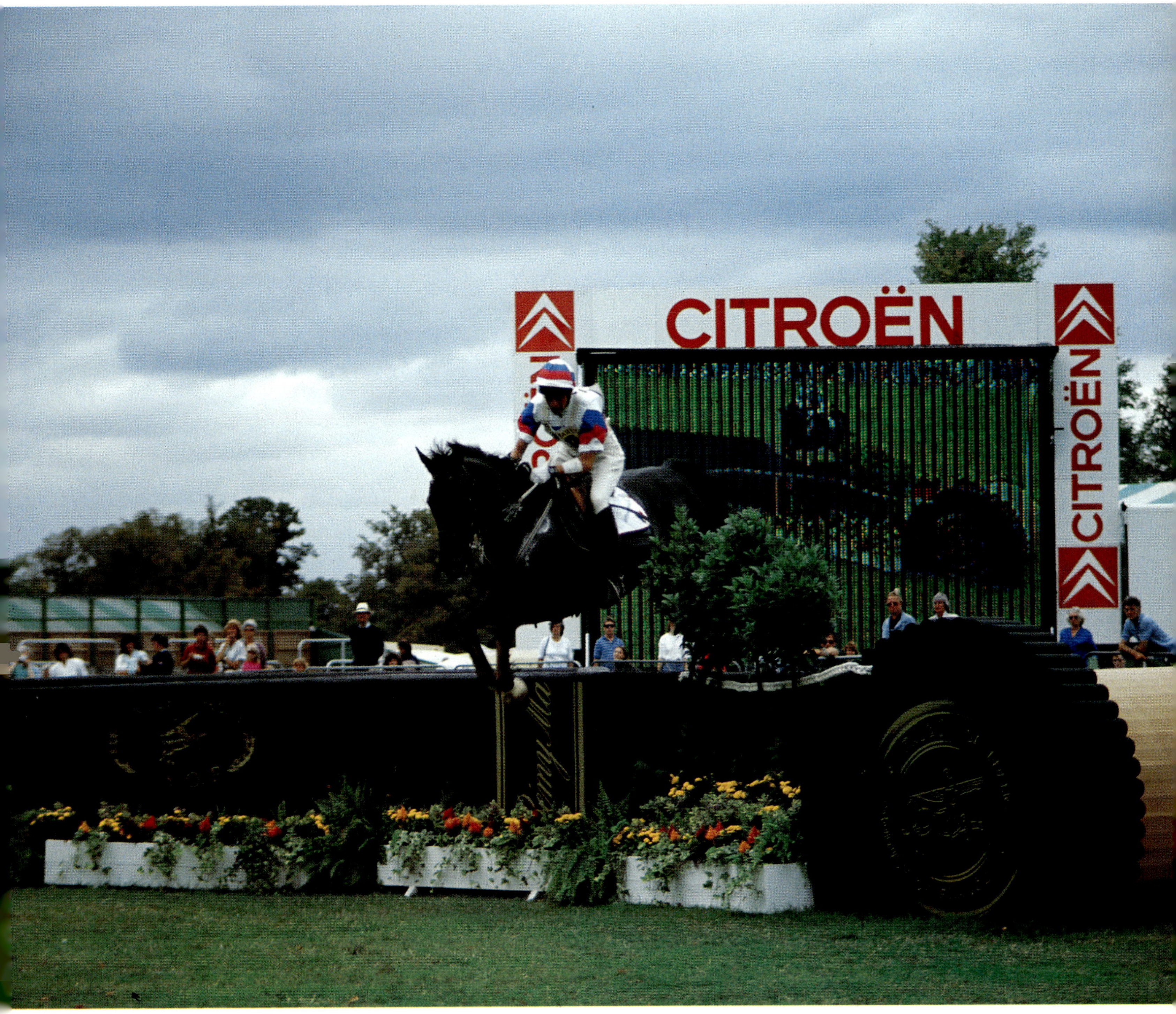
CITROËN
CITROËN

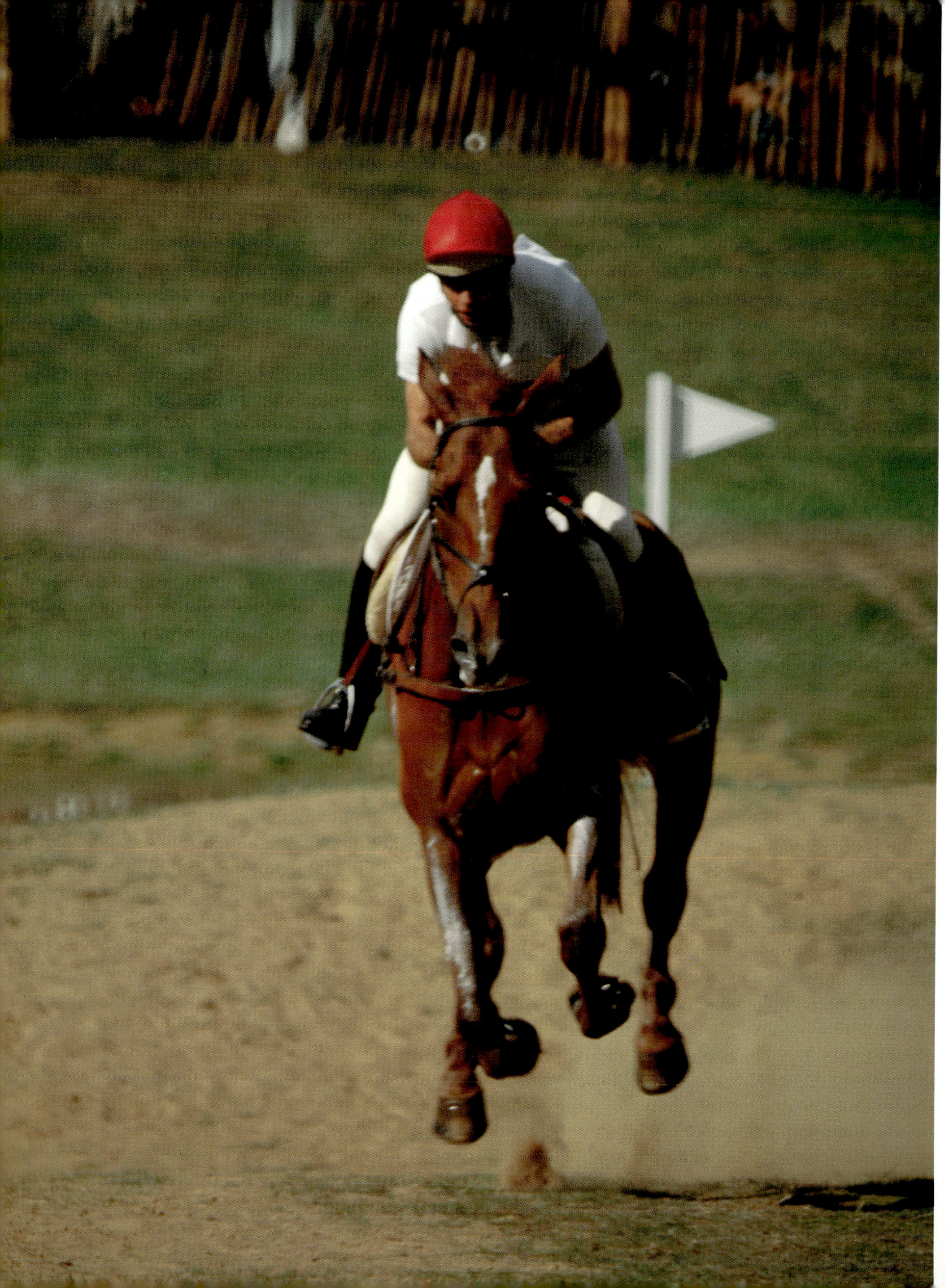

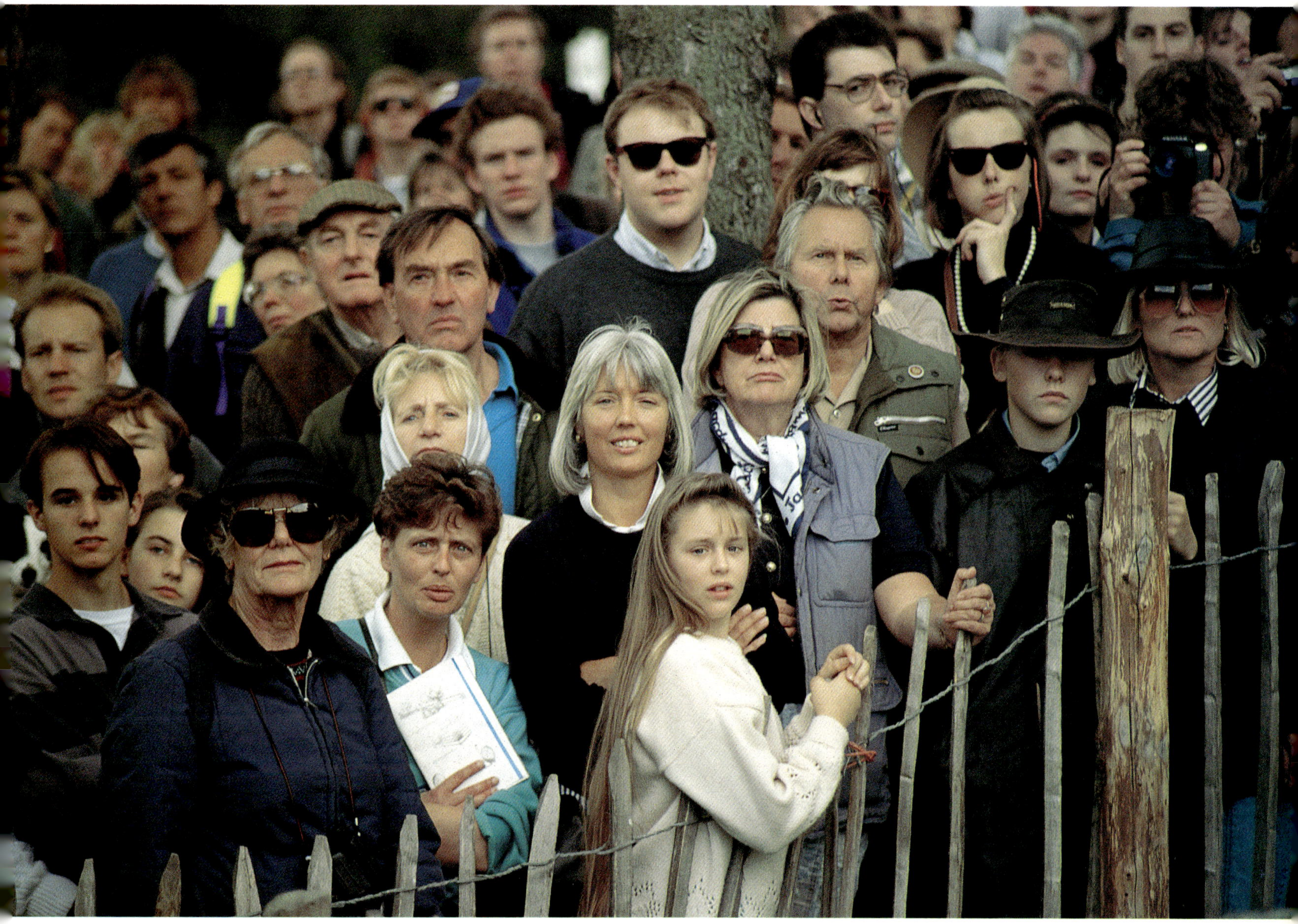

82

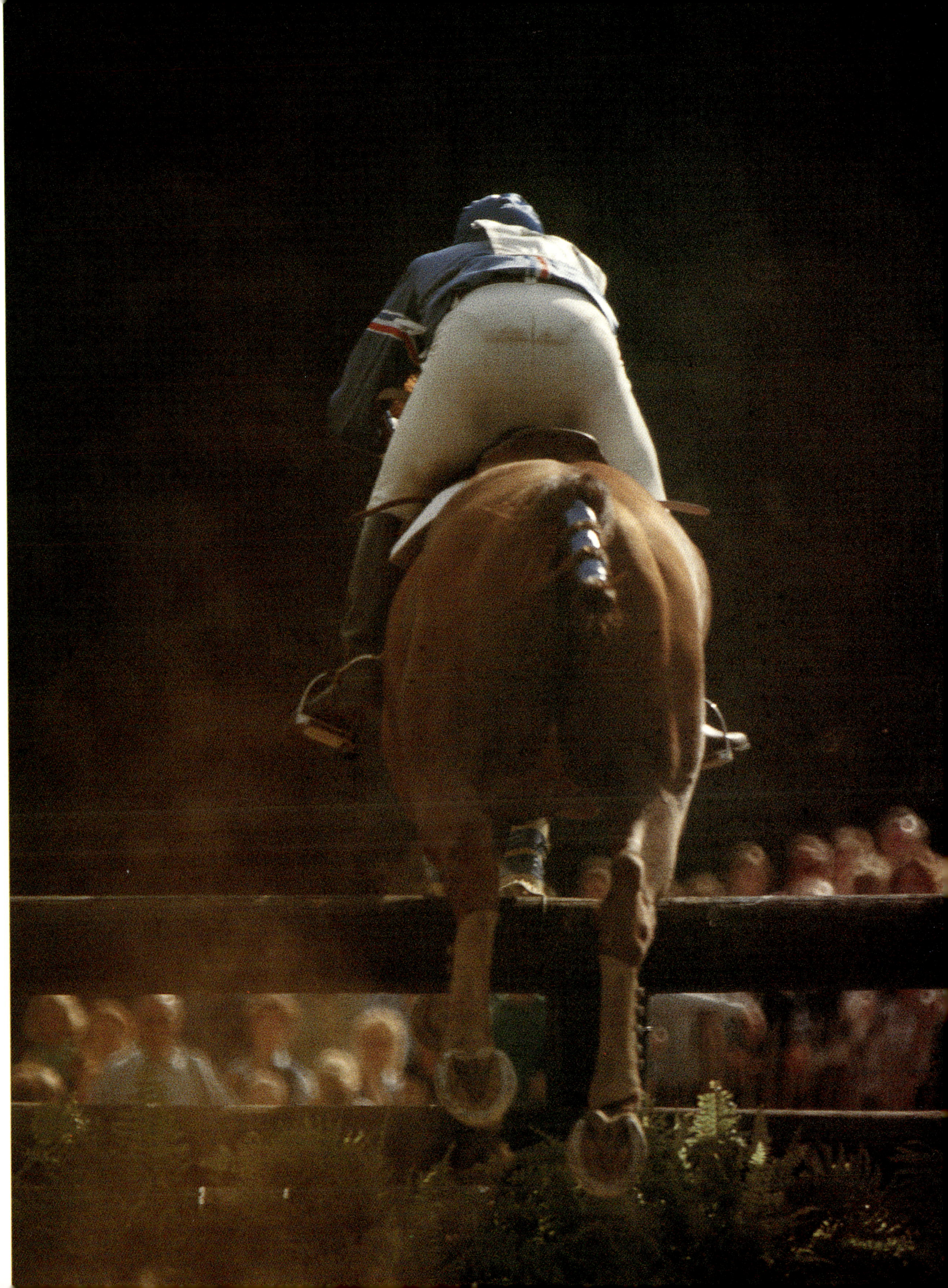

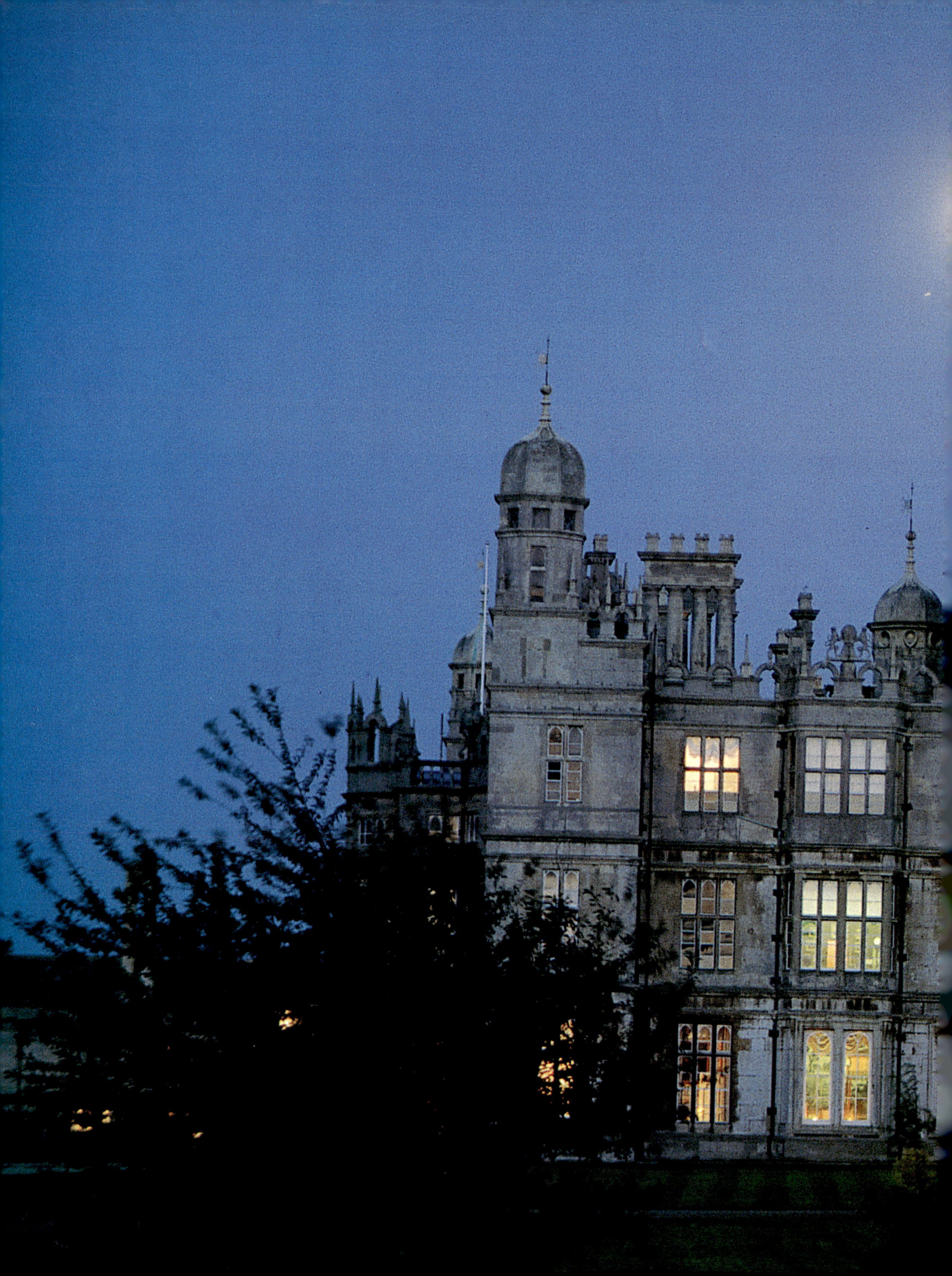

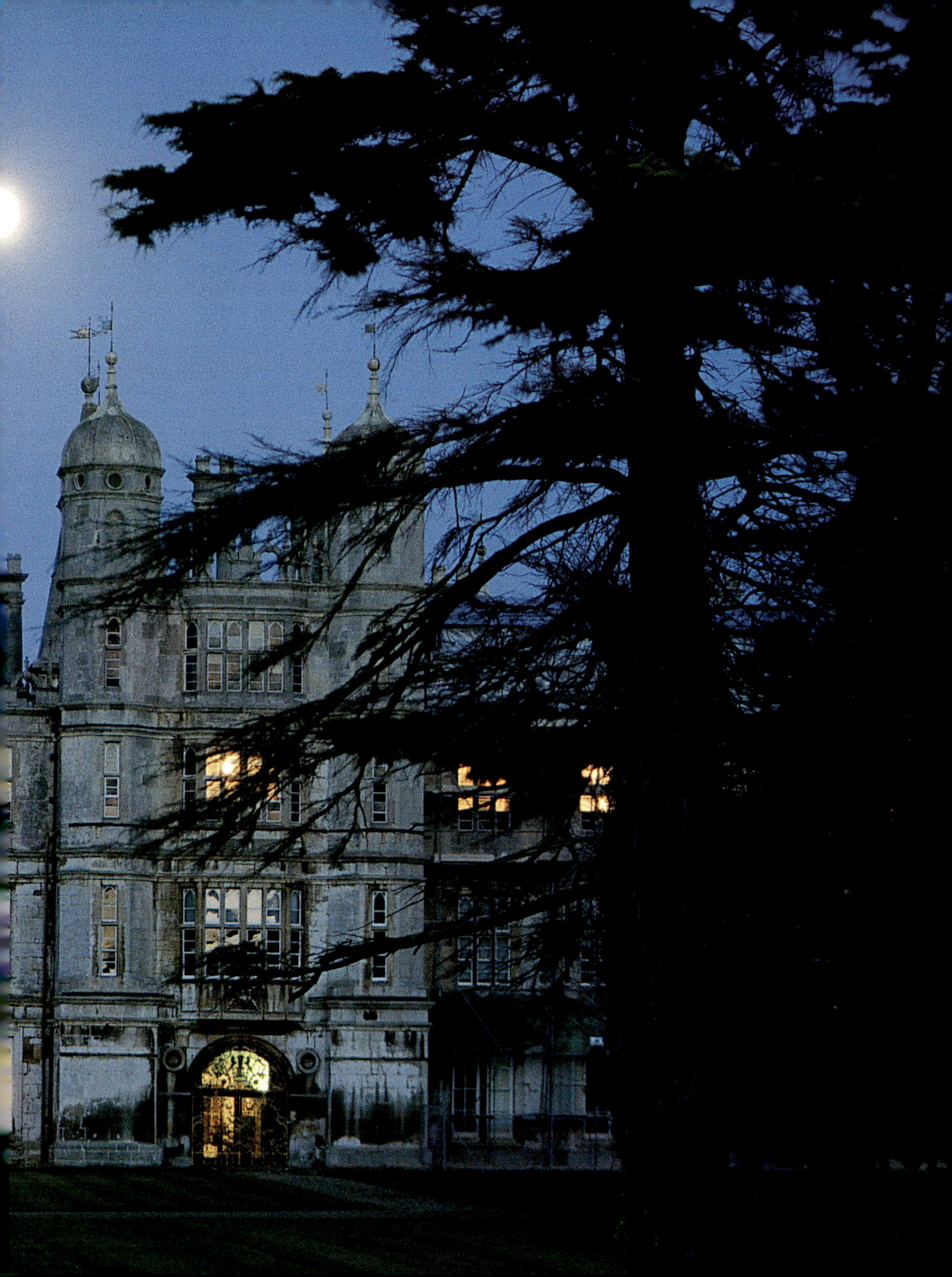

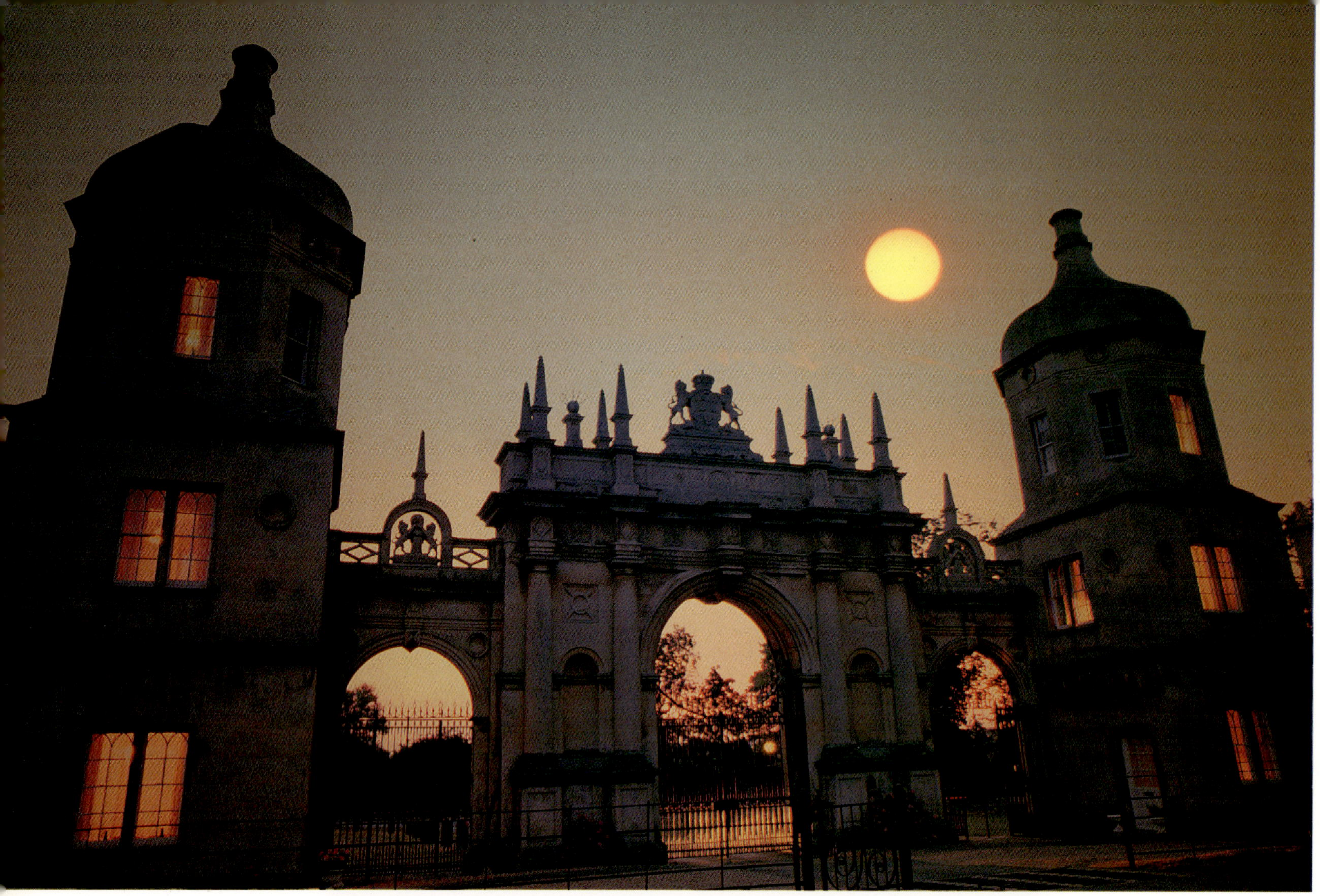

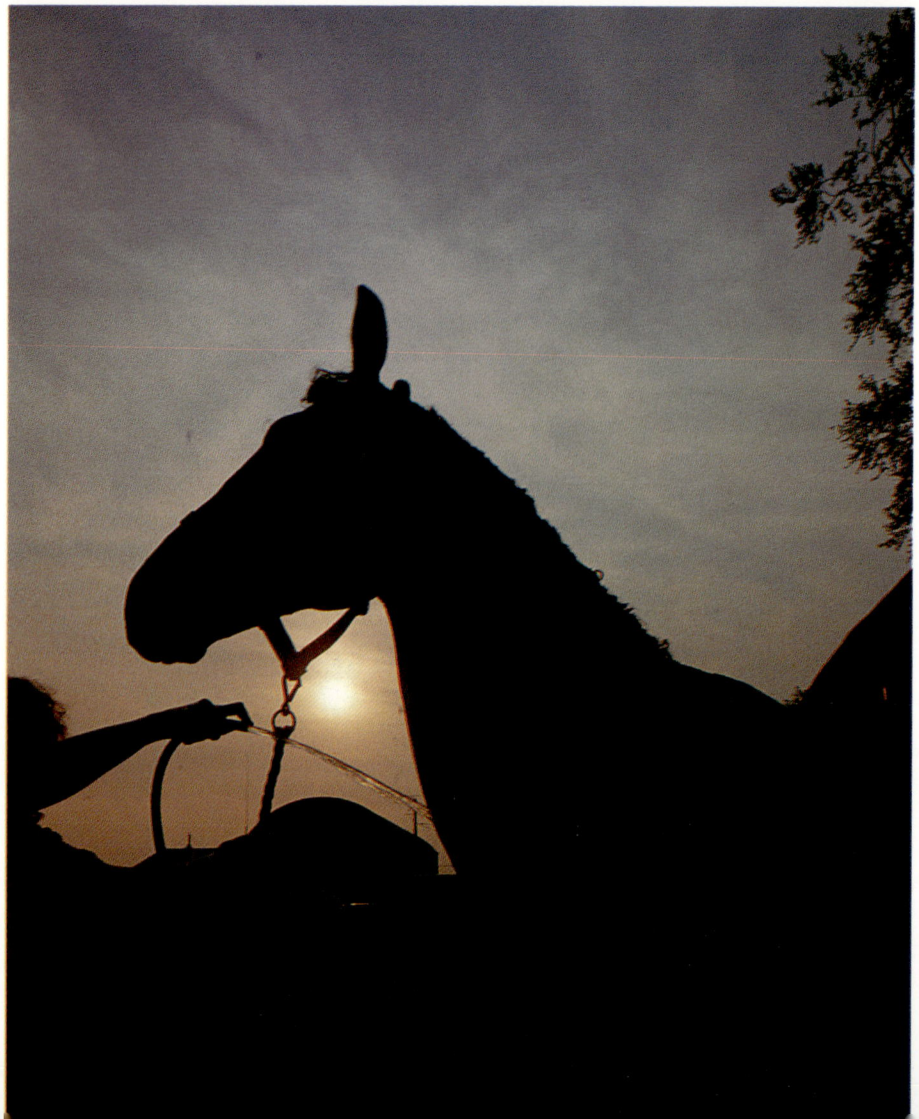

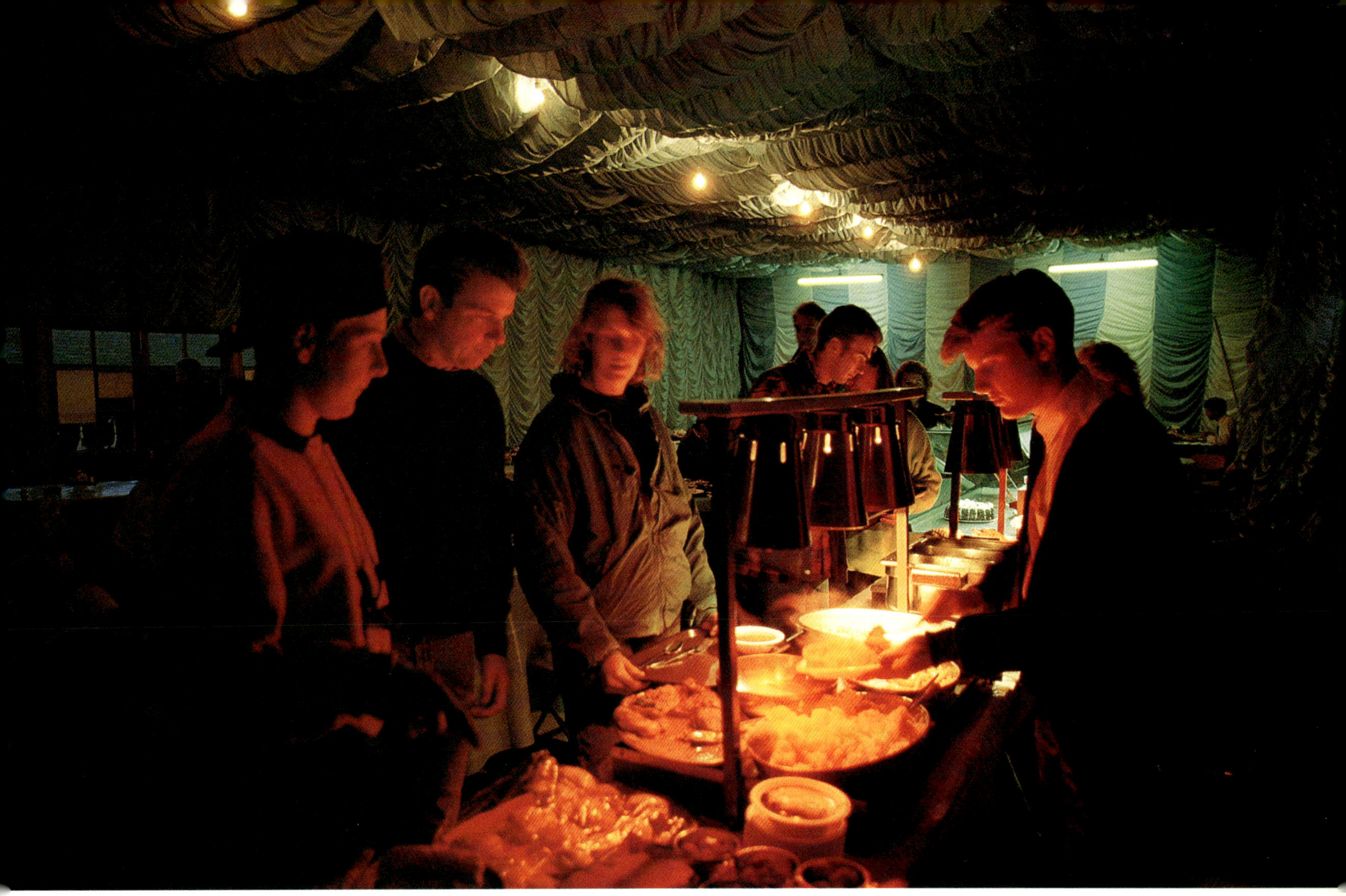

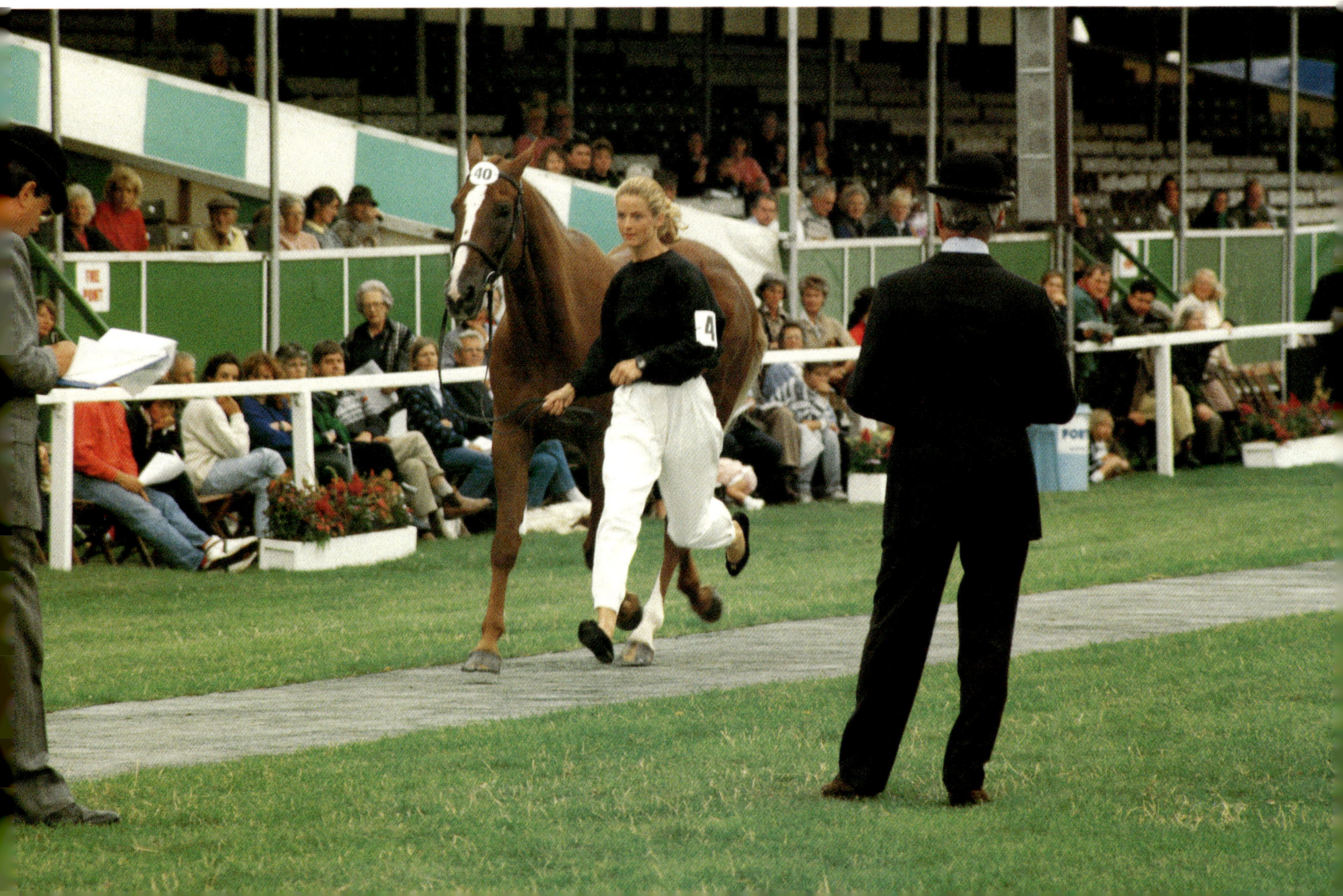
40

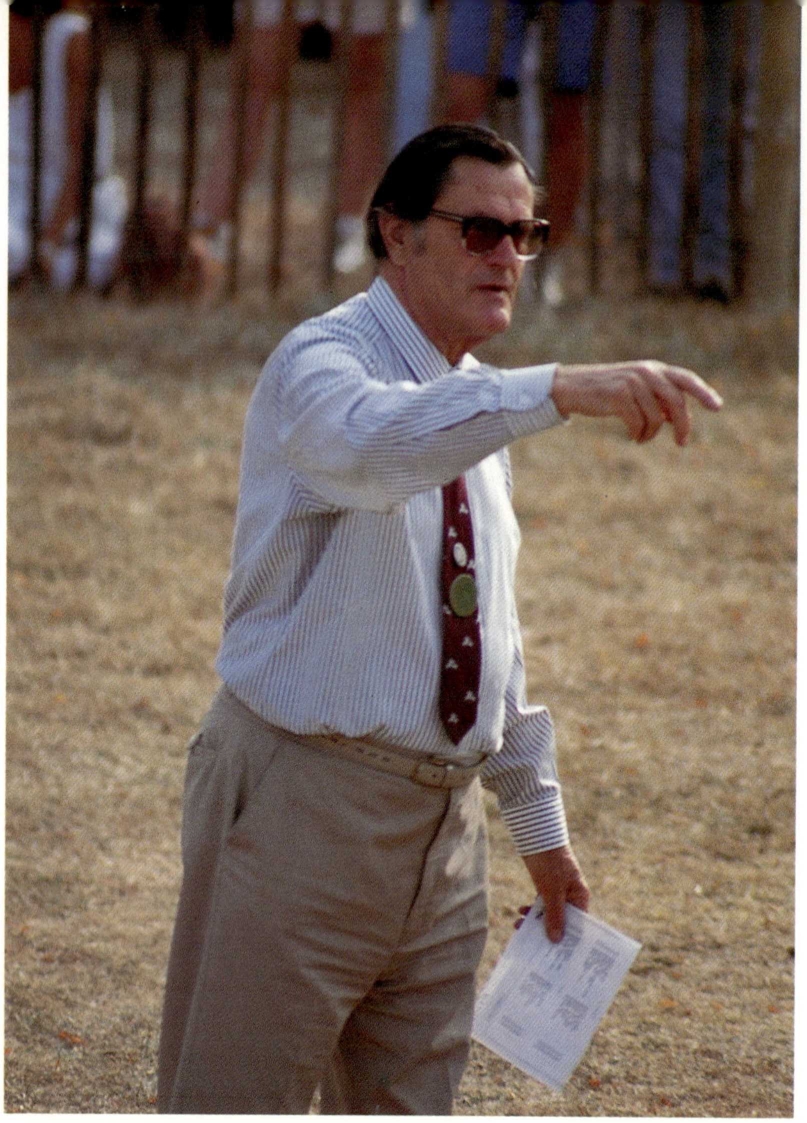
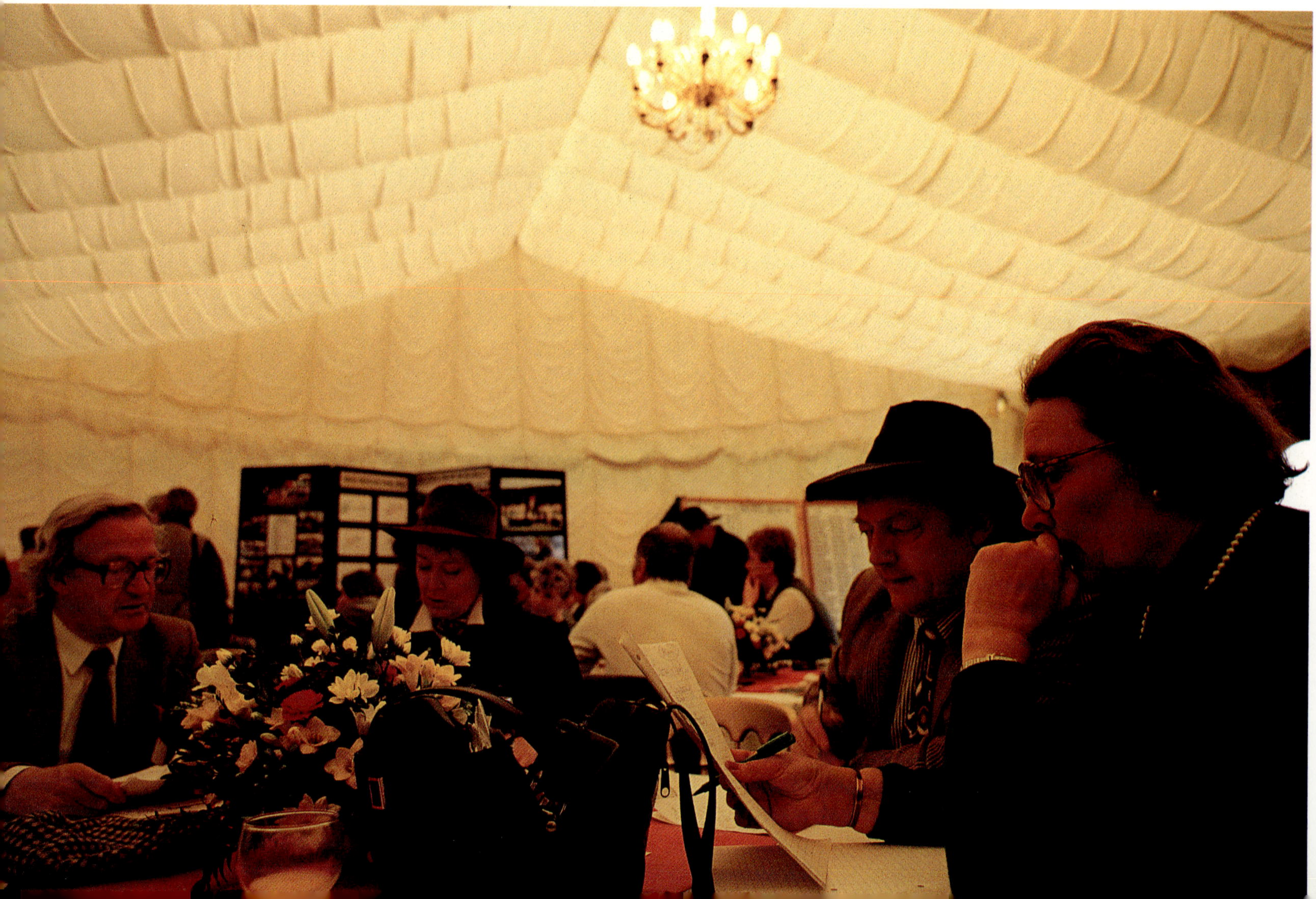

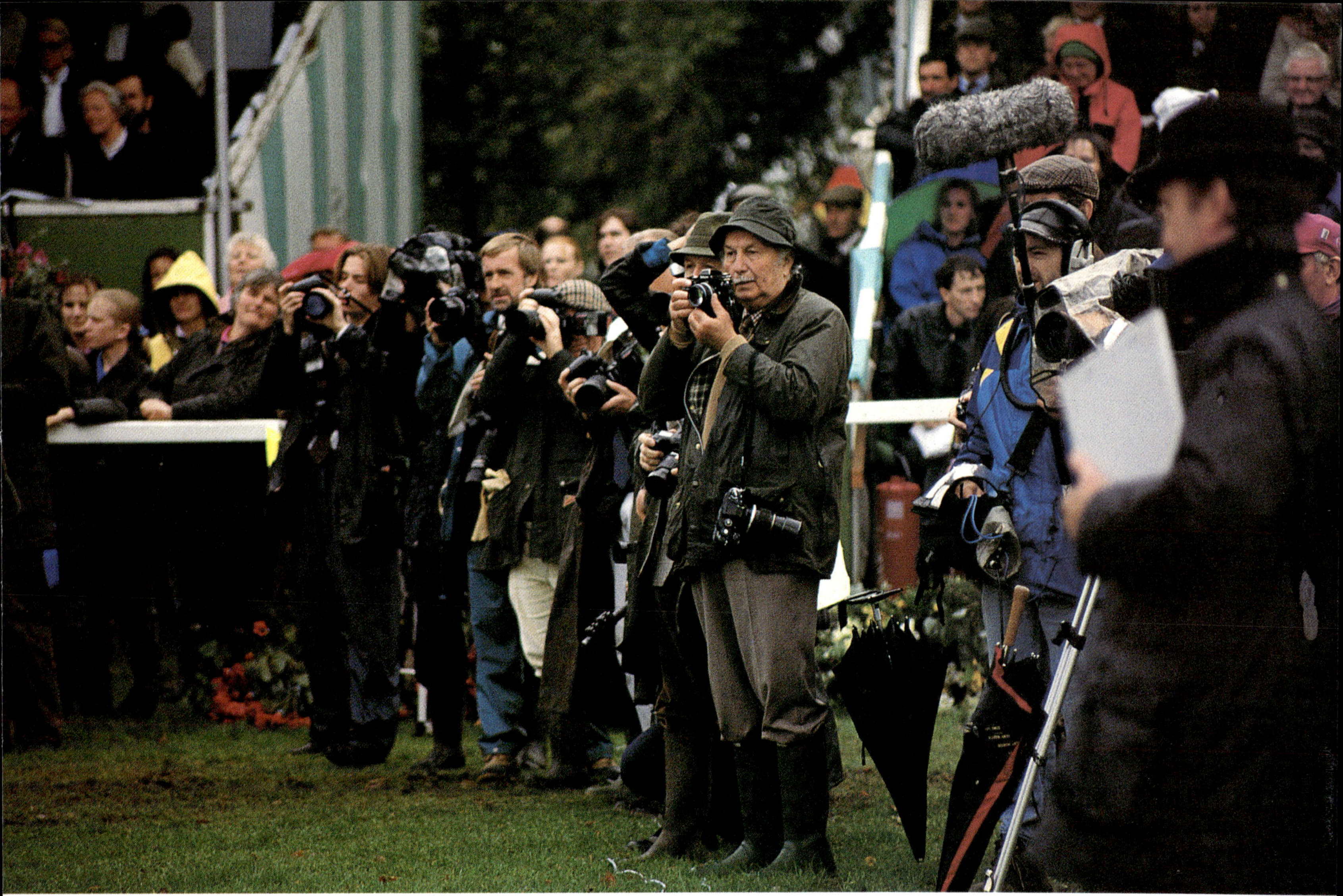

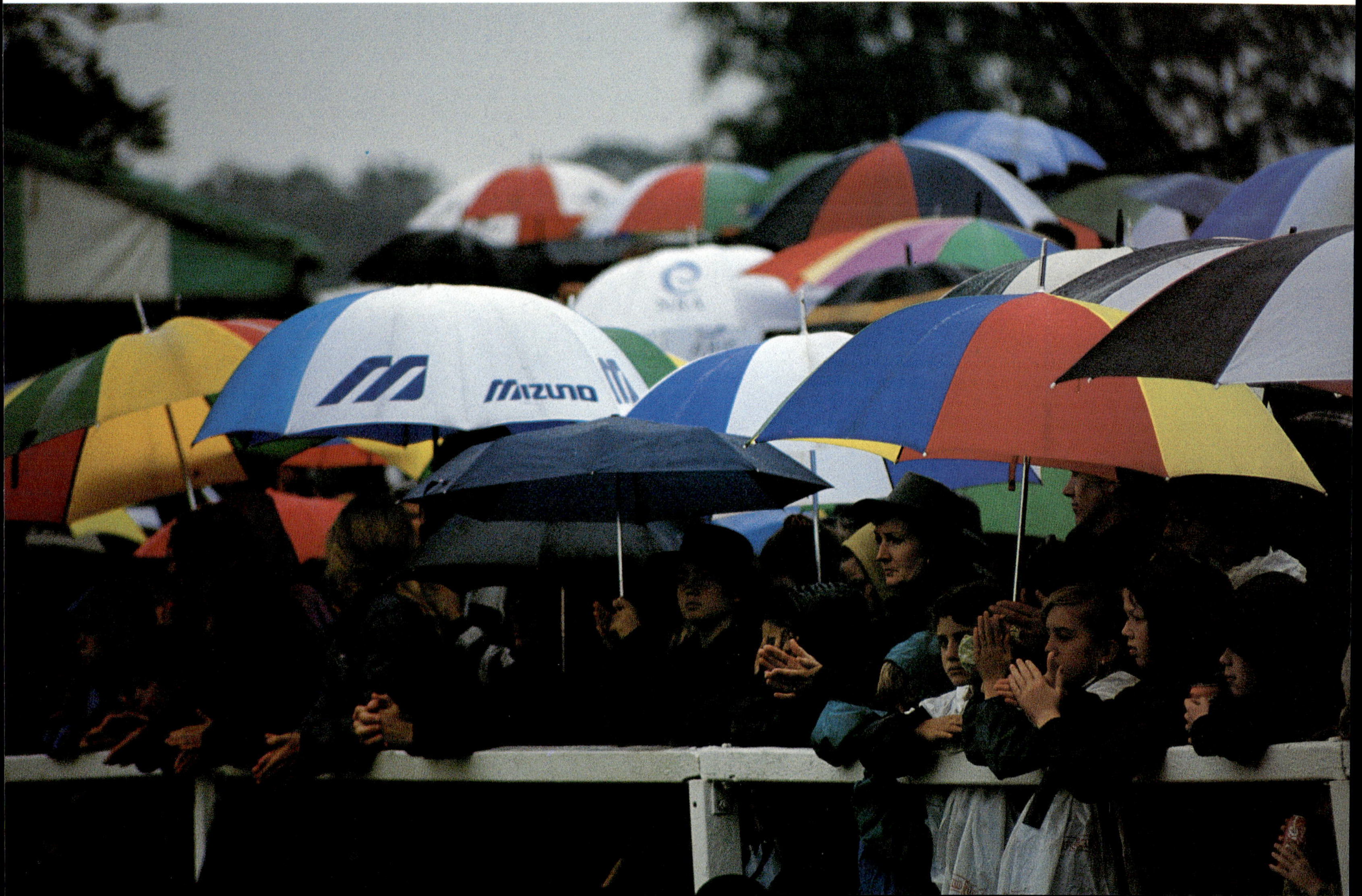
Mizuno

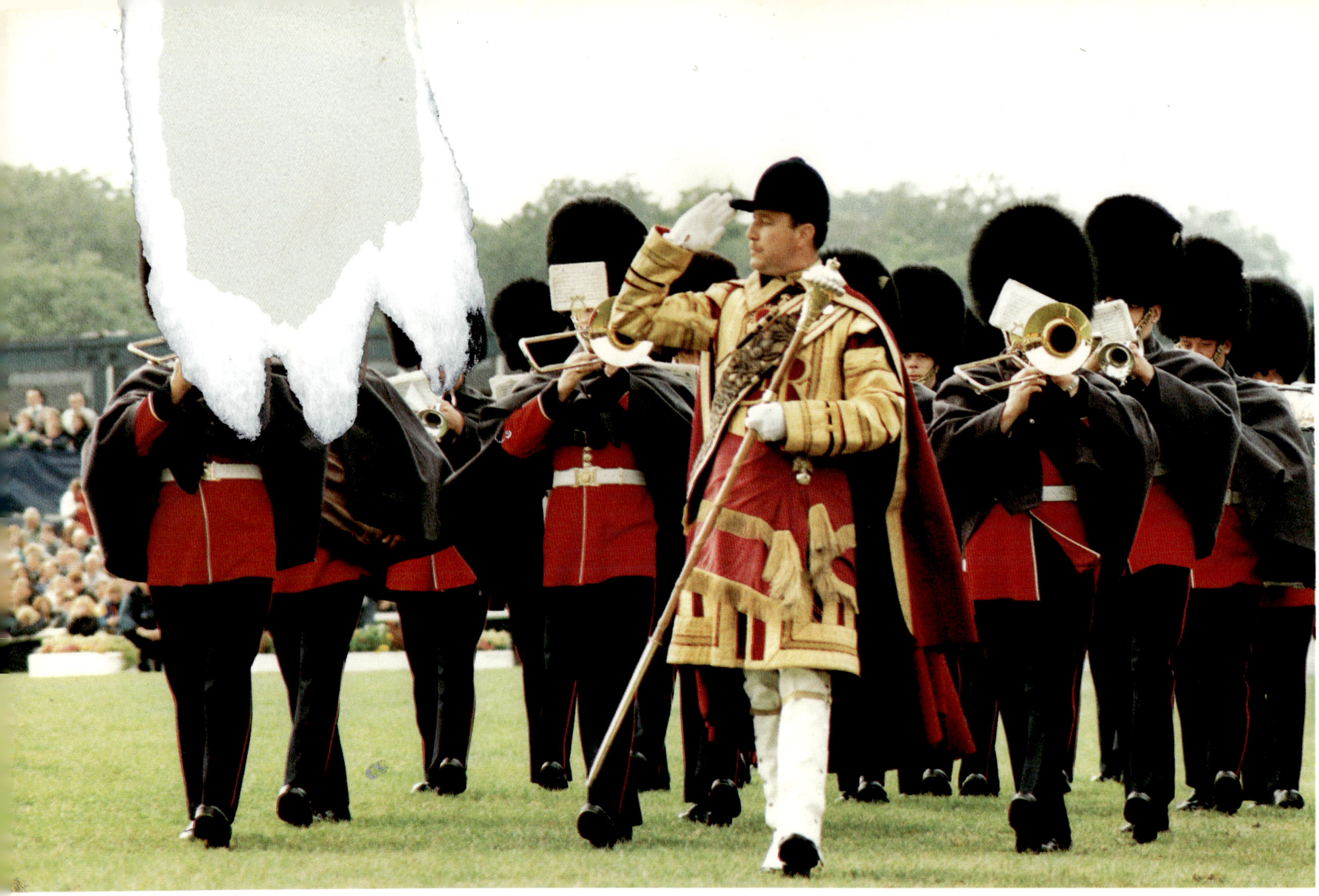

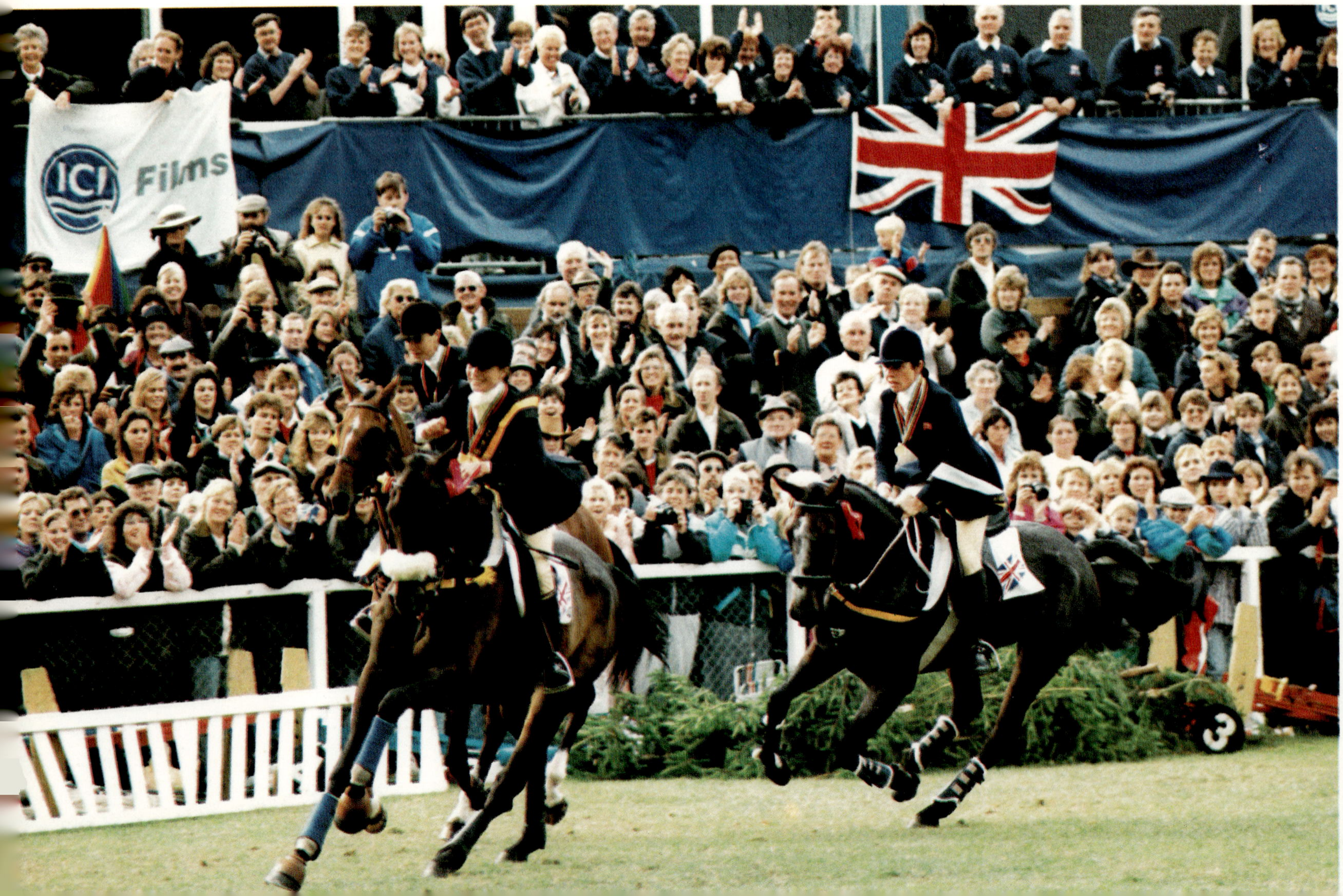
ICI Films

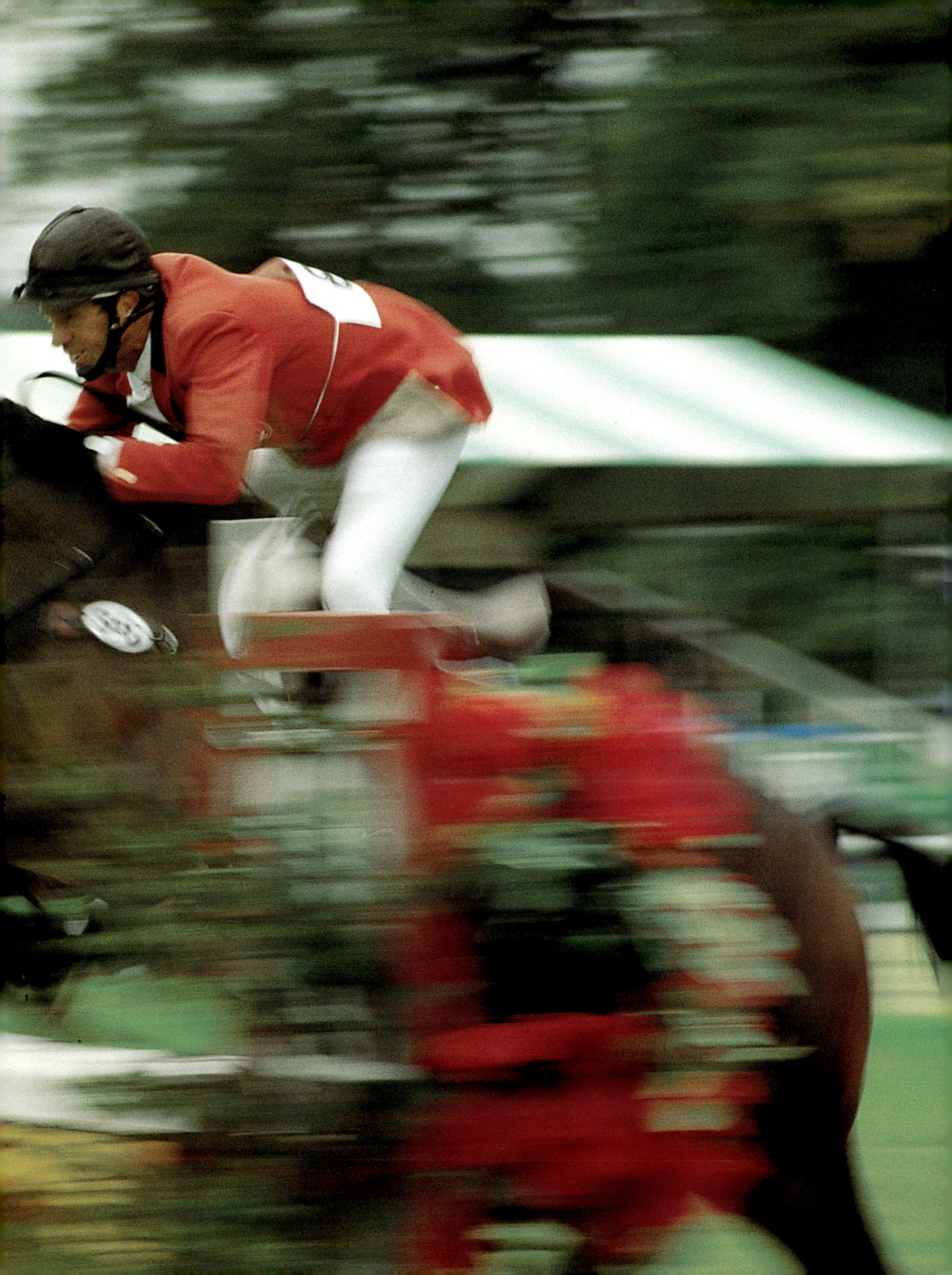

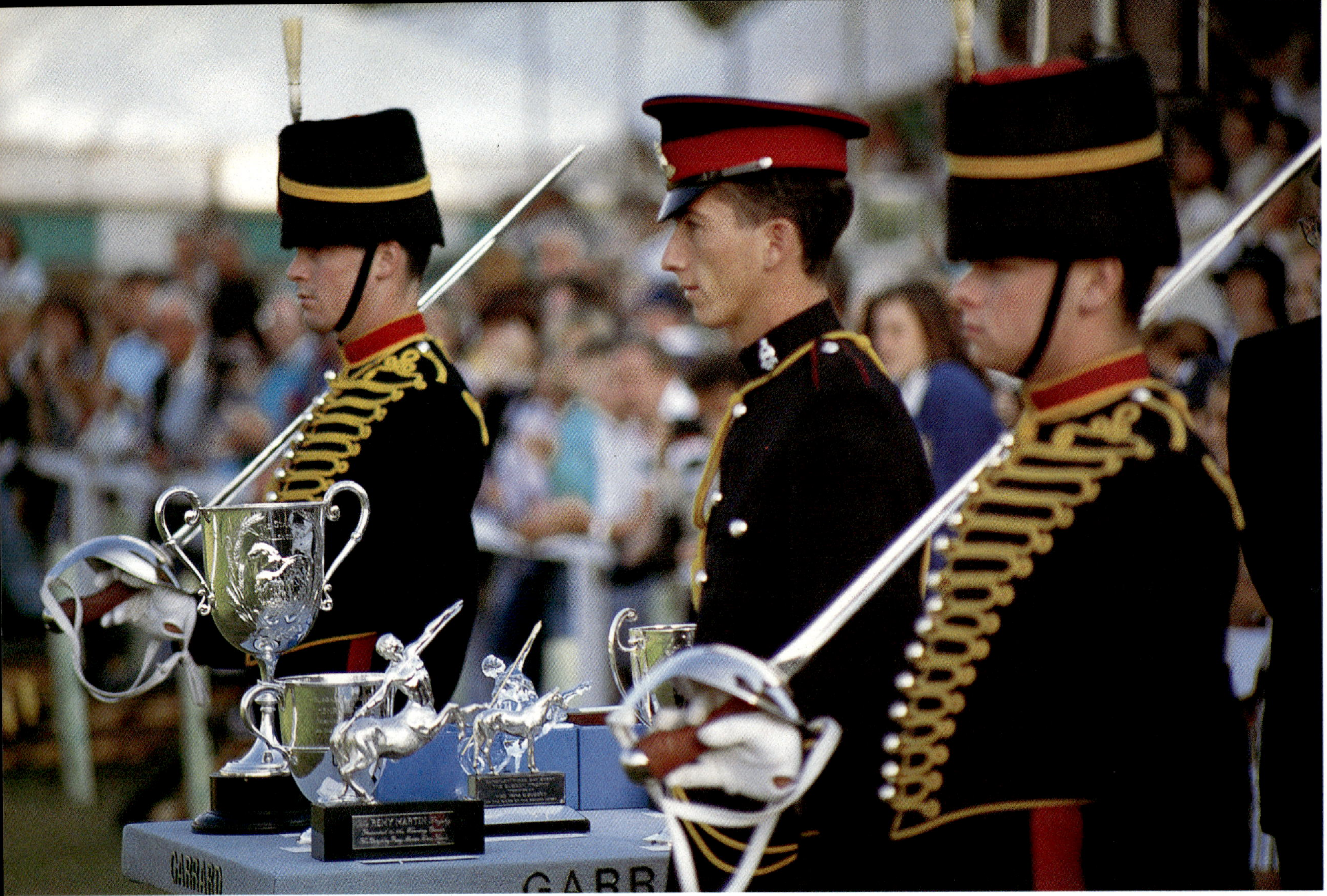
GARRARD

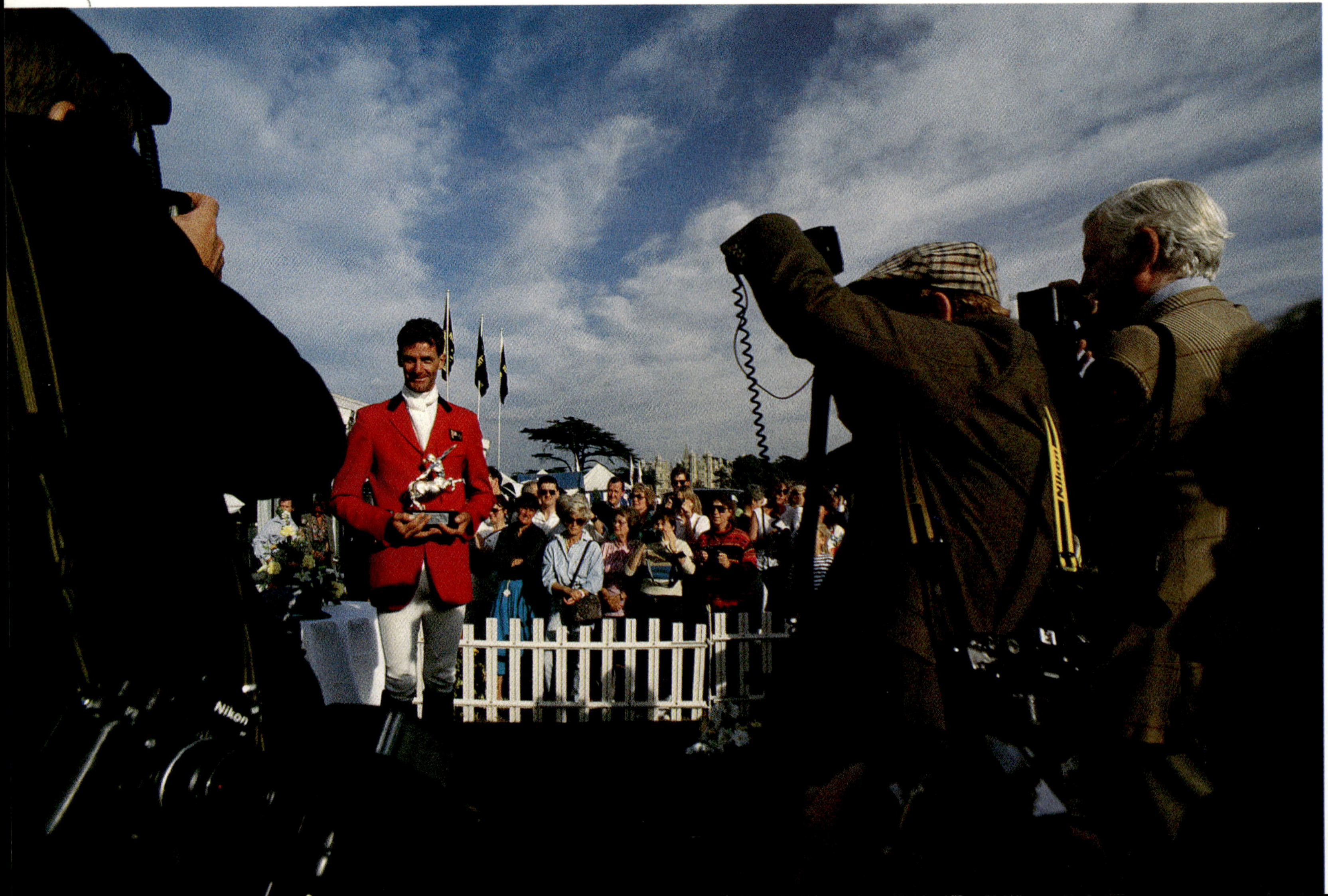
Nikon

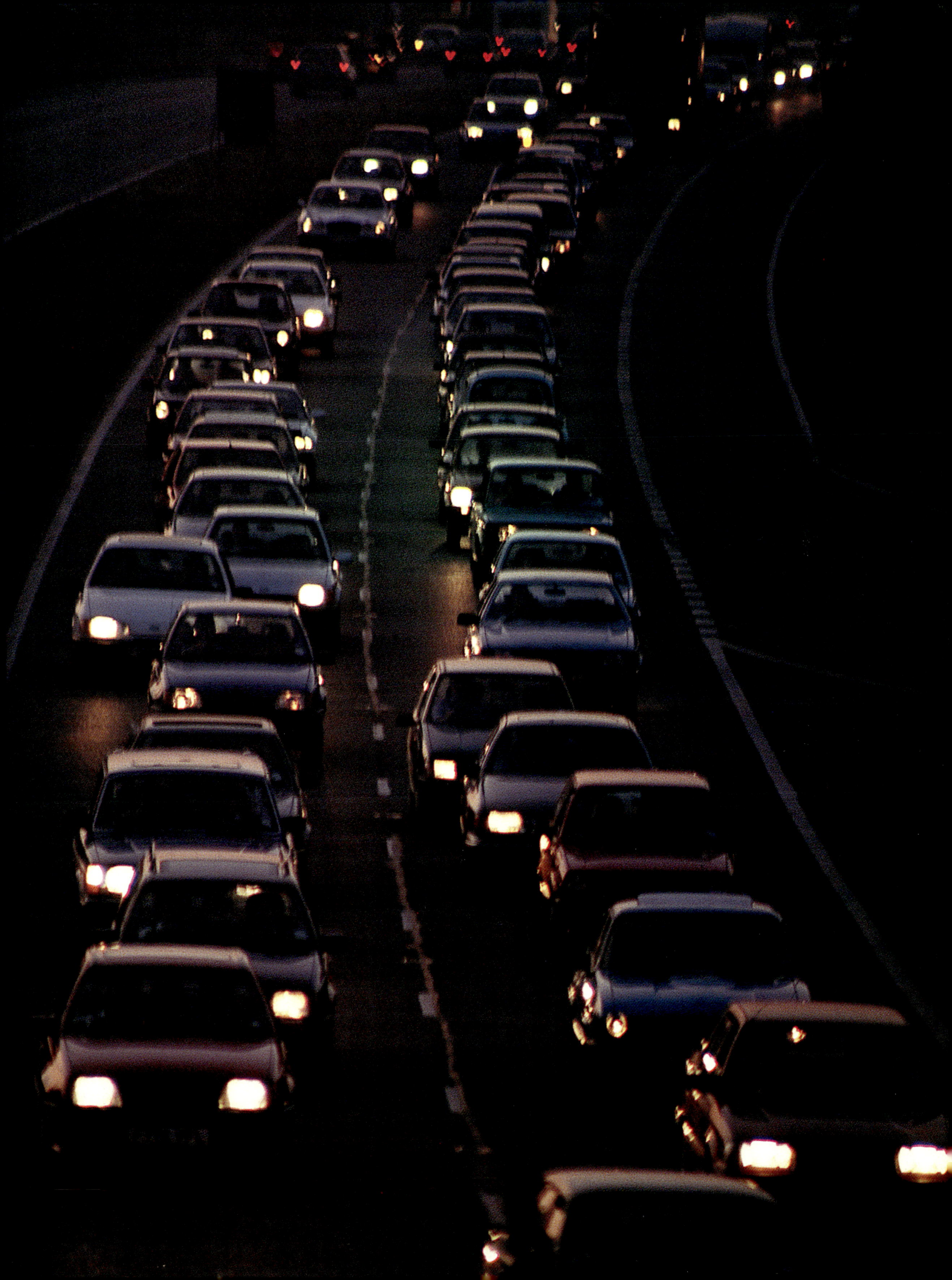

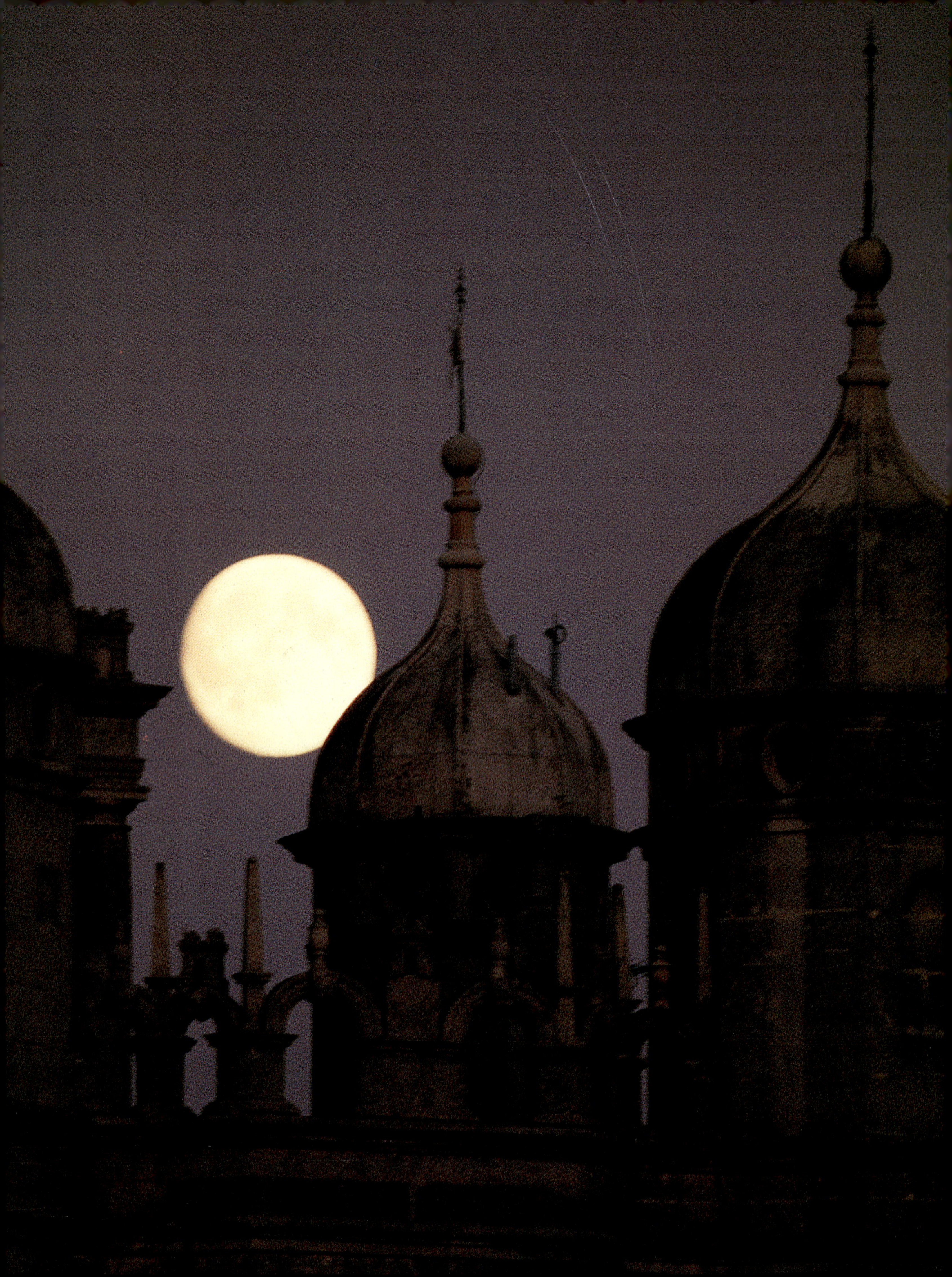

Highlights

Personal Recollections by Jane Pontifex

WITH A superb site, a generous and enthusiastic host, a first-class organiser and an experienced, percipient course designer, all the high hopes of the new event at Burghley were to be more than fulfilled. For me they were exciting times. As BHS Horse Trials executive secretary, I had been closely involved with the running of horse trials for years and chief scorer at events all over the country. Now I was to work under James Grose, newly appointed to the dual role of Director of Horse Trials and of Burghley.

I saw more of the organisation than of the competition itself, spending cross-country day in the scoring tent and catching only an occasional glimpse of the first and last cross-country fences, but I was stationed in the start and finish enclosure, at the nerve-centre of it all.

The eventing world was much smaller in those days and my job was very different from today's computerised wizardry. I typed out laborious tables of times and penalties in advance, for quick reference, but everything else was calculated 'live' by the scoring team.

In that first year there were only 19 starters, but the event itself had got off to an excellent start, with coverage by BBC Grandstand, and with Prince Philip, as President of the FEI, there to present the prizes to the line-up of a mere nine finishers.

The very next year, Burghley was host to the European Championships. We all stayed up to greet the USSR team on their arrival, the horses stumbling, stiff and swollen-legged, out into the summer night air from the cramped lorries in which they had travelled by road and sea. They looked in pretty poor shape but quickly revived, to win the team championship.

Alternative fences, an innovation of Bill Thomson's to cater for less experienced competitors, were in evidence that year, becoming known as an English speciality.

James Grose, staff officer *par excellence*, was a great man for graphs. He had graphs for everything imaginable pinned up on the walls of his office, with different colours for entries, members, ticket sales, trade stands, and so on. Whenever I arrived at Burghley I was hauled off to look at the graphs and admire their steady growth. I do not remember the coloured lines ever turning downwards!

In 1963 that great Irish campaigner, Captain Harry Freeman-Jackson, won on St. Finbarr. In his honour, a strange, shaggy, unkempt individualist, kindly but uncommunicative, known only as Nimpy – who was allowed to live in one of the permanent boxes at the event stables and took an aloof interest in the annual activity surrounding his usually peaceful home – painted 'St. Finnibar' on the wall of the Dutch barn housing the grooms' canteen. The faded name still survives.

Burghley 1964 was dramatic, because team selection was still open for the Tokyo Olympic Games. Richard Meade and Barberry had not been under serious consideration, but they won so convincingly that they were chosen. One of the competitors that year was a certain Bill Henson.

The very first World Championships were to be staged at Burghley in 1966. The bitter disappointment of learning that no horses from Europe would be allowed into the country, due to a swamp fever epidemic, may be imagined. However, a gallant band of Argentinians sailed across the world, spending a month in quarantine before moving in at Burghley. With the Irish, Russians, Americans and British, they brought the total to the required minimum of five teams.

In 1967 Lorna Sutherland (now Clarke) made the first of her record 17 appearances at Burghley and won, on Popadom – the first time a coloured horse had ever won a major event.

In 1968 Sheila Willcox, triple Badminton winner in the '50s, made an unexpected comeback to win on Fair And Square. On the strength of this she was invited to travel to Mexico with the team, but declined the role of reserve rider. The team included last-minute changes from Burghley – Richard Meade on Cornishman V and Ben Jones on The Poacher – but won the gold medal.

In 1969 I was succeeded by Eileen Thomas and moved to the Press tent. It was a completely new experience to be able to watch so much of the competition. One of my tasks was to drive the press to vantage points around the cross-country course and I became familiar with every track, every gap in the ropes, so that I could find them even in the throng of spectators and ferry my charges as quickly as possible without obstructing the paying public.

In 1971 the European Championships came to Burghley once more. What with the heavy demands of the international press and trying to keep the more intrusive newshounds at bay while Princess Anne was competing, I saw rather less of the action than usual, but it was a gratifying climax when the Princess received the championship trophy and congratulatory kisses from her royal parents for an outstanding performance on the Queen's Doublet.

In 1972 the Trout Hatchery provided thrills for the huge crowds with an unprecedented number of duckings. The unfortunate Barbara Pearson (now Hammond) appeared on television screens all over the country diving into the water and emerging backwards from the spray, action-replayed, into the saddle, only to plunge in again and again.

In the World Championships of 1974 Mark Phillips took the lead with the fastest round on Columbus, but Sunday morning brought the crushing news that the horse had slipped a hock tendon, so both individual and team gold medals were lost to the USA.

In the hot, dry summer of 1976, Jane Holderness-Roddam won on Warrior. The horse's breaststrap broke in the show jumping but Jane coolly caught one of the flying ends and kept hold of it to the end of her clear round.

I was not among those present at the European Championships in 1977. Languishing in Stamford hospital with a ruptured disc, I had to rely upon my many kind visitors each evening for an account of the proceedings. Apparently Lucinda Prior-Palmer had felt ill for most of the event, so her first Burghley and second European Championship victory was possibly the most dramatic of her career.

In 1978 Lorna Sutherland won again, on Greco, and the Junior European Championships were run concurrently, but it was one of the rare occasions when Britain's juniors won no medals.

By now the entries for Burghley were huge, but 1980 still holds the record of 79 starters.

Winner for the second time in 1981, on Beagle Bay, Lucinda Prior-Palmer presented Lord Exeter with a painting to mark the event's 21 years. It was to be his last appearance as President. Both he and Lady Exeter died within the next 12 months. In 1983 their daughter, Lady Victoria Leatham, took over the presidency of the horse trials. Her first year coincided with the Young Rider European Championships, in which Britain won team gold, and also with the advent of Remy Martin as sponsors. In their honour Bill Thomson designed a huge timber 'brandy glass' obstacle where Virginia Holgate and Priceless served notice of their future virtuosity by jumping in a dead straight line across the two curving rails of the 'bowl' and the corner where the 'stem' met the 'foot' of the glass, without any break in the rhythm of their stride.

In 1984 Philip Herbert took over as Clerk of the Course, Bill Thomson retiring to an honoured role on the Committee as Course Consultant.

In 1985 Britain cleaned up at Burghley's European Championships, winning the team gold and all three individual medals. Philip Herbert's fourth fence, a formidable bullfinch beyond a ditch, was the focus of much attention. Both the longer and the direct routes were tried, with mixed results. France's Jean Teulère riding Godelureau received a rousing cheer as the first to clear it. Then Clarissa Strachan and Delphy Dazzle negotiated it with cool perfection – making it look positively easy.

For the first time I was covering the event for *Horse and Hound*. Over the years the press facilities have improved out of all recognition and they are now superb, with up-to-the-minute computerised results and closed circuit television – essential for the daily correspondents who have to file their copy almost before the cross-country is over.

Television is the only way to get anything like a comprehensive view of the competition and I too generally end up in front of it, but I always start my day out on the course, to watch closely, absorb the atmosphere and set my own adrenalin running. The start of the cross-country at a big three-day event, the hush that falls on the crowd as a steward's whistle heralds the approach of the first competitor to one of the more challenging fences, is still, for me, most exciting.

In 1986 Ginny Leng scored her record fourth successive victory and in 1987 the cross-country course ran for the first time through the main arena. There Philip Herbert had built for the sponsors a massive timber 'RM', which had to be completely removed afterwards, ready for the morrow's show jumping.

Philip's course the following year, beautifully built as ever, presented a succession of problems. Mark Todd's 15-year-old Olympic champion, Charisma, performed with his customary brilliance, only to be overtaken in the show jumping by his younger stablemate, Wilton Fair, achieving for Mark a record first and second.

In 1989 Mark Phillips was invited to design Burghley's European Championship course. He incorporated a roofed shed in a completely revamped Trout Hatchery complex and, for the arena obstacle, built the Remy Martin Selection, a sinuous three-effort rail, filled in with barrels. Everybody was very circumspect at this fence until Ian Stark, last of the British team, rode Glenburnie through on the straight line, jumping three times at an angle. It was risky, and word had got about that Mark had bet him he wouldn't do it, but it worked and the crowd watching from the grandstand went wild.

Ian faced controversy again in 1990, falling with his last-minute ride on Sarah Bullen's Alfresco at the end of the course. I particularly remember Richard Walker's inspired ride on Jacana and the sickening clunk when Mary Thomson on King Cuthbert hit the last fence in the show jumping and lost to Mark Todd.

The following year Mark Phillips designed an elaborate Sunken Road complex where even the most dashing competitors chose the long way round and only Carolyne Ryan-Bell jumped straight through the middle on Hooray Henry.

On the last two days of the 1992 event Burghley's reputation for fantastic weather suffered a setback: but, undeterred, Charlotte Hollingsworth and The Cool Customer won at their first attempt and Ian Stark led his famous pair of greys, Murphy Himself and Glenburnie, out of the rainswept arena into retirement.

The Winners

1961 Anneli Drummond-Hay and Merely-a-Monarch at the Trout Hatchery.

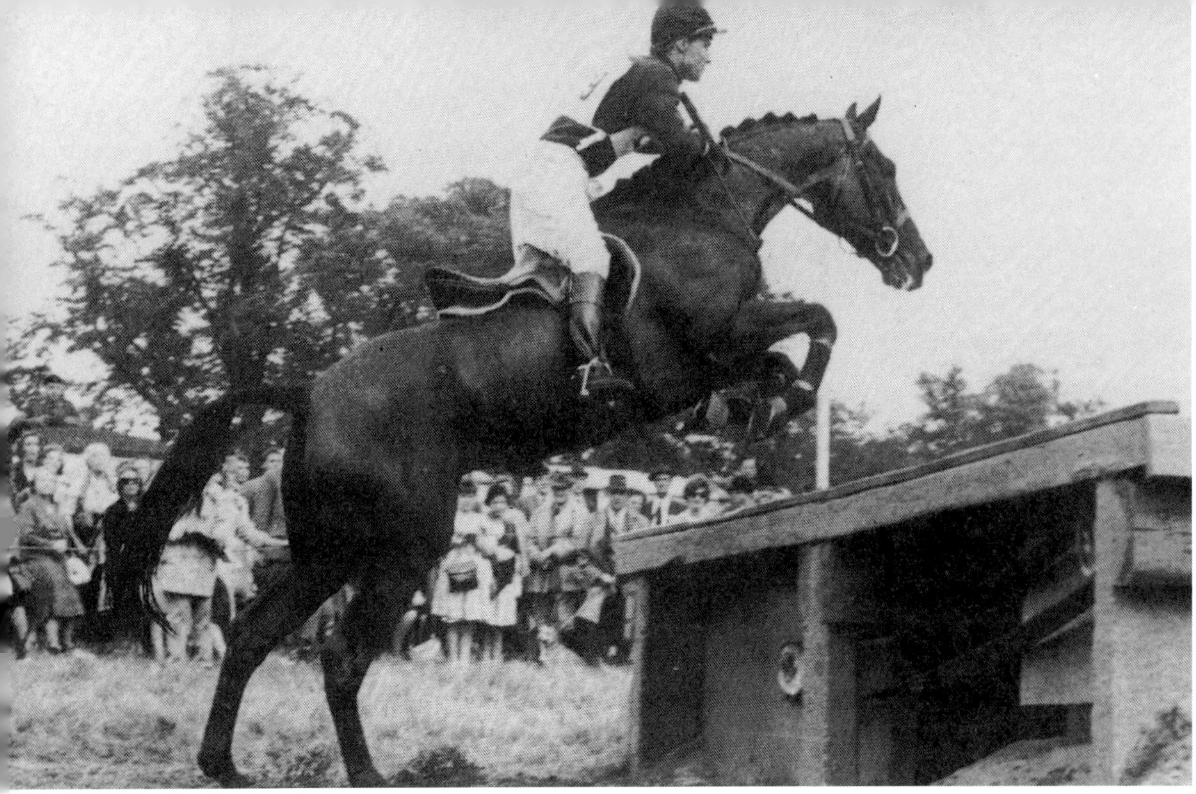

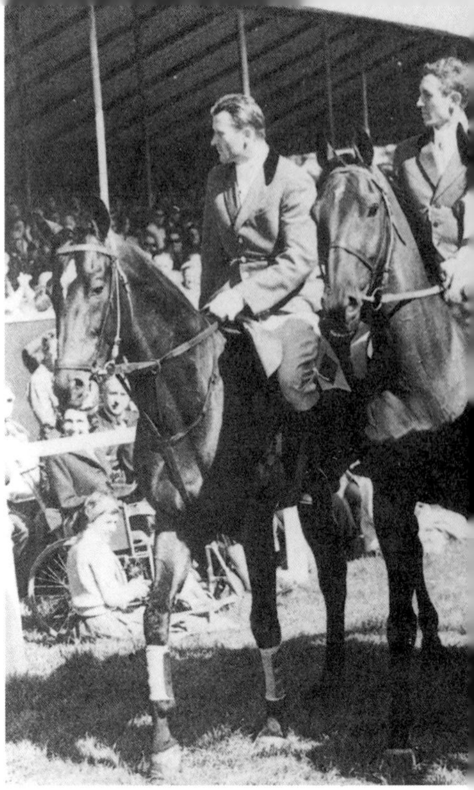

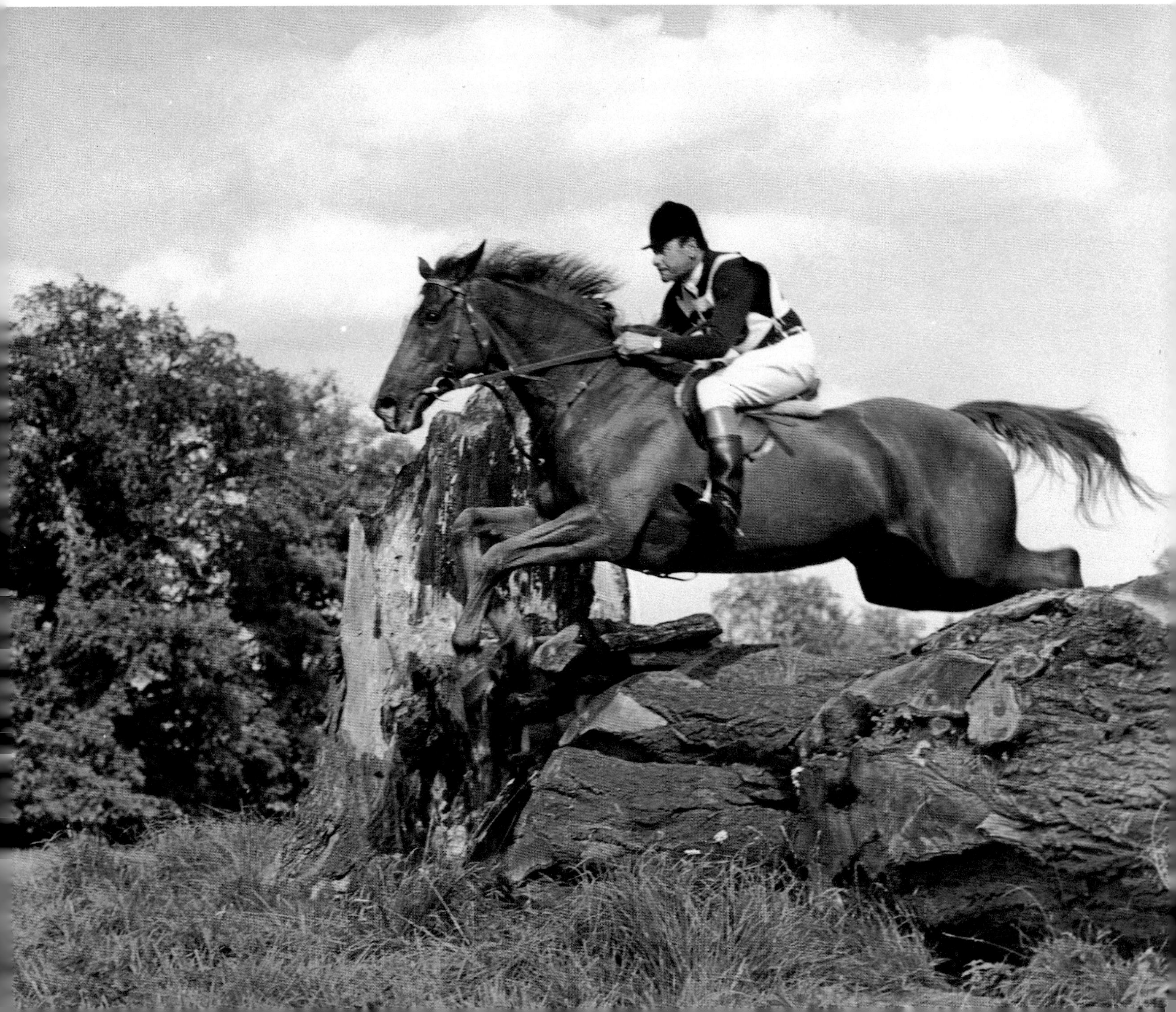

Top left and *centre* **1962 European Championships** *Individual* Captain James Templer and M'Lord Connolly. *Team* USSR: G. Gazumov/Granz; P. Deyev/Satrap; B. Konkov/Rumb; L. Baklyschkin/Khirurg.

Left **1963** Captain Harry Freeman-Jackson and St Finbarr (Ire).

Top right **1964** Richard Meade and Barberry. *Above* **1965** Captain Jeremy Beale and Victoria Bridge.

1966 World Championships, (*Right*) *Individual* Captain Carlos Moratorio and Chalan (Arg). (*Above, right*) *Team* Ireland: Major Eddie Boylan/Durlas Eile; Penny Moreton/Loughlin; Virginia Freeman-Jackson/Sam Weller; T. Brennan/Kilkenny.

Top left **1967** Lorna Sutherland and Popadom. *Top right* **1968** Sheila Willcox and Fair and Square. *Above* **1969** Gillian Watson and Shaitan. *Left* **1970** Judy Bradwell and Don Camillo.

Facing page **1971 European Championships**. (*Top*) *Individual* HRH The Princess Anne and Doublet. (*Centre*) *Team* Great Britain: Richard Meade/The Poacher; Lt. Mark Phillips/Great Ovation; Debbie West/Baccarat; Mary Gordon Watson/Cornishman V. *Far right* **1972** Janet Hodgson and Larkspur. *Right* **1973** Captain Mark Phillips and Maid Marion.

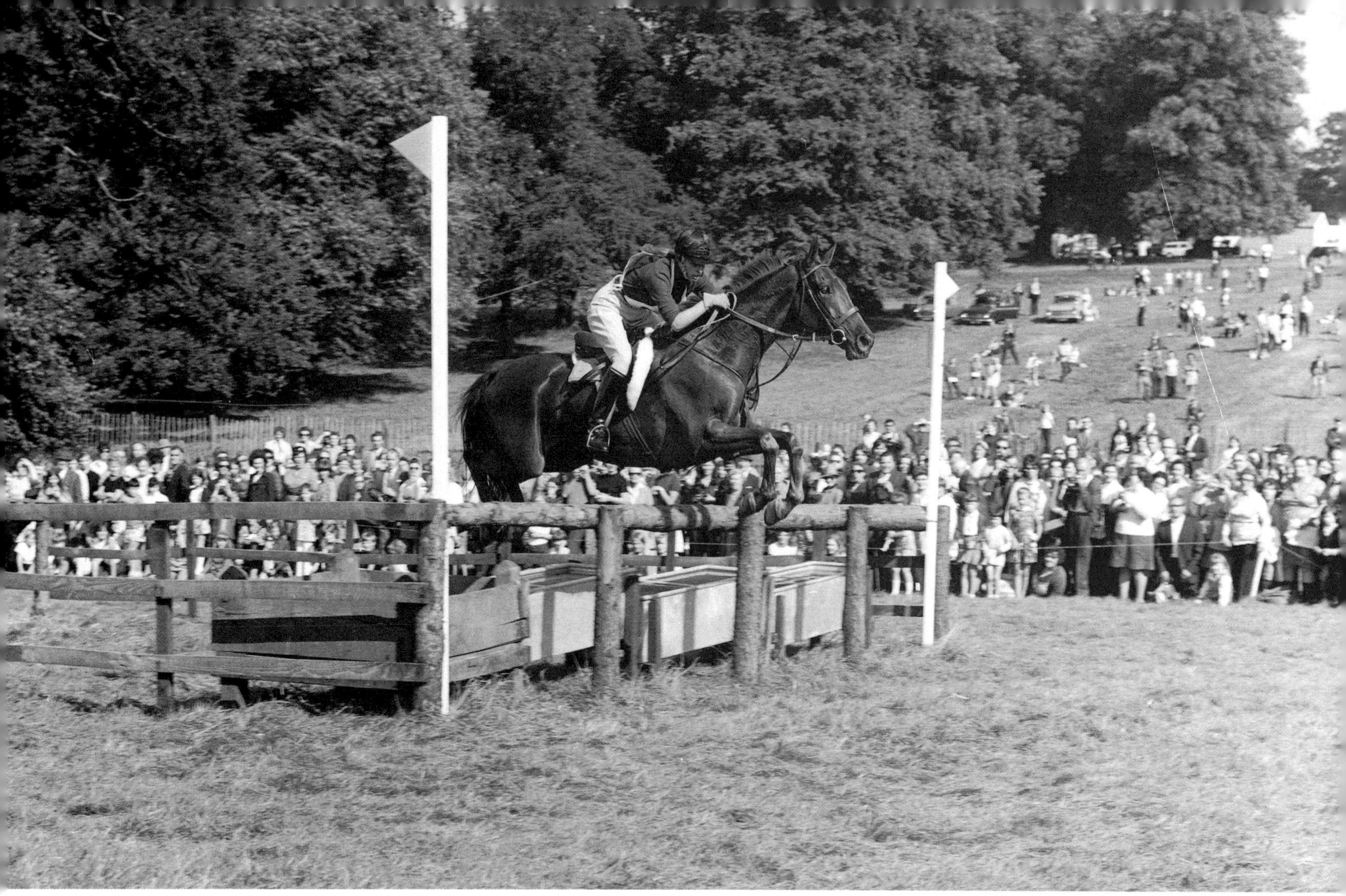

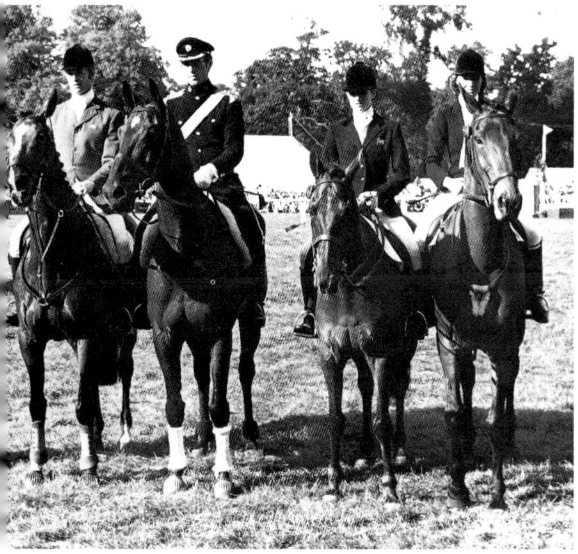

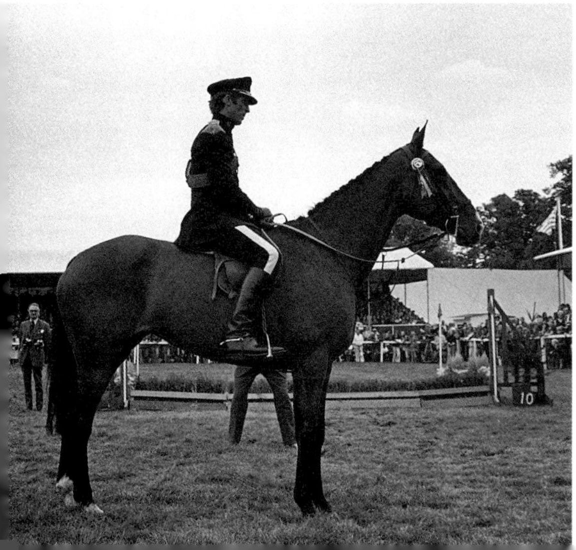
10

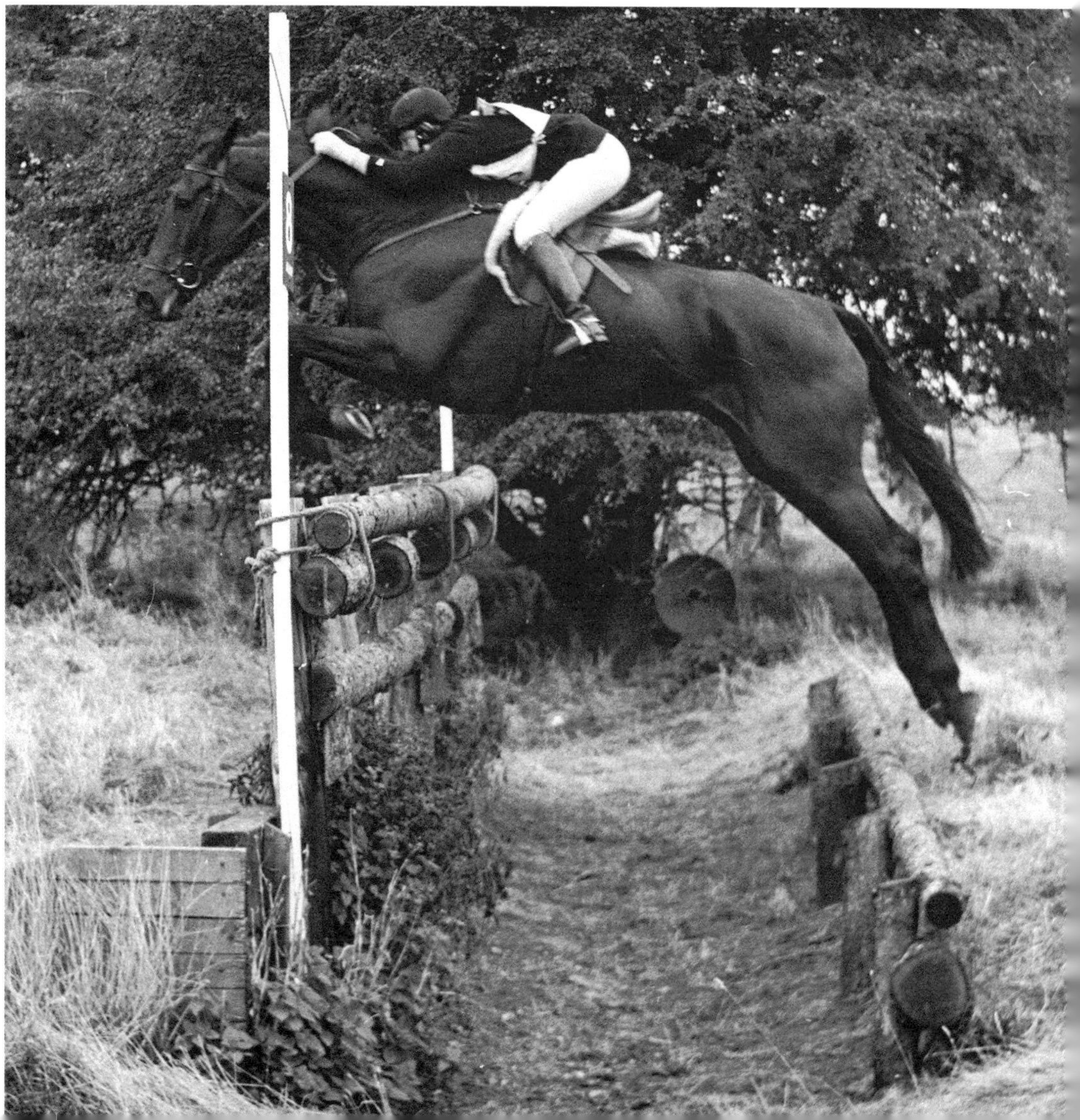

1974 World Championships. (*Right*) *Individual* Bruce Davidson and Irish Cap (USA): (*Below*) *Team* USA: J. M. Plumb/Good Mixture; E. Emerson/Victor Dakin; D. Sachey/Plain Sailing; B. Davidson/Irish Cap.

Below, right **1975** Aly Pattinson and Carawich. *Bottom* **1976** Jane Holderness-Roddam and Warrior.

1977 European Championships (*Left*) *Individual* Lucinda Prior-Palmer and George. (*Below, left*) *Team* Great Britain: Lucinda Prior-Palmer/George; Jane Holderness-Roddam/Warrior; Clarissa Strachan/Merry Sovereign; Chris Collins/Smokey VI.

1978 European Junior Championships. *Individual* (*left*) Dietrich Baumbart and Kurfurst (W. Germany). (*Above*) *Team* W. Germany: D. Baumgart/Kurfurst; R. Ehrenbrink/Huntsman; M. Hilker/Doran; Edith Schlees/Pigane.

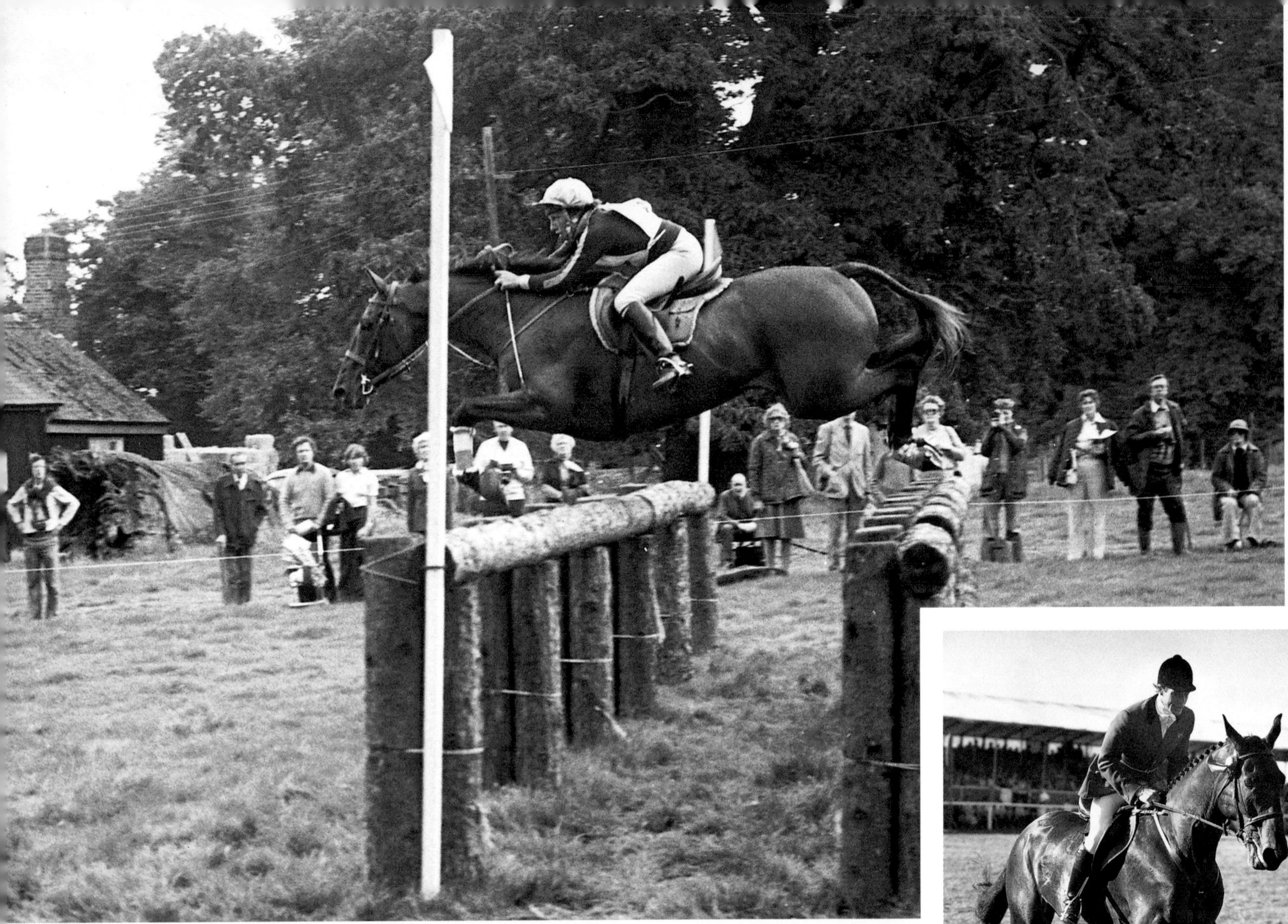

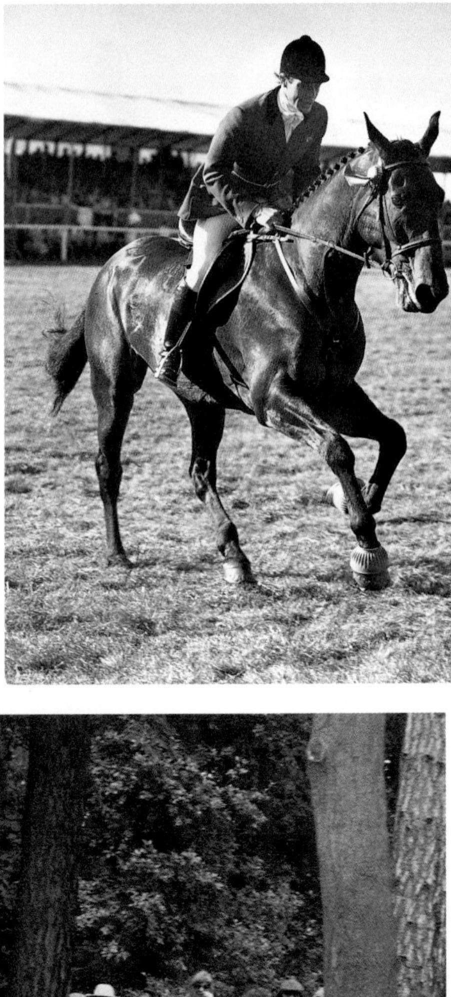

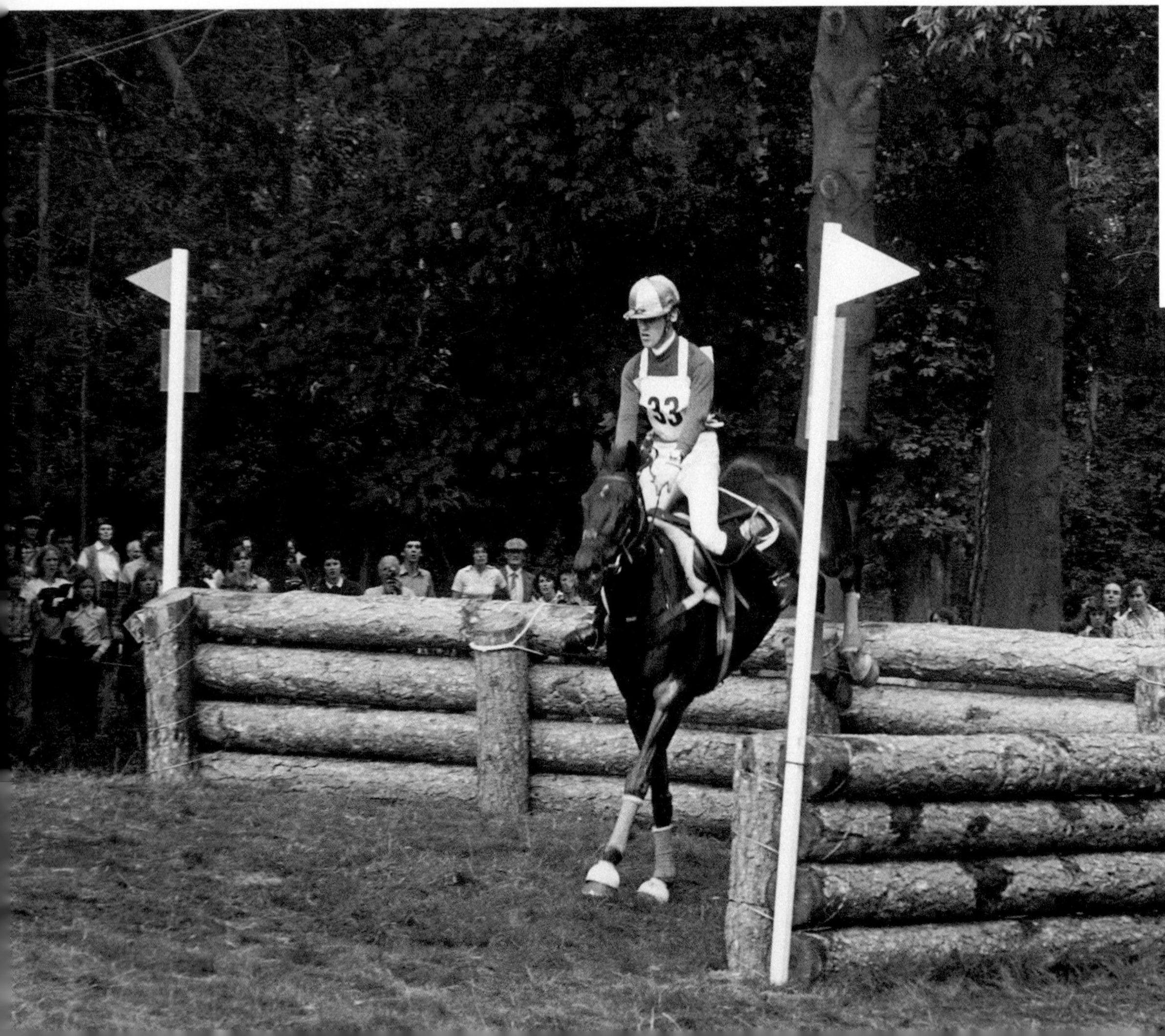
33

Left **1981** Lucinda Prior-Palmer and Beagle Bay.

Facing page: top **1978** Burghley Champions: Lorna Clarke and Greco. *Bottom* **1979** Andrew Hoy and Davey (Australia). *Centre* **1980** Richard Walker and John of Gaunt.

Right **1982** Richard Walker and Ryan's Cross.

(*Below, right*) **1983 European Young Rider Championships** *Individual* Jean-Paul St Vignes and Jocelyn A. (*Below*) *Team* Great Britain: P. Schwerdt/Dylan; C. Murdoch/Rugan; V. Strawson/Minsmore; K. Straker/Running Bear.

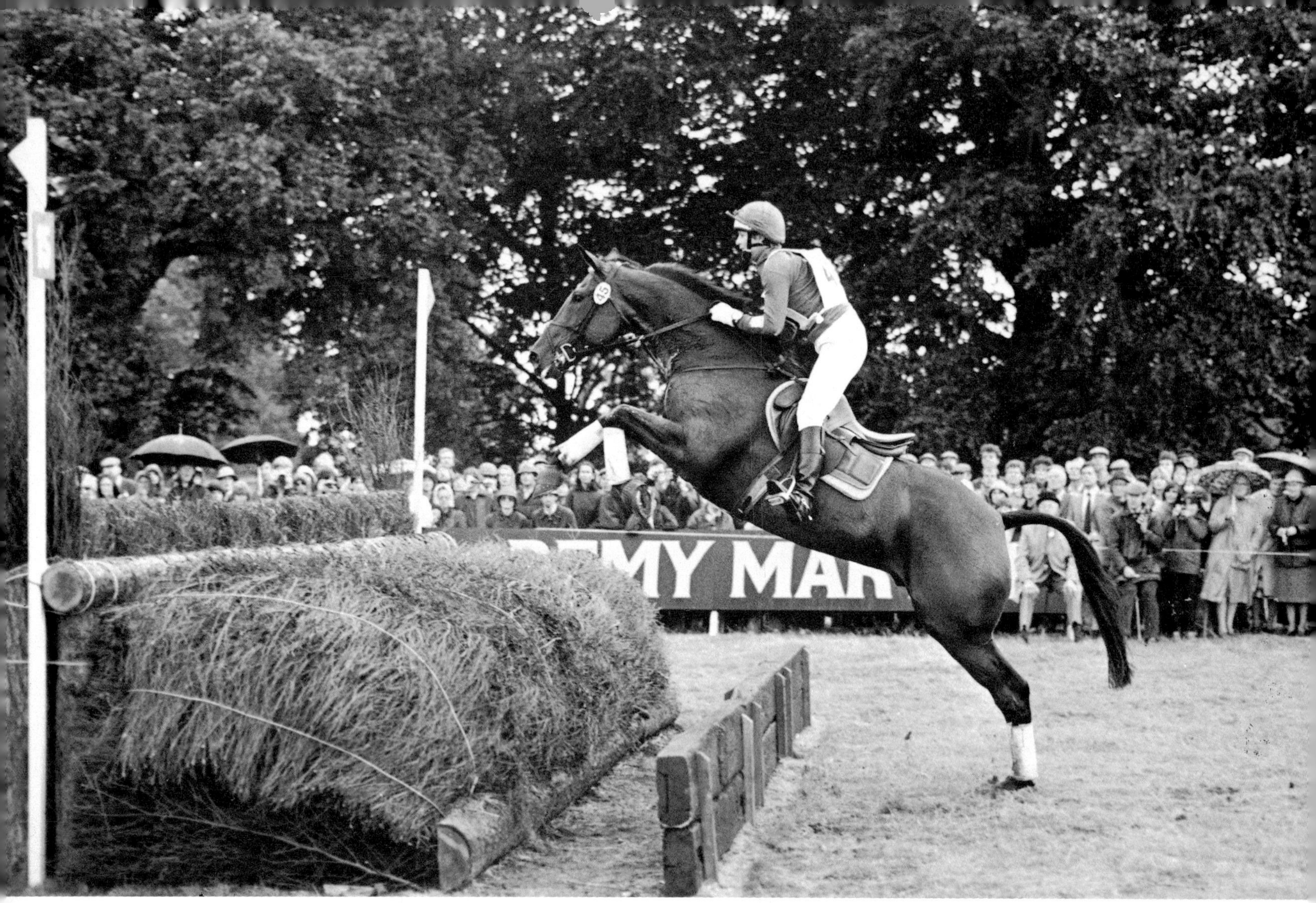

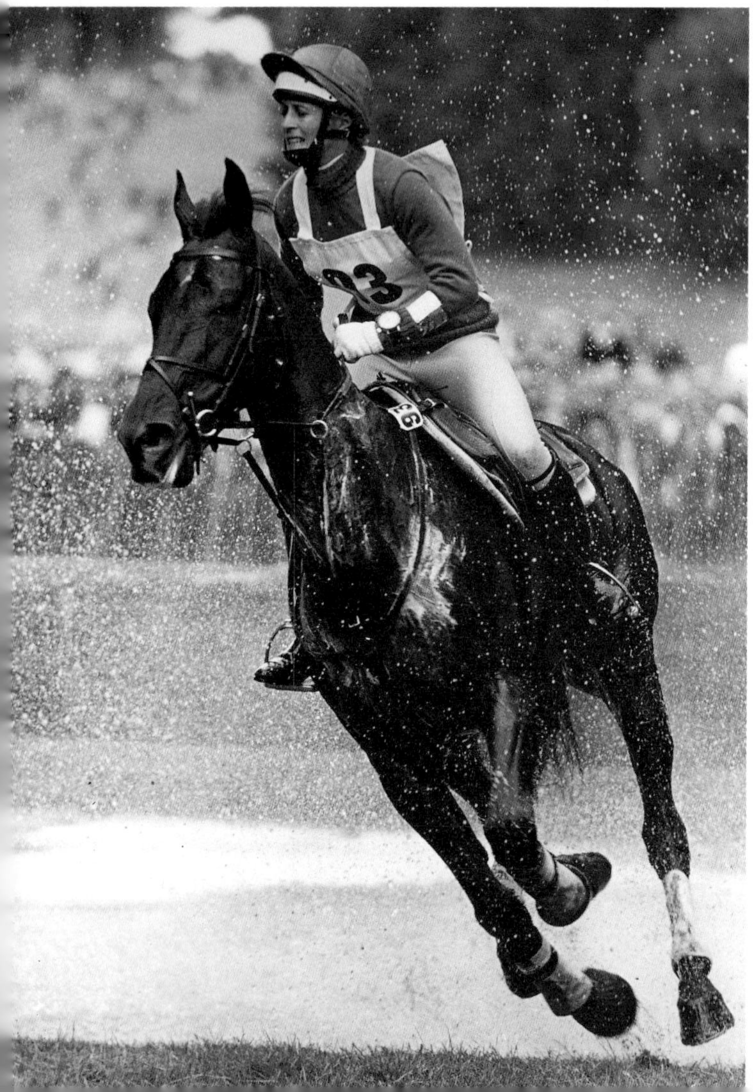

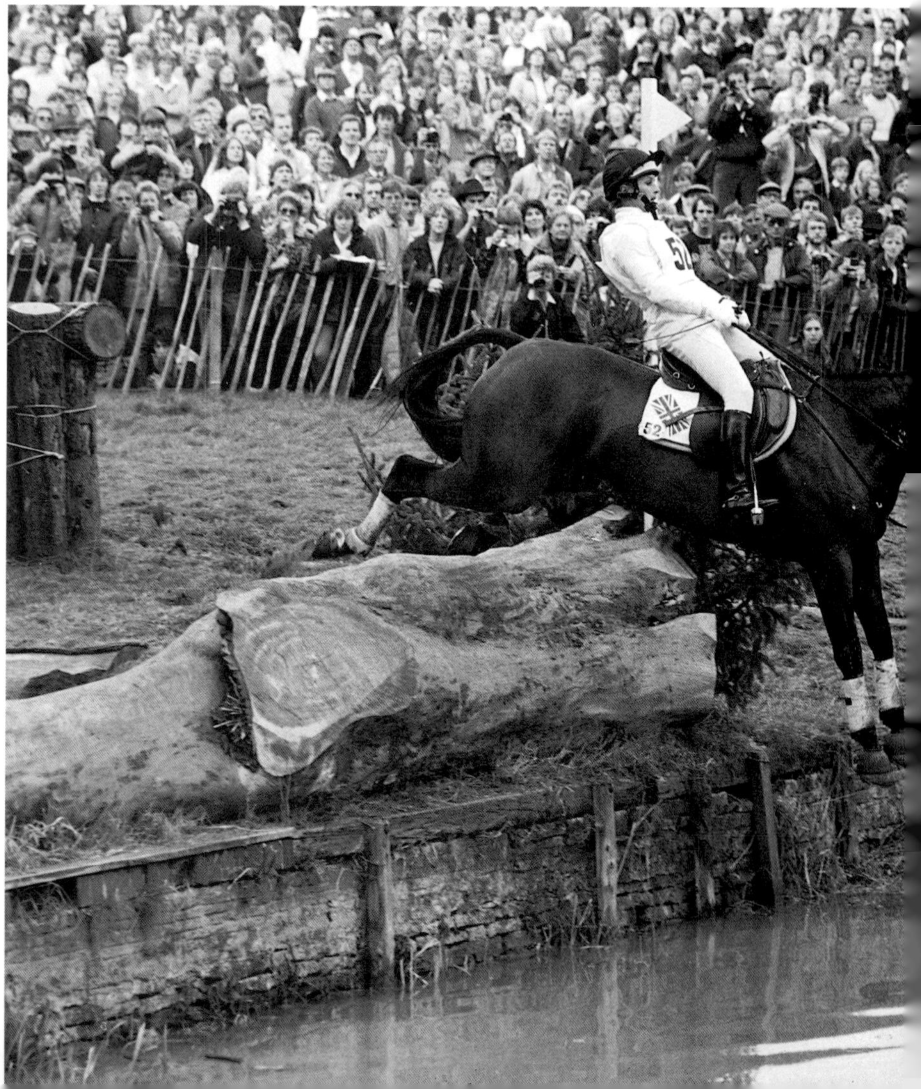

Ginny's Four-in-a-Row

With: Priceless, **1983**, *left*, and **1985**, *below*, (Winners, European Individual Gold Medal); Nightcap, **1984**, *below, left*; Murphy Himself, **1986**, *right*.

Left **1985 European Championships**
Team Great Britain: Lorna Clarke/
Myross; Ian Starke/Oxford Blue; Virginia
Holgate/Priceless; Lucinda Green/Regal
Realm. *Below, left* **1987** Mark Todd and
Wilton Fair (NZ). *Bottom left* **1988** Jane
Thelwall and King's Jester. *Below and right*
1989 European Championships.
Individual Virginia Leng and Master
Craftsman. *Team* Great Britain: Ian
Stark/Glenburnie; Virginia Leng/Master
Craftsman; Lorna Clarke/Fearliath Mor;
Rodney Powell/The Irishman. *Far right*
1990 Mark Todd and Face the Music.
Below right **1991** Mark Todd and Welton
Greylag. *Bottom right* **1992** Charlotte
Hollingsworth and The Cool Customer.

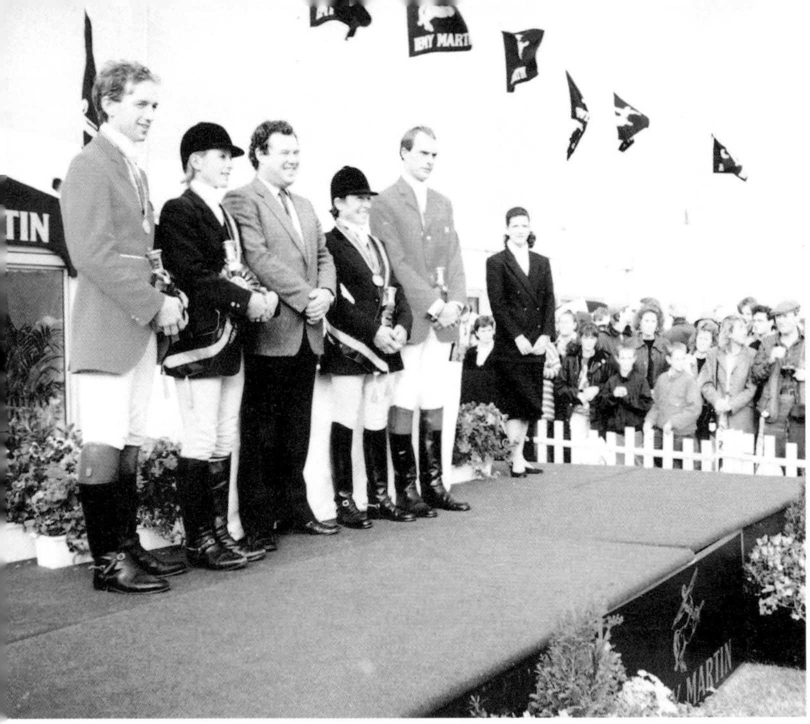

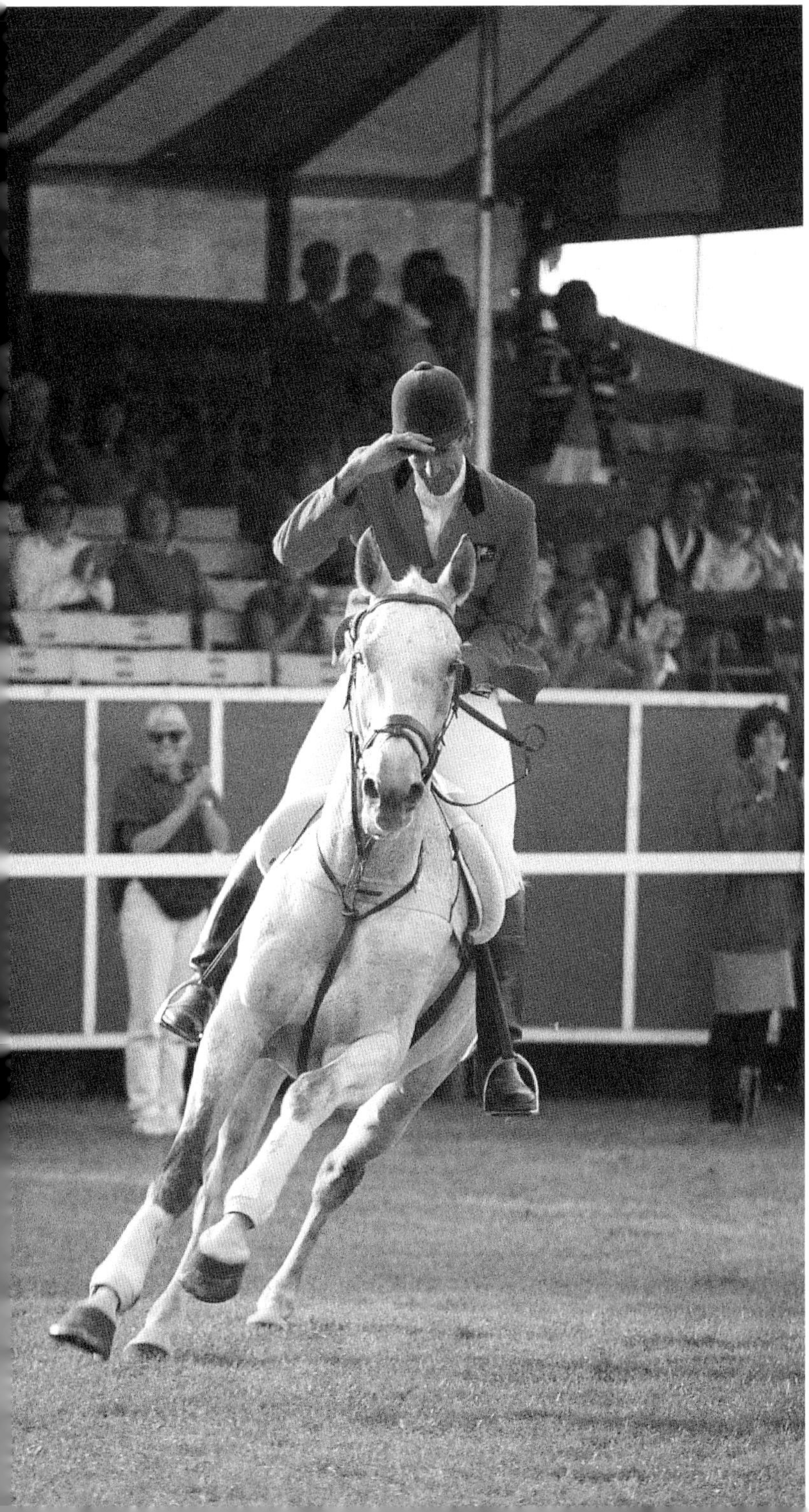

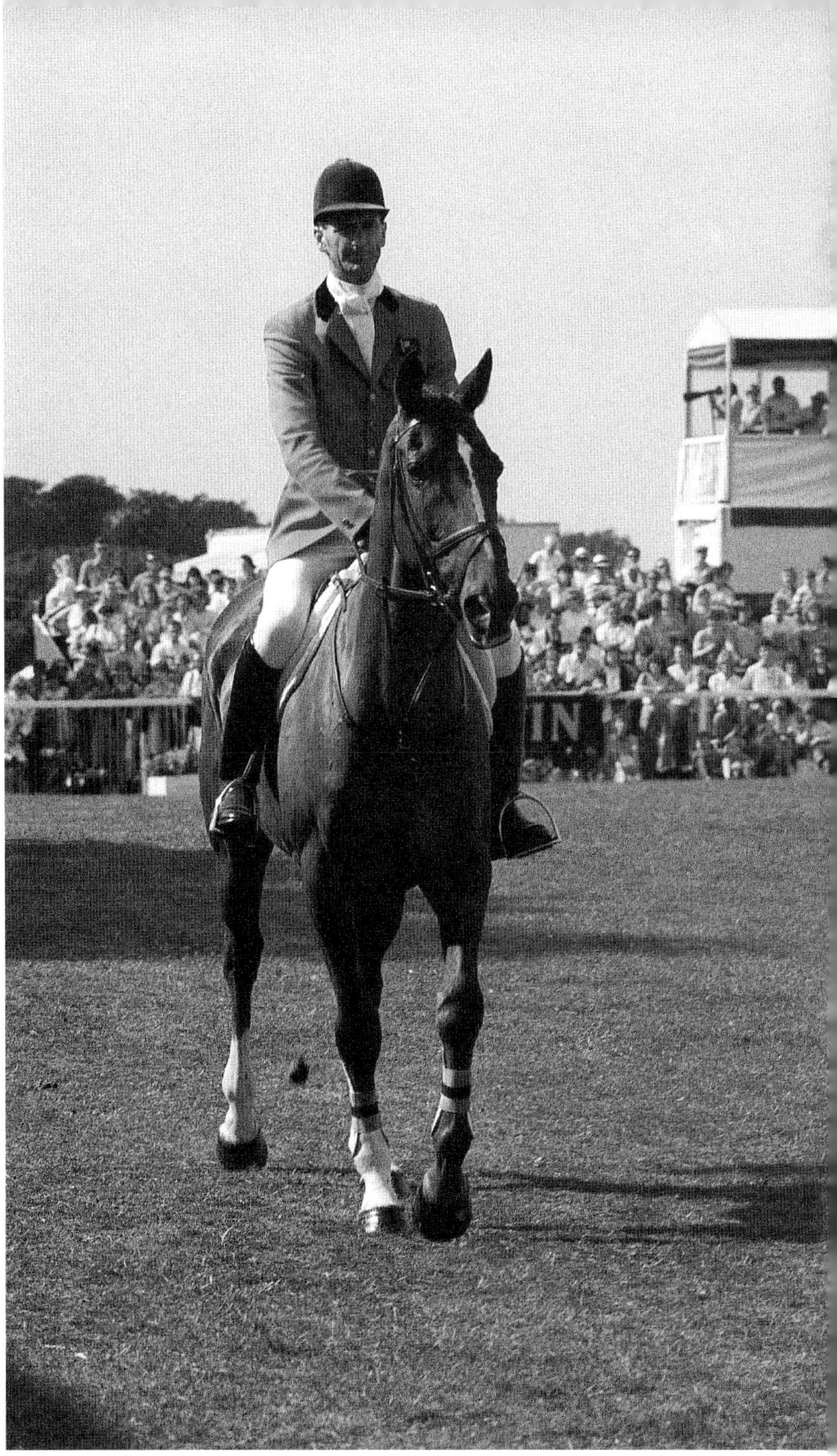

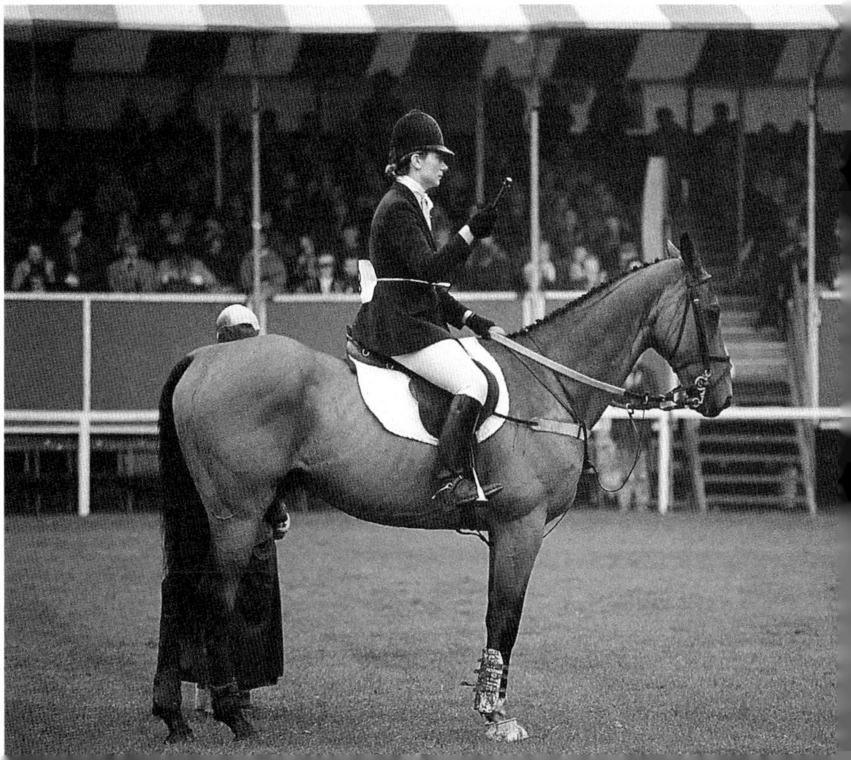

Results

1961

	FIRST DAY		SECOND DAY						THIRD DAY	
	DRESSAGE		STEEPLECHASE		CROSS-COUNTRY		END OF TWO DAYS		SHOW JUMPING	FINAL SCORE
	penalties	place	jumping penalties	time penalties	jumping penalties	time penalties	score	place	penalties	total points
1. Mrs. A. Gilroy's MERELY-A-MONARCH (Miss A. Drummond-Hay)	- 38	1st	—	+22.4	—	+46.4	+30.8	1st	—	+30.8
2. Lt. J. D. Smith-Bingham's BY GOLLY (owner)	- 79.33	4th	—	+37.6	—	+48.8	+7.07	2nd	- 10	- 2.93
3. Lt. The Hon. P. T. Conolly-Carew's BALLYHOO (owner)	- 107.33	11th	—	+22.4	- 20	+29.6	- 75.33	3rd	—	- 75.33
4. N. W. Gardiner's YOUNG PRETENDER (Lt.-Col. F. W. C. Weldon)	- 134.67	15th	—	+37.6	- 60	+59.6	- 97.47	4th	—	- 97.47
5. Captain and Mrs. J. J. Beale's ANONYMOUS (Capt. J. J. Beale)	96	8th	—	+37.6	- 60	+3.2	- 115.2	5th	- 10	- 125.2
6. Miss G. Tilney's LEANDER (owner)	- 128.67	14th	—	+37.6	- 100	+6	- 185.07	6th	- 10	- 195.07
7. Miss J. Sansome's NUTMEG (owner)	- 120.67	12th	—	+23.2	- 80	- 118.8	- 296.27	7th	—	- 296.27
8. OC The King's Troop RHA's SAVERNAKE (Capt. W. A. Dickins)	- 142	16th	—	+19.2	- 240	- 52.8	- 415.6	8th	- 20	- 435.6
9. Miss J. Sebag-Montefiore's SAMANTHA	- 125.33	13th	—	+32	- 420	- 52.4	- 565.73	9th	—	- 565.73

1962

TEAM RESULTS

1. USSR +2.2
   - Granj +34.1
   - Satrap - 12.7
   - Khirurg - 19.2
   - (Rumb Withdrawn)

2. IRELAND 93.3
   - St. Finbarr +3.4
   - Sam Weller - 35.4
   - Ballyhoo - 61.3
   - (Irish Lace - 184.1)

3. GREAT BRITAIN 160.2
   - Young Pretender - 23.9
   - Sea Breeze - 43.4
   - The Gladiator - 92.9
   - (Mr. Wilson E)

	FIRST DAY		SECOND DAY						THIRD DAY	
	DRESSAGE		STEEPLECHASE		CROSS-COUNTRY		END OF TWO DAYS		SHOW JUMPING	FINAL SCORE
	penalties	place	jumping penalties	time penalties	jumping penalties	time penalties	score	place	penalties	total points
1. Captain J. R. Templer's M'LORD CONNOLLY (owner)	- 60.5	4th	—	+37.6	- 20	+86	+43.1	2nd	—	+43.1
2. USSR Equestrian Federation's GRANJ (G. Gazjumov) (USSR)	- 89.5	17th	—	+37.6	—	+86	+34.1	3rd	—	+34.1
3. Miss J. Wykeham-Musgrave's RYEBROOKS (owner)	- 65.5	6th	—	+37.6	—	+78.8	+50.9	1st	- 20	+30.9
4. Capt. H. Freeman-Jackson's ST. FINBARR (owner)	- 79	14th	—	+33.6	—	+48.8	+3.4	6th	—	+3.4
5. USSR Equestrian Federation's SATRAP (P. Deev) (USSR)	- 61.5	5th	—	+35.2	- 20	+63.6	+17.3	4th	- 30	- 12.7
6. Mme. Le Roy's GARDEN (J. Le Roy) (France)	- 58.5	3rd	—	+29.6	- 20	+46	- 2.9	7th	- 10	- 12.9
7. USSR Equestrian Federation's KHIRURG (L. Baklyshkin) (USSR)	- 82	15th	—	+19.2	—	+73.6	+10.8	5th	- 30	- 19.2
8. N. W. Gardiner's YOUNG PRETENDER (Lt.-Col. F. W. C. Weldon)	- 113.5	25th	—	+36.8	—	+62.8	- 13.9	10th	- 10	- 23.9
9. A. Le Goupil's JACASSE B (owner) (France)	- 70	8th	—	+36	- 20	+40.8	- 13.2	9th	- 20	- 33.2
10. C. C. Cameron's SAM WELLER (A. Cameron) (Ireland)	- 107	24th	—	34.4	—	+57.2	- 15.4	11th	- 20	- 35.4
11. Col. V. D. S. Williams' SEA BREEZE (M. Bullen)	- 67	7th	—	+37.6	- 60	+86	- 3.4	8th	- 40	- 43.4
12. Miss B Pearson's ANNA'S BANNER (owner)	- 87	16th	—	+23.2	- 20	+38	- 45.8	12th	—	- 45.8

1963

	FIRST DAY		SECOND DAY						THIRD DAY	
	DRESSAGE		STEEPLECHASE		CROSS-COUNTRY		END OF TWO DAYS		SHOW JUMPING	FINAL SCORE
	penalties	place	jumping penalties	time penalties	jumping penalties	time penalties	score	place	penalties	total points
1. Capt. H. Freeman-Jackson's ST. FINBARR (owner) (Ireland)	- 63.33	5th	—	+37.6	—	+80.8	+55.07	3rd	—	+55.07
2. Maj. D. Allhusen's LOCHINVAR (Miss S. Kesler)	- 63	=3rd	—	+37.6	—	+80.8	+55.4	1st	- 10	+45.4
3. Centre National des Sports Equestres Militaires' LAURIER (Adj. J. Le Goff) (France)	- 63	=3rd	—	+37.6	—	+80.8	+55.4	2nd	- 10	+45.4
4. Mr. and Mrs. A. Kitchin's CHAR'S CHOICE (L. Sederholm)	- 62.67	2nd	—	+37.6	—	+62.8	+37.73	5th	—	+37.73
5. The King's Troop RHA's MASTER BERNARD (Sgt. R. S. Jones)	- 83.33	12th	—	+37.6	—	+80.8	+35.07	7th	- 10	+25.07
6. Capt. M. Whiteley's HAPPY TALK (owner)	- 89.33	15th	—	+28	—	+75.6	+14.27	12th	—	+14.27
7. M. Gabe's ICELUY (Capt. Landon) (France)	- 99.67	23rd	—	+37.6	—	+80.8	+18.73	9th	- 10	+8.73
8. C. C. Cameron's SAM WELLER (A. Cameron) (Ireland)	- 83.33	12th	—	+37.6	- 20	+80.8	+15.07	11th	- 10	+5.07
9. R. J. H. Meade's BARBERRY (owner)	- 86.33	14th	—	+37.6	—	+80.8	+32.07	8th	- 30	+2.07
10. Centre National des Sports Equestres Militaires' MICROBE (Lt. de Croutte) (France)	- 56.67	1st	—	+37.6	- 20	+48	+8.93	14th	- 10	- 1.07
11. The King's Troop RHA's HOT SPOT (Sgt. E. Witts)	- 65.67	7th	—	+37.6	- 20	+65.6	+17.53	10th	- 20	- 2.47
12. Mrs. R. F. Orford's SUNNY JIM (Mrs. J. J. Beale)	- 77.33	11th	—	+37.6	—	+75.2	+35.47	6th	- 40	- 4.53

1964

	FIRST DAY		SECOND DAY						THIRD DAY	
	DRESSAGE		STEEPLECHASE		CROSS-COUNTRY		END OF TWO DAYS		SHOW JUMPING	FINAL SCORE
	penalties	place	jumping penalties	time penalties	jumping penalties	time penalties	score	place	penalties	total points
•1. R. J. H. Meade's BARBERRY (owner)	- 45.5	6th	—	+31.2	—	+75.6	+61.3	1st	—	+61.3
2. J. Mehrdorf's ILTSCHI (owner) (W. Germany)	- 39.5	3rd	—	+20	—	+62.4	+42.9	3rd	—	+42.9
3. The King's Troop RHA's MASTER BERNARD (Sgt. R. S. Jones)	- 41.5	4th	*—	+31.2	—	+73.6	+45.3	2nd	- 10	+35.3*
4. Major E. A. Boylan's DURLAS EILE (owner) (Ireland)	- 64	9th	—	+25.6	—	+75.6	+37.2	5th	- 10	+27.2
5. L. Goessing's KING (owner) (W. Germany)	- 37.5	=1st	*—	+30.4	- 20	+66.4	+23.3	6th	—	23.3ƒ
6. Miss M. Macdonell's KILMACTHOMAS (owner)	- 82.5	19th	—	+27.2	—	+58.4	+3.1	7th	--	+3.1
7. Miss C. Sheppard's FENJIRAO (owner)	- 69	12th	—	+18.4	- 20	+70.8	+0.2	8th	—	+0.2
8. The King's Troop RHA's SIR FRANCIS (Capt. H. B. de Fonblanque)	- 106.5	26th	—	+30.4	—	+74.4	- 1.7	9th	- 10	- 11.7
9. H. Graham-Clark's FRENCH FROLIC (Miss J. Graham-Clark)	- 74	16th	—	+30.4	- 20	+50.4	- 13.2	10th	—	- 13.2
10. Mrs. S. Waddington's GLENAMOY (owner)	- 37.5	=1st	—	+31.2	- 80	+58.8	- 27.5	13th	—	- 27.5
11. Miss E. Meynell's QUESTION GIRL (N. Simpson)	- 128.5	34th	—	+31.2	—	+74	- 23.3	12th	- 10	- 33.3
12. The Hon. W. R. Leigh's MARSHALL TUDOR (owner)	- 101	24th	—	+31.2	- 20	+75.6	- 14.2	11th	- 20	- 34.2

* Includes 18 penalties on Phase C
ƒ Includes 16 penalties on Phase C

1965

	FIRST DAY DRESSAGE		SECOND DAY				END OF TWO DAYS		THIRD DAY SHOW JUMPING	FINAL SCORE
			STEEPLECHASE		CROSS-COUNTRY					
	penalties	place	jumping penalties	time penalties	jumping penalties	time penalties	score	place	penalties	total points
1. Capt. and Mrs. J. J. Beale's VICTORIA BRIDGE (Capt. J. J. Beale)	- 61.9	2nd	—	+36.8	—	+67.2	+42.1	1st	—	+42.1
2. Miss M. Speed's RISE AND SHINE (owner)	- 91.9	14th	—	+37.6	—	+62.8	+4.5	2nd	- 20	- 15.5*
3. Miss J. Walkington's MERRY JUDGE (owner)	- 92.5	15th	—	+18.4	—	+32	- 42.1	8th	—	- 42.1
4. H. Graham-Clark's PRIAM (Miss J. Graham-Clark)	- 86.5	12th	—	+25.6	—	+33.2	- 27.7	3rd	- 20	- 47.7
5. The Hon. Mrs. Hely-Hutchinson's COUNT JASPER (Miss P. Hely-Hutchinson)	- 75	5th	—	+18.4	—	+18.8	- 37.8	6th	- 10	- 47.8
6. Miss P. J. Cawston's CHARM (owner)	- 99.4	18th	—	+4.8	—	+60.4	- 34.2	4th	- 20	- 54.2
7. H. Graham-Clark's FRENCH FROLIC (Miss J. Graham-Clark)	- 79	7th	—	+24.8	- 20	+38.8	- 35.4	5th	- 20	- 55.4
8. Miss B. Pearson's EASTER BOUQUET (owner)	- 85.5	11th	—	+28.8	- 40	+26.8	- 69.9	11th	—	- 69.9
9. Capt. H. Freeman-Jackson's MERCURY (A. Lillingston)	- 83.5	9th	—	+30.4	- 60	+52.4	- 60.7	9th	- 10	- 70.7
10. Mrs. T. W. Kopanski's THE LITTLE MERMAID (owner)	- 73.5	3rd	—	+2.4	—	+32	- 39.1	7th	- 40.5	- 79.6
11. M. Tucker's THE VIKING (owner)	- 114	27th	—	+11.2	—	+32	- 70.8	12th	- 10	- 80.8
12. Miss F. Pearson's TAM O'TULLOCHAN (owner)	- 102.4	21st	—	+37.6	- 60	+40.8	- 84	14th	—	- 84

*Includes 4 penalties on Phase C

1966

TEAM RESULTS

1. IRELAND +80.4
   - Durlas Eile +41.2
   - Loughlin 2.4
   - Sam Weller 41.6
   - (Kilkenny 54.8)

2. ARGENTINA - 213.8
   - Gatapardo 215.7
   - Desidia 61.2
   - Chalan 63.1
   - (Hijo Manso retired)

	FIRST DAY DRESSAGE		SECOND DAY				END OF TWO DAYS		THIRD DAY SHOW JUMPING	FINAL SCORE
			STEEPLECHASE		CROSS-COUNTRY					
	penalties	place	jumping penalties	time penalties	jumping penalties	time penalties	score	place	penalties	total points
1. Capt. C. Moratorio's CHALAN (owner) (Argentina)	- 42.5	1st	—	+37.6	—	+78	+73.1	1st	- 10	+63.1
2. R. J. H. Meade's BARBERRY (owner)	- 77	20th	—	+37.6	—	- 86	+46.6	4th	—	+46.6
3. Miss V. Freeman-Jackson's SAM WELLER (owner) (Ireland)	- 62	11th	—	+37.6	—	+86	+61.6	2nd	- 20	+41.6
4. Major E. A. Boylan's DURLAS EILE (owner) (Ireland)	- 54	6th	—	+37.6	—	+67.6	+51.2	3rd	- 10	+41.2
5. M. Whiteley's THE POACHER (owner)	- 68.5	13th	—	+37.6	—	+64	+33.1	5th	—	+33.1
6. USSR Equestrian Federation's PAKET (P. Deev) (USSR)	- 55	7th	—	+37.6	- 20	+60.8	+23.4	8th	—	+23.4
7. Miss C. Sheppard's FENJIRAO (owner)	- 58	8th	—	+37.6	—	+53.2	+32.8	6th	- 10	+22.8
8. Sir John Galvin's LOUGHLIN (Miss P. Moreton) (Ireland)	- 86	28th	—	+37.6	—	+46	- 2.4	10th	—	- 2.4
9. Mrs. C. D. Plumb's M'LORD CONNOLLY (K. Freeman) (USA)	- 71	16th	—	+37.6	- 60	+82.4	- 11	12th	—	- 11
10. T. Durston-Smith's DREAMY DASHER (owner)	- 107.5	36th	—	+37.6	—	+74	+4.1	9th	- 20	- 15.9
11. Sub.-Lt. E. C. Atkinson's PRIAM (owner)	- 70	15th	—	+37.6	- 60	+83.6	- 8.8	11th	- 10	- 18.8
12. Mrs. A. B. Whiteley's FOXDOR (Mrs. A. Oliver)	- 75	20th	—	+37.6	- 60	+66.8	- 30.6	13th	- 10	- 40.6

1967

	FIRST DAY DRESSAGE		SECOND DAY						THIRD DAY	
			STEEPLECHASE		CROSS-COUNTRY		END OF TWO DAYS		SHOW JUMPING	FINAL SCORE
	penalties	place	jumping penalties	time penalties	jumping penalties	time penalties	score	place	penalties	total points
1. Miss L. Sutherland's POPADOM (owner)	- 28	1st	—	+37.6	—	+61.2	+70.8	1st	—	+70.8
2. Miss A. Roger Smith's QUESTIONNAIRE (owner)	- 51.67	6th	—	+36.8	—	+75.6	+60.73	2nd	—	+60.73
3. Miss J. Bullen's OUR NOBBY (owner)	- 58.67	15th	—	+28.8	—	+72	+42.13	8th	—	+42.13
4. M. Phillips' ROCK ON (owner)	- 76.33	36th	—	+37.6	—	+75.6	+36.87	10th	—	+36.87
5. Major D. S. Allhusen's LOCHINVAR (owner)	- 51.33	5th	—	+37.6	—	+69.6	+55.87	4th	- 20	+35.87
6. Mr. & Mrs. A. Kitchin's CHAR'S CHOICE (P. Welch)	- 66.67	24th	—	+37.6	—	+64	+34.93	11th	—	+34.93
7. W. Haggard's CHALAN (owner) (USA)	- 50	4th	—	+37.6	—	+63.2	+50.8	5th	- 20	+30.8
8. Miss S. Lord's EVENING MAIL (owner) (USA)	- 65.67	22nd	—	+37.6	—	+75.6	+47.53	7th	- 20	+27.53
9. Miss J. Jobling-Purser's JENNY (owner)	- 48.33	3rd	—	+36.8	—	+41.2	+29.67	12th	- 10	+19.67
10. J. Shedden's HEYDAY (Mrs. S. Waddington)	- 54.33	8th	—	+37.6	—	+64.8	+48.07	6th	- 30	+18.07
11. M. Herbert's ARGONAUT (owner)	- 54.67	9th	—	+37.6	—	+54.8	+37.73	9th	- 20	+17.73
12. Miss M. Macdonell's KILMACTHOMAS (owner)	- 67.67	24th	—	+37.6	—	+56.4	+26.33	13th	- 10	+16.31

1968

	FIRST DAY DRESSAGE		SECOND DAY						THIRD DAY	
			STEEPLECHASE		CROSS-COUNTRY		END OF TWO DAYS		SHOW JUMPING	FINAL SCORE
	penalties	place	jumping penalties	time penalties	jumping penalties	time penalties	score	place	penalties	total points
1. Miss S. Willcox's FAIR AND SQUARE (owner)	- 39.17	3rd	—	+37.6	—	+28.8	+27.23	2nd	- .5	+26.73
2. Miss S. Neill's PERI (owner)	- 69.33	26th	—	+37.6	—	+51.6	+19.87	3rd	- 10	+9.87
3. Miss J. Bullen's OUR NOBBY (owner)	- 78.33	33rd	—	+37.6	—	+48.4	+7.67	5th	—	+7.67
4. H. Michel's OURAGAN C (owner) (France)	- 48.67	=4th	—	+37.6	—	+28	+16.93	4th	- 20	- 3.07
5. O. Vaughan-Jones' ALL OVER (owner)	- 76	32nd	—	+36	—	+44	+4	6th	- 10	- 6
6. Executors late N. P. Gold's SHAITAN (Miss G. Watson)	- 73	30th	—	+32	—	+23.6	- 17.4	8th	—	- 17.4
7. Mrs. C. M. Parker's CORNISHMAN (S/Sgt. R. S. Jones)	- 55.33	7th	—	+37.6	- 20	+28	- 9.73	7th	—	- 29.73
8. Brig. M. Gordon-Watson's CORNISHMAN V (S/Sgt. R. S. Jones)	- 55.33	7th	—	+37.6	- 20	+28	- 9.73	7th	—	- 29.73
9. Mrs. C. M. Parker's MANX MONARCH (owner)	- 66.33	17th	—	+29.6	- 80	+48	- 68.73	13th	—	- 68.73
10. Miss C. Lockhart's GAMECOCK (owner)	- 67.67	20th	—	+18.4	- 20	- .4	- 69.67	14th	- 10	- 79.67
11. M. Whiteley's THE POACHER (owner)	- 68	21st	—	+28	- 60	+22.4	- 77.6	15th	- 20	- 97.6
12. Mrs. C. Horton's THE DARK HORSE (owner)	- 64.67	16th	—	- 4	- 20	- 3.6	- 92.27	17th	- 20	112.27

1969

	FIRST DAY DRESSAGE		SECOND DAY						THIRD DAY	
			STEEPLECHASE		CROSS-COUNTRY		END OF TWO DAYS		SHOW JUMPING	FINAL SCORE
	penalties	place	jumping penalties	time penalties	jumping penalties	time penalties	score	place	penalties	total points
1. Mrs. M. Stinton's and Mr., Mrs. and Miss Smallwood's SHAITAN (Miss G. Watson)	- 57.33	3rd	—	+37.6	—	+73.6	+53.87	1st	- 20	+33.87
2. Mrs. M. Laurent's SKYBORN (M. Tucker)	- 74.33	17th	—	+37.6	—	+72	+35.27	2nd	- 10	+25.27
3. Miss L. Sutherland's POPADOM (owner)	- 53.33	1st	—	+34.4	—	+34.8	+15.87	4th	—	+15.87
4. Miss S. Neill's PERI (owner)	- 74.67	18th	—	+37.6	- 20	+69.2	+12.13	5th	—	+12.13
5. Lt.-Col. M. A. Q. Darley's CORNCRAKE (owner)	- 61.67	7th	—	+37.6	—	+45.6	+21.53	3rd	- 10	+11.53
6. Mrs. H. Wilkin's SEA QUEST (M. Bullen)	- 72.67	15th	—	+37.6	- 20	+55.6	+.53	8th	- 10	- 9.47
7. Miss T. Martin-Bird's SPIRIDION (owner)	- 65.67	9th	—	+37.6	- 20	+54.8	+6.73	7th	- 20	- 13.27
8. T. R. Sturgis's COCO (owner)	- 98.33	31st	—	+37.6	- 20	+67.2	- 13.53	9th	—	- 13.53
9. Miss L. Sutherland's GYPSY FLAME (owner)	- 56.67	2nd	—	+37.6	- 60	+61.6	- 17.47	10th	—	- 17.47
10. Lt. E. C. Atkinson's MAGIC CARPET (owner)	- 75.33	20th	—	+37.6	—	+69.6	+11.87	6th	- 30	- 18.13
11. T. Durston-Smith's HENRY THE NAVIGATOR (owner)	- 72	14th	—	+20.8	- 20	+40.4	- 30.8	14th	—	- 30.8
12. Capt. and Mrs. C. Kendall's PJ-LL ESQ (J. Smart)	- 71.33	13th	- 60	+37.6	—	+72	- 21.73	11th	- 10	- 31.73

1970

	FIRST DAY DRESSAGE		SECOND DAY						THIRD DAY	
			STEEPLECHASE		CROSS-COUNTRY		END OF TWO DAYS		SHOW JUMPING	FINAL SCORE
	penalties	place	jumping penalties	time penalties	jumping penalties	time penalties	score	place	penalties	total points
1. R. Smith's DON CAMILLO (Miss J. Bradwell)	- 28.67	1st	—	+37.6	—	+54.8	+63.73	2nd	- 10	+53.73
2. Mr. and Mrs. Compton-Bracebridge's UPPER STRATA (R.D. Walker)	- 53.67	13th	—	+37.6	—	+61.6	+45.53	4th	—	+45.53
3. W. Goldie's REMBRANDT (D. Goldie)	- 42.67	3rd	—	+37.6	—	+68.8	+63.73	1st	- 20	+43.73
4. Miss J. Hodgson's LARKSPUR (owner)	- 52	11th	—	+37.6	—	+63.6	+49.2	3rd	- 10	+39.2
5. Miss D. West's BACCARAT (owner)	- 69	27th	—	+37.6	—	+72	+40.6	5th	- 10	+30.6
6. Miss A. Sowden's MOONCOIN (owner)	- 58.67	16th	—	+37.6	—	+50.4	+29.33	7th	—	+29.33
7. M. Moffett's DEMERARA (owner)	- 53	12th	—	+37.6	—	+38	+22.6	8th	—	+22.6
8. Miss J. Neill's PERI (Miss S. Neill)	- 65	21st	—	+37.6	—	+59.6	+32.2	6th	- 10	+22.2
9. W. Powell-Harris's SMOKEY (owner) (Ireland)	- 92	32nd	—	+36	—	+75.6	+19.6	9th	—	+19.6
10. J. B. Eastwood's SLIEVE NAMON (Miss A. Fenwick)	- 72	28th	—	+32.8	- 20	+49.6	- 9.6	15th	—	- 9.6
11. Mrs. A. Franks' SAM (Miss B. Chambers)	- 54.67	14th	—	+37.6	- 60	+69.6	- 7.47	14th	- 10	- 17.47
12. Miss F. Lochore's THE YOUNG LAIRD (owner)	- 49	9th	—	+28	—	+29.6	+8.6	10th	- 30	- 21.4

1971

	FIRST DAY		SECOND DAY						THIRD DAY	FINAL SCORE
	DRESSAGE		STEEPLECHASE		CROSS-COUNTRY		END OF TWO DAYS		SHOW JUMPING	
	penalties	place	jumping penalties	time penalties	jumping penalties	time penalties	score	place	penalties	total points
1. HRH the Princess Anne's DOUBLET (owner)	- 41.5	1st	—	—	—	- 18.8	- 60.3	1st	—	- 60.3
2. Miss D. West's BACCARAT (owner)	- 62.5	10th	—	—	—	- 25.6	- 88.1	2nd	- 10	- 98.1
3. The Hon. Mrs. F. Westenra's CLASSIC CHIPS (S. Stevens)	- 98.5	35th	—	—	—	- 4.4	- 102.9	4th	- 10	- 112.9
4. Brig. M. Gordon-Watson's CORNISHMAN V (Miss M. Gordon-Watson)	- 71	15th	—	—	—	- 26	- 97	3rd	- 20	- 117
5. The Combined Training Committee's THE POACHER (R. J. H. Meade)	- 59	6th	—	—	- 20	- 29.2	- 108.2	5th	- 10	- 118.2
6. Miss F. and Lt. M. Phillips' GREAT OVATION (Lt. M. Phillips)	- 64.5	12th	—	—	- 20	- 32.4	- 116.9	7th	- 10	- 126.9
7. Miss J. Hodgson's LARKSPUR (owner)	- 84.5	23rd	—	—	—	- 31.2	- 115.7	6th	- 20	- 135.7
8. Miss A. Sowden's MOONCOIN (owner)	- 84	22nd	—	—	—	- 52	- 136	8th	—	- 136
9. Col. H. Buehler's WUKARI (1st Lt. A. Buehler) (Switz)	- 73.5	17th	—	- 18.4	—	- 52	- 143.9	9th	—	- 143.9
10. USSR Equestrian Federation's RESFEDER (Mr. Muhin) (USSR)	- 49	2nd	—	- .8	- 80	- 30.8	- 160.6	10th	—	- 160.6
11. Swedish Army's SARAJEVO (J. Jonsson) (Sweden)	- 59.5	8th	- 60	—	—	- 55.6	- 175.1	12th	—	- 175.1
12. T. Durston-Smith's and Miss M. Rock's HENRY THE NAVIGATOR (T. Durston-Smith)	- 85.5	25th	—	—	- 60	- 39.6	- 185.1	14th	—	- 185.1

TEAM RESULTS

1. GREAT BRITAIN - 333.3
   - Baccarat - 98.1
   - Cornishman V - 117
   - The Poacher - 118.2
   - (Great Ovation - 126.9)

2. USSR - 755.5
   - Resfeder - 160.6
   - Obzor - 262.6
   - Farkhad - 332.3
   - (Rashod Eliminated)

3. IRELAND - 795.6
   - Ballangarry - 193
   - Broken Promise - 290.6
   - Smokey VI - 312
   - (San Carlos Withdrawn)

1972

	FIRST DAY		SECOND DAY						THIRD DAY	FINAL SCORE
	DRESSAGE		STEEPLECHASE		CROSS-COUNTRY		END OF TWO DAYS		SHOW JUMPING	
	penalties	place	jumping penalties	time penalties	jumping penalties	time penalties	score	place	penalties	total points
1. Miss J. Hodgson's LARKSPUR (owner)	- 47	=11th	—	—	—	- 8	- 55	1st	—	- 55
2. Miss D. West's BACCARAT (owner)	- 48	13th	—	—	—	- 10	- 58	2nd	—	- 58
3. Mrs. D. Brentnall's MARY POPPINS II (Miss H. Booth)	- 43	7th	—	—	—	- 16.4	- 59.4	3rd	—	- 59.4
4. Miss L. Prior-Palmer's BE FAIR (owner)	- 47	=11th	—	- 2.4	—	- 10.4	- 59.8	4th	—	- 59.8
5. Mrs. H. Wilkin's WAYFARER II (R. J. H. Meade)	- 38	4th	—	—	—	- 24.4	- 62.4	5th	- 10	- 72.4
6. W. Baldus' SIOUX (H. Karsten) (W. Germany)	- 38.67	5th	—	—	—	- 56	- 94.67	9th	—	- 94.67
7. The Hon. Mrs. F. Westenra's CLASSIC CHIPS (S. Stevens)	- 58	17th	—	—	20	- 21.6	- 94.6	8th	- 10	- 104.6
8. Mr. and Mrs. M. Tucker's MOONCOIN (Mrs. M. Tucker)	- 59	21st	—	—	—	- 46	- 105	10th	—	- 105
9. Lt.-Col and Mrs. C. and Miss A. Siewright's ALSEDELL (Miss A. Siewright)	- 66.33	29th	—	—	—	- 39.6	- 105.93	-11th	—	- 105.93
10. Miss L. Sutherland's PEER GYNT (owner)	- 27.33	1st	—	—	40	- 43.6	- 110.93	12th	—	- 110.93
11. Miss E. Profumo's WESTERN MORN (Miss J. Bullen)	- 71	31st	—	- .8	—	- 41.2	- 113	13th	- 10	- 123
12. Miss A. L. C. Daybell's WITCH GIRL (J. Marsden)	- 85	58th	—	- 16.8	—	- 37.2	- 139	18th	—	- 139

1973

	FIRST DAY DRESSAGE		SECOND DAY STEEPLECHASE		CROSS-COUNTRY		END OF TWO DAYS		THIRD DAY SHOW JUMPING	FINAL SCORE
	penalties	place	jumping penalties	time penalties	jumping penalties	time penalties	score	place	penalties	total points
1. A. E. and A. G. Hill's MAID MARION (Captain M. Phillips)	- 41.57	2nd	—	—	—	- 15.6	- 57.27	1st	- 10	- 67.27
2. Mrs. M. J. and Miss D. Thorne's THE KINGMAKER (Miss D. Thorne)	- 71.33	29th	—	—	—	- 5.2	- 76.53	3rd	—	- 76.53
3. Mrs. A. H. and Miss S. Hatherly's HARLEY (Miss S. Hatherly)	-62.67	14th	—	—	—	- 8.4	- 71.07	2nd	- 10	- 81.07
4. C. Collins' CENTURIAN (owner)	- 54.33	4th	—	- 8	—	- 24.4	- 86.73	6th	—	- 86.73
5. Miss L. Sutherland's PEER GYNT (owner)	- 47.33	3rd	—	- 3.2	- 20	- 27.6	- 98.13	9th	—	- 98.13
6. Mrs. and Miss J. Starkey's ACROBAT (Miss J. Starkey)	- 75	33rd	—	—	—	- 24.8	- 99.8	10th	—	- 99.8
7. C. Wares' GAVELACRE (owner)	- 64.67	18th	—	—	—	- 36	- 100.67	12th	—	- 100.67
8. W. Powell-Harris's SMOKEY VI (owner) (Ireland)	- 81.33	39th	—	—	—	—	- 81.33	5th	- 21	- 102.33
9. Miss J. Crossland's TOUCH AND GO III (Miss M. Frank)	- 65.33	19th	—	—	—	- 28	- 93.33	8th	- 20	- 113.33
10. Mr. and Mrs. T. R. Sturgis' DEMI-DOUZAINE (T. R. Sturgis)	- 79.67	36th	—	- 5.6	—	- 15.2	- 100.47	11th	- 21	- 121.47
11. Miss K. Hill's DAY RETURN (owner)	- 67.33	24th	—	—	—	- 10	- 77.33	4th	- 44.25	- 121.58
12. M. Moffett's DEMERARA (owner)	- 75	32nd	—	—	- 20	- 8	- 103	13th	- 20	- 123

1974

TEAM RESULTS

1. U.S.A. - 288.07
   - Irish Cap - 71.67
   - Good Mixture - 71.93
   - Victor Dakin - 144.47
   - (Plain Sailing - 192.45)

2. GREAT BRITAIN - 458.6
   - Wayfarer II - 115.13
   - Cornish Gold - 123.27
   - Smokey VI - 220.2
   - (Columbus Withdrawn)

3. GERMANY - 519.53
   - Virginia - 162.07
   - Albrant - 165.07
   - Sioux - 191.73
   - (Vaibel Eliminated)

	FIRST DAY DRESSAGE		SECOND DAY STEEPLECHASE		CROSS-COUNTRY		END OF TWO DAYS		THIRD DAY SHOW JUMPING	FINAL SCORE
	penalties	place	jumping penalties	time penalties	jumping penalties	time penalties	score	place	penalties	total points
1. B. O. Davidson's IRISH CAP (owner) (USA)	- 45.67	2nd	—	—	—	- 26	- 71.67	2nd	—	- 71.67
2. U.S. Equestrian Team's GOOD MIXTURE (J. M. Plumb) (USA)	- 58.33	=16th	—	—	—	- 13.6	- 71.93	3rd	—	- 71.93
3. H. Thomas's PLAYAMAR (owner)	- 59.67	21st	—	—	—	- 12.8	- 72.47	4th	—	- 72.47
4. Miss J. Hodgson's LARKSPUR (owner)	- 54.67	8th	—	- 4	—	- 30.8	- 89.47	5th	—	- 89.47
5. Minister for Defence's BOTHAR BUI (Capt. R. MacMahon) (Ireland)	- 72.67	50th	—	—	—	- 26.4	- 99.07	7th	—	- 99.07
6. R. Perkins' FURTIVE (Miss E. T. Perkins) (USA)	- 50.3	35th	—	—	—	- 46.4	- 96.73	6th	- 10	- 106.73
7. Mrs. H. Wilkin's WAYFARER II (R. J. H. Meade)	- 58.33	=16th	--	- 9.6	—	- 47.2	- 115.13	11th	—	- 115.13
8. Mr. and Mrs. E. B. Graham's SUMATRA (Miss J. Graham) (Canada)	- 74.67	53rd	—	—	—	- 47.6	- 122.27	12th	- .75	- 123.02
9. Mrs. C. M. Parker's CORNISH GOLD (owner)	- 63.67	31st	—	—	- 20	- 29.6	- 113.27	9th	- 10	- 123.27
10. Miss L. Prior-Palmer's BE FAIR (owner)	- 66	39th	—	- 28	—	- 33.6	- 127.6	13th	—	- 127.6
11. Mr. and Mrs. T. R. Sturgis' DEMI-DOUZAINE (T. R. Sturgis)	- 70.67	46th	—	- 4	—	- 36.4	- 111.07	8th	- 20.5	- 131.57
12. HM the Queen's GOODWILL (HRH the Princess Anne, Mrs. M. Phillips)	- 69	42nd	—	- 4	- 20	- 45.6	- 138.6	15th	- .5	- 139.1

1975

	FIRST DAY DRESSAGE		SECOND DAY STEEPLECHASE		CROSS-COUNTRY		END OF TWO DAYS		THIRD DAY SHOW JUMPING	FINAL SCORE
	penalties	place	jumping penalties	time penalties	jumping penalties	time penalties	score	place	penalties	total points
1. A. Colquhoun's CARAWICH (Miss A. Pattinson)	- 54.67	7th	—	—	—	—	- 54.67	1st	- 10	- 64.67
2. Mrs. J. R. Hodgson's GRETNA GREEN (Captain M. Phillips)	- 64.33	15th	—	—	—	- 7.2	- 71.53	6th	—	- 71.53
3. M. D. Abrahams' TOMMY BUCK (R. J. H. Meade)	- 60.33	12th	—	- .8	—	- 2.4	- 63.53	2nd	- 10	- 73.53
4. Mr. and Mrs. R. D. S. Carpendale's FAVOUR (J. Kersley)	- 74.33	31st	—	—	—	—	- 74.33	7th	—	- 74.33
5. Mrs. R. B. Lunger's TOUCH AND GO (Miss M. Frank)	- 46.33	3rd	—	—	—	- 21.6	- 67.93	4th	- 10	- 77.93
6. Mrs. and Miss J. Starkey's ACROBAT (Miss J. Starkey)	- 70	28th	—	—	—	- 9.2	- 79.2	11th	—	- 79.2
7. Miss P. Biden's LITTLE EXTRA (owner)	- 69.67	27th	—	—	—	—	- 69.67	5th	- 10	- 79.67
8. The Viscountess Brookeborough's VILLAGE GOSSIP (Miss K. O'Hara)	- 66	19th	—	—	—	—	- 66	3rd	- 20	- 86
9. M. Moffett's DEMERARA (owner)	- 80.67	44th	—	—	—	—	- 80.67	12th	- 10	- 90.67
10. Miss D. Thorne's THE KINGMAKER (owner)	- 82	45th	—	—	—	—	- 82	13th	- 10	- 92
11. Mrs W. and Miss D. West's BENJIE (Miss D. West)	- 55	8th	—	—	- 20	- 8	- 83	14th	- 10	- 93
12. Mrs. P. Gormley's MASTER QUESTION (J. Seaman)	- 68.67	23rd	—	- 2.4	—	- 13.2	- 84.27	15th	- 10	- 94.27

1976

	FIRST DAY DRESSAGE		SECOND DAY STEEPLECHASE		CROSS-COUNTRY		END OF TWO DAYS		THIRD DAY SHOW JUMPING	FINAL SCORE
	penalties	place	jumping penalties	time penalties	jumping penalties	time penalties	score	place	penalties	total points
1. Mrs. S. Howard's WARRIOR (Mrs. T. Holderness-Roddam)	- 67	13th	—	- 9.6	—	- 18.4	- 95	2nd	—	- 95
2. C. A. Cyzer's KILLAIRE (Miss L. Prior-Palmer)	- 68.33	15th	—	- 26.4	—	- 5.6	- 100.33	5th	—	- 100.33
3. Mr. and Mrs. G. Brookes' WELTON PLAYBOY (Miss S. Brookes)	- 66.33	11th	—	- 17.6	—	- 16	- 99.93	4th	- 10	- 109.93
4. Mrs. and Miss J. Starkey's TOPPER TOO (Miss J. Starkey)	- 59.67	6th	—	- 21.6	—	- 30.4	- 111.67	8th	—	- 111.67
5. Mr. and Mrs. T. R. Sturgis's DEMI-DOUZAINE (T. R. Sturgis)	- 74	25th	—	16	—	- 4	- 94	1st	- 20	- 114
6. Mrs. J. Geekie's COPPER TIGER (Miss C. Geekie)	- 61.33	8th	—	- 24.8	—	- 21.6	- 107.73	7th	- 10	- 117.73
7. Miss J. Thorne's SPARTAN BOY (owner)	- 76	31st	—	- 13.6	—	- 25.2	- 114.8	9th	- 10	- 124.8
8. Captain M. Phillips PERSIAN HOLIDAY (owner)	- 52	1st	—	- 8.8	60	- 6.4	- 127.2	12th	—	- 127.2
9. R. Clarke's ALOOF (Miss S. Hatherly)	- 89	50th	—	- 16	—	- 24	- 129	14th	—	- 129
10. N. Engert's MILLE TONNERRES (owner)	- 79	38th	—	- 16.8	—	- 27.2	- 123	10th	10	- 133
11. Miss P. M. Maher's BALLANGARRY (owner) (Ireland)	- 74.67	27th	—	- 32.8	—	- 38	- 145.47	21st	—	- 145.47
12. Miss E. Boone's FELDAY FARMER (owner)	- 87.67	48th	—	- 8.8	—	- 9.6	- 106.07	6th	- 40	- 146.07

1977

TEAM RESULTS

1. GREAT BRITAIN - 151.25
   - George - 37.35
   - Smokey - 60
   - Warrior - 53.9
   - (Merry Sovereign W.)

2. GERMANY - 221.9
   - Madrigal - 39
   - Sioux - 48.2
   - Akzent - 134.7
   - (El Paso Retired)

3. IRELAND - 247.9
   - Cambridge Blue - 58.05
   - Pontoon - 91.75
   - Ballangarry - 98.1
   - (Blue Tom Tit Retired)

	FIRST DAY DRESSAGE penalties	place	SECOND DAY STEEPLECHASE jumping penalties	time penalties	CROSS-COUNTRY jumping penalties	time penalties	END OF TWO DAYS score	place	THIRD DAY SHOW JUMPING penalties	FINAL SCORE total points
1. Mrs. H. C. Straker's GEORGE (Miss L. Prior-Palmer)	31.75	3rd	—	—	—	- 5.6	- 37.35	2nd	—	- 37.35
2. Gestüt Nehmten's MADRIGAL (K. Schultz) (W. Germany)	- 21	1st	—	—	—	- 8	- 29	1st	- 10	- 39
3. Dr. Baldus and G. Weyhausen SIOUX (H. Karsten) (W. Germany)	- 35	7th	—	—	—	- 3.2	- 38.2	3rd	- 10	- 48.2
4. Mrs. M. J. and Miss D. Thorne's THE KINGMAKER (Miss D. Thorne)	- 47.5	23rd	—	—	—	- 4.8	- 52.3	5th	—	- 52.3
5. Mrs. T. Holderness-Roddam's WARRIOR (owner)	- 43.5	19th	—	—	—	- 10.4	- 53.9	6th	—	- 53.9
6. Major G. T. Ponsonby's CAMBRIDGE BLUE (J. Watson) (Ireland)	- 57.25	38th	—	—	—	- .8	- 58.05	8th	—	- 58.05
7. C. Collins' SMOKEY VI (owner)	- 40	16th	—	—	—	—	- 40	4th	- 20	- 60
8. Mme. A. Souchon BEGIUN CHARRIERE (A. Souchon) (France)	- 47	22nd	—	—	—	- 21.6	- 68.6	9th	—	- 68.6
9. USSR Equestrian Federation's BALADZHAR (M. Gubarev) (USSR)	- 48.75	28th	—	- 7.2	—	- 14.8	- 70.75	10th	—	- 70.75
10. A. Colquhoun's CARAWICH (Mrs. A. Adsetts)	- 34.75	6th	—	—	—	- 20.4	- 55.15	7th	- 20	- 75.15
11. C. F. Harrison's CHEAL CLOUD (Mrs. M. Comerford)	- 48.75	28th	—	—	—	- 22.8	- 71.55	11th	- 10	- 81.55
12. Mrs. and Miss J. Starkey's TOPPER TOO (Miss J. Starkey)	- 36	8th	—	—	—	- 46	- 82	14th	—	- 82

1978

EUROPEAN JUNIOR CHAMPIONSHIPS

1. D. Baumgart	FRG	Kurfurst	- 37	—	—		- 37
2. R. Ehrenbrink	FRG	Huntsman	- 37.8	—	—		- 37.8
3. P. Cronier	FRA	Danseur II G	- 47	—	—		- 47
4. J. Le Goupil	FRA	Godeleureau	- 52.8	—	—		- 52.8
5. J. Dermody	IRL	Heathdliffe	- 54.6	—	—		- 54.6
6. O. Depagne	FRA	Bobineau	- 46	—	- 10		- 56
7. J. Bobik	POL	Optyk	- 46.2	—	- 10		- 56.2
8. C. Bealby	GBR	Jack Be Nimble	- 58.8	—	—		- 58.8
9. R. Funder	AUT	Dac	- 40.4	- 20	—		- 60.4
10. N. van Nieuwenhuyse	FRA	Boutantrin	- 60.6	—	—		- 60.6
11. H. van der Brink	NED	Mr. Solo B	- 67.2	—	—		- 67.2
12. Miss J. King	GBR	Hinton Admiral	- 57.6	- 2	- 10		- 69.6

TEAM RESULTS
1. West Germany - 151.4
2. France - 155.8
3. Ireland - 202.0

	FIRST DAY DRESSAGE penalties	place	SECOND DAY STEEPLECHASE jumping penalties	time penalties	CROSS-COUNTRY jumping penalties	time penalties	END OF TWO DAYS score	place	THIRD DAY SHOW JUMPING penalties	FINAL SCORE total points
1. Mrs. L. J. Clarke's GRECO (owner)	- 62	8th	—	—	—	- 12	- 74	1st	—	- 74
2. Miss R.M. and Mr. T.L. Bayliss's GURGLE THE GREEK (Miss R.M. Bayliss)	- 58.6	3rd	—	—	—	- 20	- 78.6	4th	—	- 78.6
3. Miss A. Cassagrande's DALEYE (owner) (Italy)	- 72.6	20th	—	—	—	- 3.6	- 76.2	3rd	- 5	- 81.2
4. Mr. and Mrs. G. Brookes's WELTON PLAYBOY (Miss S. Brookes)	- 72	18th	—	—	—	- 13.2	- 85.2	6th	—	- 85.2
5. Mr. G. Pons's ENSORCELEUSE (J. Pons) (France)	- 71.2	17th	—	—	—	- 17.6	- 88.8	7th	—	- 88.8
6. Mrs. H. Butler's MERGANSER II (owner)	- 75	27th	—	—	—	—	- 75	2nd	- 15	- 90
7. Miss D. Clapham's MARTHA (owner)	- 65.2	12th	—	- 0.8	—	15.6	- 81.6	5th	- 10	- 91.6
8. Mrs. D. Henderson & Mrs. M.J. Thorne's THE KINGMAKER (Mrs. D. Henderson)	- 78	30th	—	—	—	- 17.2	- 95.2	8th	—	- 95.2
9. Mr. R. Brake's BAMPTON FAIR (A. Brake)	- 74.8	26th	—	—	—	- 24.8	- 99.6	9th	—	- 99.6
10. Miss C. Geppart's JERRICHO IV (owner)	- 65.6	26th	—	—	—	- 36.8	- 102.4	10th	- 0.5	- 102.9
11. Miss P. Gilbert's CONTAGO II (owner)	- 80	32nd	—	—	—	- 22.8	- 102.8	11th	- 10	- 112.8
12. Mrs. P. Gormley's MASTER QUESTION (J. Seaman)	- 74	23rd	—	- 10.4	- 20	- 19.6	- 124	15th	- 5	- 129

1979

	FIRST DAY DRESSAGE		SECOND DAY				END OF TWO DAYS		THIRD DAY SHOW JUMPING	FINAL SCORE
			STEEPLECHASE		CROSS-COUNTRY					
	penalties	place	jumping penalties	time penalties	jumping penalties	time penalties	score	place	penalties	total points
1. Mr. A. Hoy's DAVEY (owner) (Australia)	-53.8	6th	—	-2.4	—	—	-56.2	1st	—	-56.2
2. Miss K. Marra's POLTROON (Miss T. Watkins) (U.S.A.)	-52.2	4th	—	—	—	-5.6	-57.8	2nd	—	-57.8
3. Mrs. H. Butler's MERGANSER (owner)	-58	11th	—	—	—	-4.8	-62.8	3rd	-11.75	-74.55
4. Mrs. L. J. Clarke's GRECO (owner)	-62.6	20th	—	—	—	-7.6	-70.2	4th	-5	-75.2
5. Mr. G. Breisner's ULTIMUS (owner) (Sweden)	-74.2	49th	—	—	—	—	-74.2	5th	-2	-76.2
6. Miss T. and Mrs. N. Martin-Bird's THE MOUNTAINEER (Miss T. Martin-Bird)	-76.8	59th	—	—	—	-9.2	-86	8th	-0.75	-86.75
7. Mr. N. Tabor's SIRDAR II (owner)	-86.2	71st	—	—	—	-4.4	-90.6	10th	-2	-92.6
8. Mr. and Mrs. G. Brookes's SCRIPT (Miss J. Brookes)	-67.2	=30th	—	—	—	-11.6	-78.8	6th	-15.25	-94.05
9. Mr. C. Collins's RADWAY (owner)	-68.6	35th	—	-3.2	—	-20.8	-92.6	12th	-5.25	-97.85
10. Mr. E. A. Thomas's MYTHIC LIGHT (H. Thomas)	-78.6	61st	—	—	—	-21.6	-100.2	15th	—	-100.2
11. Miss J. Wilson's FLYING SOLO (owner)	-68.4	=33rd	—	—	-20	-13.6	-102	17th	—	-102
12. Captain R. L. Seaman's THE REVEREND (J. Seaman)	-49.2	1st	—	-4.8	—	-35.6	-89.6	9th	-15	-104.6

1980

	FIRST DAY DRESSAGE		SECOND DAY				END OF TWO DAYS		THIRD DAY SHOW JUMPING	FINAL SCORE
			STEEPLECHASE		CROSS-COUNTRY					
	penalties	place	jumping penalties	time penalties	jumping penalties	time penalties	score	place	penalties	total points
1. Kent Leather Distributors Ltd.'s JOHN OF GAUNT (R. Walker)	-45.2	4th	—	—	—	-1.2	-46.4	2nd	-5	-51.4
2. Range Rover Team's PERSIAN HOLIDAY (Capt. M. Phillips)	-43.6	1st	—	—	—	-0.8	-44.4	1st	-10	-54.4
3. Mrs. S. Howard & Mrs. J. Holderness-Roddam's WARRIOR (Mrs. J. Holderness-Roddam)	-55	9th	—	-0.8	—	—	-55.8	3rd	—	-55.8
4. Miss J. McKnight's COUNTRY FROST Miss B. Perkins (U.S.A.)	-49.6	6th	—	—	—	-8.4	-58	4th	-5	-63
5. Mrs. L. J. Clarke's GRECO (owner)	-57	13th	—	—	—	-13.2	-70.2	6th	—	-70.2
6. Major J. Rice and Miss V. Holgate's PRICELESS (Miss V. Holgate)	-44.2	2nd	—	—	—	-27.2	-71.4	7th	-0.5	-71.9
7. Dr. B. Springorum's CLIPPIE (M. Plewa) (Germany)	-48.8	5th	—	-0.8	—	-18	-67.6	5th	-5	-72.6
8. Planters Peanuts's GEMMA JAY (Mrs. S. Benson)	-60.4	18th	—	—	—	-18.8	-79.2	10th	-5	-84.2
9. British Equestrian Federation's FOXY BUBBLE (Miss L. Prior-Palmer)	-66.4	34th	—	-4.8	—	-15.2	-86.4	12th	-5.75	-92.15
10. Mrs. E. Purbrick's PETER THE GREAT (owner)	-79.8	61st	—	—	—	-12.8	-92.6	19th	—	-92.6
11. Mrs. J. R. Hodgson's GRETNA GREEN (Mrs. J. Norton)	-58.4	16th	—	—	—	-30	-88.4	13th	-5.75	-94.15
12. Mrs. H. M. Douglas & Mr. D. Douglas's OUR MR. TWINK (D. Douglas)	-75	52nd	—	-2.4	—	-12.4	-89.8	14th	-5	-94.8

1981

	FIRST DAY DRESSAGE		SECOND DAY						THIRD DAY	
			STEEPLECHASE		CROSS-COUNTRY		END OF TWO DAYS		SHOW JUMPING	FINAL SCORE
	penalties	place	jumping penalties	time penalties	jumping penalties	time penalties	score	place	penalties	total points
1. Overseas Containers Ltd.'s BEAGLE BAY (Miss L. Prior-Palmer)	-47.25	13th	—	—	—	-2.4	-49.65	1st	—	-49.65
2. George Wimpey Ltd.'s SPECULATOR III (R. Meade)	-44.85	8th	—	—	-20	—	-64.85	3rd	—	-64.85
3. Mrs. H. Holgate and Major J. Rice's NIGHT CAP II (Miss V. Holgate)	-47.1	12th	—	—	—	-8.4	-55.5	2nd	-10	-65.5
4. Collins Wine's KINALLEN (R. Walker)	-43.35	5th	—	—	-20	-4.4	-67.75	4th	-5	-72.75
5. Mrs. M. F. Strawson's GREEK HERB (Miss V. Strawson)	-54	=27th	—	—	—	-16	-70	5th	-5	-75
6. Mr. H. Klugmann's VEBEROD (owner) (Germany)	-46.05	10th	—	—	—	-24.8	-70.85	6th	-5	-75.85
7. Monocle Equestrian Syndicate's MONOCLE II (Mrs. S. Benson)	-44.4	7th	—	—	-20	-11.2	-75.6	7th	-5	-80.6
8. Newark Equestrian Centre's CLAUGHTON (J. Marsden)	-52.8	=22nd	—	—	-20	-5.6	-78.4	9th	-5	-83.4
9. Mrs. I. Price's QUEEN HILL (Miss L. Moir)	-75.9	63rd	—	—	—	—	-75.9	8th	-10	-85.9
10. Mr. J. Conifey's TOREADOR (owner)	-53.85	26th	—	-7.2	—	-20.8	-81.85	10th	-10	-91.85
11. The Hon. R. Cayzer's FIGHTING FIFTH (owner)	-56.1	32nd	—	-7.2	-20	-4.8	-88.1	11th	-5	93.1
12. Mrs. G. M. White's SOLDIER BLUE (Mrs. W. Hollinshead)	-54.9	30th	—	—	-40	—	-94.9	13th	-5	-99.9

1982

	FIRST DAY DRESSAGE		SECOND DAY						THIRD DAY	
			STEEPLECHASE		CROSS-COUNTRY		END OF TWO DAYS		SHOW JUMPING	FINAL SCORE
	penalties	place	jumping penalties	time penalties	jumping penalties	time penalties	score	place	penalties	total points
1. Mr. J. Ambler's RYAN'S CROSS (R. Walker)	-48	4th	—	—	—	—	-48	1st	—	-48
2. Mrs. S. A. Collins's BIG FRY (Mrs. E. Purbrick)	-51.2	7th	—	—	—	—	-51.2	2nd	-5	-56.2
3. Miss J. Wilson's FLYING SOLO (owner)	-60.4	=15th	—	—	—	—	-60.4	5th	—	-60.4
4. Miss F. Moore's SQUIRES HOLT (owner)	-62.8	22nd	—	—	—	—	-62.8	8th	-0.75	-63.55
5. British National Insurance's NIGHT CAP II (Miss V. Holgate)	-55.8	8th	—	—	—	—	-55.8	3rd	-10	-65.8
6. Mr. R. Ilsley's THREE CUPS (R. Meade)	-61.2	19th	—	—	—	—	-61.2	7th	-5	-66.2
7. Mrs. J. Arden's DALWHINNIE (M. Tucker)	-57.2	9th	—	—	—	—	-57.2	4th	-10	-67.2
8. R.H.M. Pegus Horse Feeds's CROWN OF CROWNS (Miss V. Oliver)	-60.4	=15th	—	—	—	-3.2	-63.6	9th	-10	-73.6
9. Overseas Containers Ltd.'s BEAGLE BAY (Mrs. L. Green)	-46.2	2nd	—	—	-20	-3.2	-69.4	11th	-5	-74.4
10. Mrs. J. G. Stirrat's MR. FINCH (J. Conifey)	-64	27th	—	—	—	-7.2	-71.2	12th	-5	-76.2
11. George Wimpey Ltd.'s SPECULATOR III (R. Meade)	-48.2	5th	—	—	-20	-8.8	-77	14th	—	-77
12. Mrs. T. Harding's CASTLEBLAYNEY III (D. Hancock)	-72.4	47th	—	—	—	—	-72.4	13th	-5	-77.4

1983

	FIRST DAY DRESSAGE		SECOND DAY STEEPLECHASE		CROSS-COUNTRY		END OF TWO DAYS		THIRD DAY SHOW JUMPING	FINAL SCORE
	penalties	place	jumping penalties	time penalties	jumping penalties	time penalties	score	place	penalties	total points
1. British National Insurance's PRICELESS (Miss V. Holgate)	-25.6	1st	—	—	—	—	-25.6	1st	—	-25.6
2. George Wimpey Ltd.'s KILCASHEL (R. Meade)	-31.8	=14th	—	—	—	—	-31.8	3rd	—	-31.8
3. Mrs. C. W. S. Dreyer's THE APOSTLE (Mrs. E. de Haan)	-32.2	18th	—	—	—	—	-32.2	4th	-0.25	-32.45
4. Miss A. Baille and Miss M. Hunter's BUGSY MALONE (Miss M. Hunter)	-35	=37th	—	—	—	—	-35	5th	—	-35
5. Mrs. R. Thompson's CASTLEWELLAN (J. C. Wofford) (U.S.A.)	-26.1	3rd	—	—	—	-9.2	-35.3	6th	—	-35.3
6. Mrs. E. Purbrick's FREDERICK THE GREAT (owner)	-29.9	12th	—	—	—	-1.6	-31.5	2nd	-5	-36.5
7. Mr. M. Bouquet's PERIGOURDON (owner) (France)	-26.5	4th	—	—	—	-12	-38.5	7th	-10	-48.5
8. S. R. Direct Mail's SUPER SALESMAN (D. Green) (Australia)	-38.1	53rd	—	—	—	-12.4	-50.5	10th	—	-50.5
9. Schroder Life Assurance's MILTON TYSON (N. Taylor)	-36.6	44th	—	—	—	-8.4	-45	9th	-6.75	-51.75
10. Mrs. J. F. Brignall's CLAUGHTON (N. Harland)	-40	=61st	—	—	—	—	-40	8th	-15.75	-55.75
11. Mr. and Mrs. B. Davidson's J. J. BABU (B. Davidson) (U.S.A.)	-25.7	2nd	—	—	—	-30.8	-56.5	13th	—	-56.5
12. Mrs. P. Denton's THE DARK IMP (Mrs. M. Lucey)	-33.9	=25th	—	-2.4	—	-17.6	-53.9	12th	-5	-58.9

EUROPEAN YOUNG RIDERS CHAMPIONSHIPS

1.	J. Paul St. Vignes	FRA	Jocelyn A	-66.6	—	-5	-71.6
2.	Miss. K. Straker	GBR	Running Bear	-62.8	—	-10	-72.8
3.	Miss P. Schwerdt	GBR	Dylan II	-73.2	-4.4	—	-77.6
4.	Miss A. Nilsson	SWE	Noon Star	-57.8	-20	-5	-82.8
5.	Miss J. Sainsbury	GBR	Mr. Moon	-61.8	-22.8	—	-84.6
6.	R. Breul	FRA	Javelot de L'Ile	-65.4	-20.8	—	-86.2
7.	Miss S. Gordon	IRL	Rathkenny	-77	-20	—	-97
8.	Miss M. Gurdon	GBR	The Done Thing	-64.8	-29.6	-5.25	-99.65
9.	Miss M. Orchard	GBR	Venture Busby	-78	-27.6	—	-105.6
10.	A. Kennedy	IRL	Coppit	-80.2	-20	-10	-110.2
11.	L. Joubert	FRA	Glauber du Vilmer	-63.8	-51.2	-10	-125
12.	Miss V. Strawson	GBR	Minsmore	-60.8	-60.4	-15	-136.2

TEAM RESULTS
1. Great Britain -286.6
2. France -340.8
3. Ireland -391.6

1984

	FIRST DAY DRESSAGE		SECOND DAY STEEPLECHASE		CROSS-COUNTRY		END OF TWO DAYS		THIRD DAY SHOW JUMPING	FINAL SCORE
	penalties	place	jumping penalties	time penalties	jumping penalties	time penalties	score	place	penalties	total points
1. British National Life Assurance's NIGHT CAP II (Miss V. Holgate)	-35.25	4th	—	—	—	—	-35.25	1st	—	-35.25
2. Hedderwick Consultants & Mrs. L. J. Clarke's DANVILLE (Mrs. L. J. Clarke)	-37.2	6th	—	—	—	-1.6	-38.8	3rd	—	-38.8
3. Roxton's Sporting's THE GROUSEBEATER (Mrs. E. Purbrick)	-39.45	12th	—	—	—	—	-39.45	4th	—	-39.45
4. Lanz Hotels of Bournemouth Ltd's ALOAF (Miss R. Hunt)	-41.4	20th	—	—	—	—	-41.4	5th	—	-41.4
5. Mrs. P. Orchard's VENTURE BUSBY (Miss M. Orchard)	-38.55	10th	—	—	—	—	-38.55	2nd	-5	-43.55
6. S. R. Direct Mail Ltd.'s SHANNAGH (Mrs. L. Green)	-37.5	=7th	—	—	—	-7.6	-45.1	7th	—	-45.1
7. Towerlands Ltd.'s MILTON GENERAL (R. Meade)	-41.55	21st	—	-0.8	—	—	-42.35	6th	-5	-47.35
8. Mrs. C. W. S. Dreyer's THE APOSTLE (Mrs. E. de Haan)	-44.4	28th	—	—	—	-4.4	-48.8	8th	-5	-53.8
9. Mrs. P. Denton's THE DARK IMP (Mrs. M. Lucey)	-48.9	46th	—	-1.6	—	-2.4	-52.9	9th	-5	-57.9
10. M. P. Kent p.l.c.'s POMEROY (R. Powell)	-47.7	=37th	—	—	—	-6	-53.7	10th	-10	-63.7
11. Mrs. V. Christie's THE MAGISTRATE (R. Stewart Christie)	-60.9	66th	—	—	—	-5.6	-66.55	16th	—	-66.55
12. Gateway Foodmarkets Ltd's DELPHY DAZZLE (Miss C. Strachan)	-42.75	24th	—	—	—	-20.8	-63.55	13th	-5	-68.55

1985

TEAM RESULTS

1. GREAT BRITAIN - 172.80
   - Priceless — - 49.00
   - Myross — - 61.80
   - Oxford Blue — - 62.00
   - (Regal Realm — - 83.60)

2. FRANCE - 353.80
   - Harley — - 90.80
   - Godelureau HN — - 103.40
   - Gulliver B — - 159.60
   - (Kopino HN Retired)

3. WEST GERMANY - 372.60
   - Fair Lady — - 69.20
   - Bettina — - 113.20
   - Phillip — - 190.20
   - (Frosty Bay Eliminated)

	FIRST DAY DRESSAGE penalties	place	SECOND DAY STEEPLECHASE jumping penalties	time penalties	CROSS-COUNTRY jumping penalties	time penalties	END OF TWO DAYS score	place	THIRD DAY SHOW JUMPING penalties	FINAL SCORE total points
1. British National Life Assurance's PRICELESS (Miss V. Holgate)	- 49	9th	—	—	—	—	- 49	1st	—	- 49
2. Miss D. Watson's MYROSS (Mrs. L. J. Clarke)	- 57	= 17th	—	—	—	- 4.8	- 61.8	3rd	—	- 61.8
3. The Edinburgh Woollen Mill Ltd.'s OXFORD BLUE (I. Stark)	- 54.2	12th	—	—	—	- 2.8	- 57	2nd	- 5	- 62
4. Miss M. Orchard VENTURE BUSBY (owner)	- 53.6	11th	—	—	—	- 15.2	- 68.8	6th	—	- 68.8
5. Use Leykam's FAIR LADY (C. Erhorn) (Germany)	- 44.2	3rd	—	—	—	- 20	- 64.2	4th	- 5	- 69.2
6. S. R. Direct Mail Ltd.'s REGAL REALM (Mrs. L. Green)	- 60	28th	—	—	- 20	- 3.6	- 83.6	8th	—	- 83.6
7. Mr. Bourgeoise's HARLEY (Mrs. M. C. Duroy) (France)	- 44.4	4th	—	—	- 20	- 26.4	- 90.8	9th	—	- 90.8
8. Federation Equestre Française's GODELUREAU HN (J. Teulere) (France)	- 71.2	= 46th	—	—	—	- 27.2	- 98.4	11th	- 5	- 103.4
9. Mr. P. Wagner's TIPPERARY (owner) (Austria)	- 62.8	31st	—	—	- 20	- 22.8	- 105.6	12th	- 5.25	- 110.85
10. Gateway Foodmarkets Ltd's DELPHY DAZZLE (Miss C. Strachan)	- 71.4	48th	—	—	- 20	- 19.6	- 111	14th	—	- 111
11. D. O. K. R.'s BETTINA (R. Ehrenbrink) (Germany)	- 46	5th	—	—	- 20	- 47.2	- 113.2	15th	—	- 113.2
12. Mr. E. Koczorski's GAJAL (owner) (Poland)	- 56	16th	—	—	- 20	- 51.2	- 127.2	17th	—	- 127.2

1986

	FIRST DAY DRESSAGE penalties	place	SECOND DAY STEEPLECHASE jumping penalties	time penalties	CROSS-COUNTRY jumping penalties	time penalties	END OF TWO DAYS score	place	THIRD DAY SHOW JUMPING penalties	FINAL SCORE total points
1. British National Life Assurance's MURPHY HIMSELF (Mrs. V. Leng)	- 42.2	1st	—	—	—	—	- 42.2	1st	—	- 42.2
2. Mr. and Mrs. B. Davidson's J. J. BABU (B. Davidson) (U.S.A.)	- 43	2nd	—	—	—	—	- 43	2nd	—	- 43
3. Mr. A. Birchall's ACCUMULATOR (R. Walker)	- 46.6	3rd	—	—	—	—	- 46.6	3rd	—	- 46.6
4. The Edinburgh Woollen Mill Ltd.'s GLENBURNIE (I. Stark)	- 50.4	6th	—	—	—	—	- 50.4	6th	—	- 50.4
5. Beefeater Steak House's THE GAMESMASTER (R. Lemieux)	- 55.4	9th	—	—	—	—	- 55.4	7th	—	- 55.4
6. Miss D. Watson & Mrs. L. J. Clarke's MYROSS (Mrs. L. J. Clarke)	- 56	11th	—	—	—	—	- 56	9th	—	- 56
7. Team Subaru (UK) Ltd.'s GENERAL BUGLE (M. Tucker)	- 53.2	8th	—	—	—	- 0.4	- 53.6	5th	- 5.5	- 59.1
8. Mrs. V. Ogden's STREETLIGHTER (Miss H. Ogden)	- 53.6	9th	—	—	—	- 0.8	- 54.4	6th	- 5	- 59.4
9. Merrill Lynch Europe Ltd.'s MICHAELMAS DAY (M. Todd) (New Zealand)	- 60.6	32nd	—	—	—	—	- 60.6	10th	—	- 60.6
10. Mr. M. E. Lanz and Mrs. S. J. Hunt's ALOAF (Miss R. Hunt)	- 60.2	31st	—	—	—	- 2.4	- 62.6	13th	—	- 62.6
11. Team Subaru (UK) Ltd.'s GOOD VALUE (Mrs. A. Tucker)	- 49.4	5th	—	—	—	- 14.4	- 63.8	14th	—	- 63.8
12. Catactin Stud Inc.'s LUTIN V (Miss K. Lende) (U.S.A.)	- 64.4	= 55th	—	—	—	—	- 64.4	15th	—	- 64.4

124

1987

	FIRST DAY		SECOND DAY						THIRD DAY	
	DRESSAGE		STEEPLECHASE		CROSS-COUNTRY		END OF TWO DAYS		SHOW JUMPING	FINAL SCORE
	penalties	place	jumping penalties	time penalties	jumping penalties	time penalties	score	place	penalties	total points
1. Merrill Lynch Europe Ltd.'s WILTON FAIR (M. Todd) (New Zealand)	-44.2	3rd	—	—	—	—	-44.2	2nd	—	-44.2
2. Merrill Lynch Europe Ltd.'s CHARISMA (M. Todd) (New Zealand)	-35.2	1st	—	—	—	—	-35.2	1st	-10	-45.2
3. Col. H. Selby's JIMNEY CRICKET III (Miss D. Clapham)	-40	2nd	—	—	—	-5.6	-45.6	3rd	—	-45.6
4. Arpac International Ltd.'s VOLUNTEER (Mrs. T. Pottinger) (New Zealand)	-52.6	=26th	—	—	—	—	-52.6	6th	—	-52.6
5. Carphone Team Cellnet's THE IRISHMAN II (R. Powell)	-47.2	7th	—	—	—	-1.6	-48.8	4th	-5	-53.8
6. Arpac International Ltd.'s GRAPHIC (Mrs. T. Pottinger) (New Zealand)	-59.2	50th	—	—	—	—	-59.2	10th	—	-59.2
7. S. R. International's REGAL REALM (Mrs. L. Green)	-48.2	11th	—	—	—	-10.8	-59	9th	-0.25	-59.25
8. Mrs. L. J. Clarke's FEARLIATH MOR (owner)	-61.2	54th	—	—	—	—	-61.2	11th	—	-61.2
9. Carphone Team Cellnet's KING BORIS (Miss M. Thomson)	-51.6	=21st	—	—	—	-10.8	-62.4	13th	—	-62.4
10. Happy Eater Ltd.'s MCDUFF III (Miss N. May)	-50.6	=17th	—	—	—	-7.6	-58.2	7th	-5	-63.2
11. Mrs. J. Elliot's MIDDLE ROAD (Mrs. N. McIrvine)	-53.8	=31st	—	—	—	-4.8	-58.6	8th	-6	-64.6
12. Mrs. E. F. Straker's GET SMART (Miss K. Straker)	-50.2	15th	—	—	—	-12.0	-62.2	12th	-5	-67.2

1988

	FIRST DAY		SECOND DAY						THIRD DAY	
	DRESSAGE		STEEPLECHASE		CROSS-COUNTRY		END OF TWO DAYS		SHOW JUMPING	FINAL SCORE
	penalties	place	jumping penalties	time penalties	jumping penalties	time penalties	score	place	penalties	total points
1. Mr. and Mrs. J. Huntridge's KING'S JESTER (Mrs. J. Thelwall)	-50.2	7th	—	—	—	-0.8	-51	1st	-1	-52
2. The Done Thing Ltd.'s MIDNIGHT MONARCH (Miss M. Gurdon)	-53.4	13th	—	—	—	—	-53.4	3rd	-5	-58.4
3. Happy Eater Ltd.'s MCDUFF III (Miss N. May)	-50.4	10th	—	—	—	-2.4	-52.8	2nd	-10.25	-63.05
4. The Horton Point Syndicate's HORTON POINT (Miss R. Bevan)	-50.2	7th	—	—	—	-8	-58.2	4th	-5	-63.2
5. Miss P. Muir's BARNABUS BROWN (owner)	-41.8	2nd	—	—	—	-30.8	-72.6	9th	—	-72.6
6. Mrs. K. Jenman's THE COMFORTER (owner)	-63.4	=33rd	—	—	—	—	-63.4	5th	-15	-78.4
7. Mr. T. Gwyn-Jones's PRIVATE DEAL (J. McGowan) (Ireland)	-66.8	41st	—	—	—	-6.8	-73.6	10th	-5.5	-79.1
8. Mr. G. Longson's WATKINS (Miss T. Longson)	-63.4	=33rd	—	—	—	-7.2	-70.6	8th	-10	-80.6
9. Mrs. C. Murdoch's RUGAN (owner)	-68.4	43rd	—	—	—	-10	-78.4	11th	-5	-83.4
10. Gateway Foodmarkets Ltd.'s DELPHY DAZZLE (Miss C. Strachan)	-66.2	40th	—	—	—	-17.2	-83.4	14th	—	-83.4
11. Mr. L. Evans's EARL GREY V (Miss L. Evans)	-69.6	47th	—	—	—	-10.8	-80.4	12th	-10.25	-90.65
12. Ecole Nationale d'Equitation's MARCENAT (P. Galloux) (France)	-57.8	25th	—	—	—	-30.4	-88.2	17th	-5	-93.2

1989

TEAM RESULTS

1. GREAT BRITAIN - 187.65
   - Master Craftsman — 46.25
   - Fearliath Mor — 62.40
   - Glenburnie — 79.00
   - (The Irishman II W.)

2. HOLLAND - 333.30
   - Just A Gamble — 74.05
   - Bristol's Autumn Bronze — 96.50
   - Bristol's Autumn Fantasy — 162.75

3. IRELAND - 363.10
   - Private Deal — 68.05
   - Homer — 129.05
   - Rusticus — 166.00
   - (Rathlin Roe Retired)

		FIRST DAY DRESSAGE penalties	place	SECOND DAY STEEPLECHASE jumping penalties	time penalties	CROSS-COUNTRY jumping penalties	time penalties	END OF TWO DAYS score	place	THIRD DAY SHOW JUMPING penalties	FINAL SCORE total points
1.	Citibank Savings's MASTER CRAFTSMAN (Mrs. V. Leng)	-44	2nd	—	—	—	—	-44	1st	-22.25	-46.25
2.	Mr. and Mrs. J. Huntridge's KING'S JESTER (Mrs. J. Thelwall)	-56.4	10th	—	—	—	-2.8	-59.2	4th	—	-59.2
3.	Clarendon Equestrian Ltd.'s FEARLIATH MOR (Mrs. L. J. Clarke)	-62.4	=19th	—	—	—	—	-62.4	6th	—	-62.4
4.	Range Rover Team's GET SMART (Miss K. Straker)	-58	11th	—	—	—	—	-58	3rd	-5	-63
5.	Mr. T. Gwyn-Jones's PRIVATE DEAL (J. McGowan) (Ireland)	-65.8	28th	—	—	—	—	-65.8	9th	-2.25	-68.05
6.	Mr. C. Cuyver's CITA (M. Rigouts) (Belgium)	-54.4	8th	—	—	—	-7.6	-62	5th	-10	-72
7.	Miss F. van Tuyll's JUST A GAMBLE (owner) (Holland)	-67.6	30th	—	—	—	-1.2	-68.8	10th	-5.25	-74.05
8.	The Edinburgh Woollen Mill Ltd.'s GLENBURNIE (I. Stark)	-64	=24th	—	—	—	—	-64	7th	-15	-79
9.	Miss S. Marius's MASTER MARIUS (owner)	-62.4	=19th	—	—	—	-10.8	-73.2	11th	-10	-83.2
10.	Mr. J. Laporte's NEWLOT (D. Seguret) (France)	-62.4	=19th	—	—	—	-1.6	-64	8th	-20	-84
11.	Cotton Signs Ltd.'s MORAG (Miss S. Cotton)	-65.4	26th	—	—	—	-10	-75.4	12th	-11.25	-86.65
12.	Strong and Fisher Group's TOMBO (Miss A.-M. Taylor)	-71.4	=37th	—	—	—	-13.2	-84.6	15th	-11.75	-96.35

1990

		FIRST DAY DRESSAGE penalties	place	SECOND DAY STEEPLECHASE jumping penalties	time penalties	CROSS-COUNTRY jumping penalties	time penalties	END OF TWO DAYS score	place	THIRD DAY SHOW JUMPING penalties	FINAL SCORE total points
1.	Mr. and Mrs. P. J. Davies's FACE THE MUSIC (M. Todd) (New Zealand)	-61	30th	—	—	—	-7.6	-68.6	2nd	—	-68.6
2.	Mrs. G. Thomas's KING CUTHBERT (Miss M. Thomson)	-55.2	10th	—	—	—	-11.6	-66.8	1st	-5	-71.8
3.	Mr. R. Walker's JACANA (owner)	-57.2	=16th	—	—	—	-14.4	-71.6	4th	-0.5	-72.1
4.	Mrs. G. Thomas's KING BORIS (Miss M. Thomson)	-44.8	2nd	—	-1.6	—	-24.4	-70.8	3rd	-5	-75.8
5.	Mr. P. Vaughan's RICOCHET (B. Tait) (New Zealand)	-57.2	=16th	—	—	—	-18.8	-76	6th	—	-76
6.	Haras Nationaux's QUART DU PLACINEAU (Ms. M.-C. Duroy) (France)	-44.2	1st	—	—	—	-37.2	-81.4	8th	—	-81.4
7.	Miss K. Gracey's GENTLE SEBASTIAN (owner)	-67.2	38th	—	—	—	-12.4	-79.6	7th	-5	-84.6
8.	Mrs. D. Longson's WATKINS (Miss. T. Longson)	-60	27th	—	—	—	-25.6	-86.6	9th	-0.25	-85.85
9.	Hydrophane Event Team's WELTON FAIRGAME (Miss L. Murray)	-52.6	8th	—	—	—	-34	-86.6	10th	-5	-91.6
10.	Mr. V. Ogden's TROUBLESHOOTER (Mrs. H. Bell)	-53.2	9th	—	—	—	-18.4	-71.6	5th	-22.75	-94.35
11.	Strong and Fisher Holdings p.l.c.'s BELMONT BOUNCER (Mrs. A.-M. Taylor-Evans)	-57.6	18th	—	—	—	-33.6	-91.2	13th	-5.75	-96.95
12.	Mr. D. Clothier's BADGER BOY (Mrs. J. Marsh-Smith)	-56.4	11th	—	—	—	-35.2	-91.6	14th	-12.5	-104.1

1991

	FIRST DAY DRESSAGE		SECOND DAY STEEPLECHASE		CROSS-COUNTRY		END OF TWO DAYS		THIRD DAY SHOW JUMPING	FINAL SCORE
	penalties	place	jumping penalties	time penalties	jumping penalties	time penalties	score	place	penalties	total points
1. Kimberly Clark Ltd. & Mr. & Mrs. M. Welman's WELTON GREYLAG (M. Todd) (New Zealand)	-45.2	2nd	—	—	—	—	-45.4	1st	-5.25	-50.65
2. Sir Michael Turner's CHAKA (G. Watson) (Australia)	-47.4	4th	—	—	—	—	-47.4	2nd	-5	-52.4
3. Mr. and Mrs. R. Thomas's MR. MAXWELL (Miss K. Lende) (U.S.A.)	-45.6	3rd	—	-2.4	—	-1.6	-49.6	3rd	-5	-54.6
4. Miss R. McMullen and Modern Alarms's SIR BARNABY (Miss P. Nolan)	-55	19th	—	—	—	—	-55	4th	—	-55
5. Mrs. A. Stibbe-Peereboom & Mr. E. Stibbe's BAHLUA (E. Stibbe) (Holland)	-60.4	31st	—	—	—	—	-60.4	9th	—	-60.4
6. Mr. and Mrs. A. Nicholson's APPLAUSE (A. Nicholson) (New Zealand)	-56.2	=20th	—	—	—	—	-56.2	5th	-5	-61.2
7. Mrs. K. Dobbie's LOCOMOTION (O. Moore)	-57.4	24th	—	—	—	-4.8	-62.2	12th	—	-62.2
8. Miss J. Bishop's ARCTIC CIRCLE (owner)	-63.6	41st	—	—	—	—	-63.6	13th	—	-63.6
9. Mr. and Mrs. P. J. Randle's LEGS ELEVEN (T. Randle)	-56.6	22nd	—	—	—	—	-56.6	6th	-7	-63.6
10. Kimberly Clark Ltd.'s FACE THE MUSIC (M. Todd) (New Zealand)	-60.8	32nd	—	—	—	—	-60.8	10th	-10	-70.8
11. Miss C. Hollingsworth's THE COOL CUSTOMER (owner)	-56.2	=20th	—	—	—	-4.8	-61	11th	-15.75	-76.75
12. Countryside Insurance Frizzell's FAIR SHARE (Miss C. Bowley)	-59.6	=28th	—	—	—	—	-59.6	8th	-17.75	-77.35

1992

	FIRST DAY DRESSAGE		SECOND DAY STEEPLECHASE		CROSS-COUNTRY		END OF TWO DAYS		THIRD DAY SHOW JUMPING	FINAL SCORE
	penalties	place	jumping penalties	time penalties	jumping penalties	time penalties	score	place	penalties	total points
1. Mrs. M. Hollingsworth's THE COOL CUSTOMER (Miss C. Hollingsworth)	-52.2	9th	—	—	—	-8.8	-61	1st	-5	-66
2. Team Toggi and Miss J. Shepherd's DELTA (B. Tait) (New Zealand)	-61.6	45th	—	—	—	-1.6	-63.2	3rd	-5	-68.2
3. Mr. & Mrs. P. J. and Mr. T. Randle's LEGS ELEVEN (T. Randle)	-59.2	=35th	—	—	—	-12.4	-71.6	5th	—	-71.6
4. I.C.I.'s SMITHSTOWN LAD (Miss K. Gifford)	-55.2	13th	—	—	—	-18.4	-73.6	7th	—	-73.6
5. Miss F. Golding's SPIDERMAN III (B. Powell)	-61.8	46th	—	—	—	—	-61.8	2nd	-12.75	-74.55
6. Mr. A. le Goupil's MAIRIACHI (P. le Goupil) (France)	-51.8	=7th	—	—	—	-23.6	-75.4	8th	—	-75.4
7. Mr. D. and Mrs. K. Butterworth's BALLYCOTTON (A. Harris)	-50.8	4th	—	—	—	-26	-76.8	9th	-1	-77.8
8. Miss D. Trapp's MOLOKAI (owner) (U.S.A.)	-56.2	=16th	—	—	—	-11.6	-67.8	4th	-15	-82.8
9. Miss C. Scarlett's THE OXFORD DON (owner) (U.S.A.)	-57.8	=28th	—	—	—	-21.6	-79.4	11th	-5	-84.4
10. Mr. R. Edberg & Mrs. M. Hermann's MR. PUNCH (Miss A. Hermann) (Sweden)	-57	21st	—	-5.6	—	-24.4	-87	15th	—	-87
11. Mrs. B. Ritchie's JOSHUA (owner) (New Zealand)	-62.4	=50th	—	—	—	-16.4	-78.8	10th	-10	-88.8
12. Horton Point Syndicate's HORTON POINT (Miss L. Bevan)	-63.8	=55th	—	—	—	-25.6	-89.4	18th	-2.25	-91.65

Picture References and Credits

Picture references for colour sections, pages 40 to 96

40 Lady Victoria receiving guests at the cocktail party, held in the Great Hall (**41**). **42** (Above) Horse arriving at dawn. (Below) Deer in their temporary pasture. **43** Settling in at the stables. **44/45** First inspection by Ground Jury. **46** (Above) The Clerk of the Course briefing fence judges. (Below) Competitors setting off for course inspection. **47** (Above) Judges inspecting their fence. (Below) Course Designer briefing the Ground Jury on course. **48** (Above) Rider at fence on course-walk. (Below) Programme seller at work. **49** Dogs. **50** Dressage judges at start of test. **51** Dressage steward with rider. **52/53** Dressage action shot. **54** Stable scenes. **55** Spectators walking the course. **56** Cars and happy owners. **57** Rider and official at roads and tracks checkpoint. **58** Groom with friends. **59** (Above) Luncheon, Members' enclosure, with (below) band playing. **60/61** View from the roof of Burghley House, late afternoon. **62** Spectators watching cross-country. **63** (Above) Shoppers among trade stands. (Below) Control centre on cross-country day. **64/65** View from helicopter on cross-country day. **66** Spectators resting by signpost. **67** Start of Phase B: steeplechase. **68/69** Steeplechase action shot. **70** Start of Phase D: cross-country. **71** Fence steward in action. **72** (Above) Rider passing supporters. (Below) Crowd watching closed-circuit TV on course. **73** Grooms at work in the Box. **74** (Above) Fence judges' friends. (Below) Pony Club messenger collecting score from fence judge. **75** Rider on Phase C: 2nd roads and tracks. **76/77** Cross-country action shot. **78** Picnicking in the park, and farrier at work. **79** The Big Screen. **80** Flat-out on the flat. **81** Spectators at the Trout Hatchery. **82** (Left) 'I made it!' (Right) Virtue rewarded. **83** Tail-piece. **84/85** Burghley House by moonlight. **86** (Above) The Bottle Lodges at sunset. (Below) Night-time at the stables, cross-country day. **87** (Above) Grooms' canteen, end of the day. (Below) Beginning of the next day: horse inspection. **88** (Above) Press arena steward on duty. (Below) Equestrian journalists in the press tent. **89** (Above) Press photographers at prize-giving. (Below) 'Les Parapluies' 1992. **90** (Above) Band of the Welsh Guards, with Drum-Major. (Below) British team, lap of honour, 1989. **91** (Above) Parade of foxhounds. (Below) Braving the mud, 1992. **92/93** Show jumping action shot. **94** (Above) King's Troop guarding trophies. (Below) Winner takes the stand. **95** Going home. **96** Burghley magic.

Picture Credits

All colour photographs by **Mark A. L. Scott**.

Monochrome *Introduction* **Cyril Diamond** pages 16, 17, 22, 23, 24, 27 and 34. Gipsy Joe p. 33. *The Winners* **Cyril Diamond** 1961, '63, '64, '65, '67, '68, '69, '71 (individual), '73, '75, '76, '78 (Burghley winner), '79, '82. **Findlay Davidson** 1966 (individual and team), '70, '71 (team), '72, '74 (individual and team), '77 (team), '78 (European Juniors, individual and team), '81, '83 (European Young Riders, individual and team). **Kit Houghton** 1983, '84, '85, '86, '87. **Frank Meads** 1977 (individual). **Jim Meads** 1980, '85 (team). **Mark Scott** 1989 (individual and team), '90, '91, '92.